Mishkan Moeid

A Guide to the Jewish Seasons

Mishkan Moeid
A Guide to the Jewish Seasons

אֵלֶּה מוֹעֲדֵי יְיָ מִקְרָאֵי קֹדֶשׁ
אֲשֶׁר־תִּקְרְאוּ אֹתָם בְּמוֹעֲדָם

These are the set times of the Eternal, the sacred occasions,
which you shall celebrate each at its appointed time.
—LEVITICUS 23:4

EDITED BY Rabbi Peter S. Knobel, *Ph.D.*

ILLUSTRATED BY Michael J. Silber

WITH NOTES BY Rabbi Bennett M. Hermann
& Rabbi Peter S. Knobel

Central Conference of American Rabbis
5773 New York 2013

The original edition of this book, *Shaarei Moeid: Gates of the Seasons*, was produced by the Committee on Reform Jewish Practice of the Central Conference of American Rabbis:

Rabbi W. Gunther Plaut, Chairman, 1972–1981
Rabbi Simeon J. Maslin, Chairman, 1981–

Rabbi Norman J. Cohen	Rabbi Michael A. Signer
Rabbi Joan S. Friedman	Rabbi Michael S. Stroh
Rabbi Peter S. Knobel	Rabbi Brooks R. Susman
Rabbi Seymour Prystowsky	Rabbi Eric H. Yoffie
Rabbi Aaron Rosenberg	

Ex Officio:

Rabbi Herbert Bronstein	Rabbi Walter Jacob
Rabbi Lawrence A. Hoffman	

ISBN 978-0-88123-177-9

Library of Congress Cataloging-in-Publication Data

Mishkan moeid : a guide to the Jewish seasons / edited by Rabbi Peter S. Knobel ; Illustrated by Michael J. Silber ; with notes by Rabbi Bennett M. Hermann & Rabbi Peter S. Knobel.

p. cm.

Revised and updated edition.

Includes bibliographical references and index.

1. Reform Judaism—Customs and practices. 2. Fasts and feasts—Judaism. I. Knobel, Peter S., 1943–, editor. II. Silber, Michael J., illustrator. III. Hermann, Bennett M., author of added commentary. IV. Gates of season. V. Title: Guide to the Jewish seasons.

BM700.G35 2013
296.4′3—dc23

2013024987

CCAR Press, 355 Lexington Avenue, New York, NY 10017
(212) 972-3636
www.ccarpress.org
Printed in U.S.A.
17 16 15 14 13   6 5 4 3 2 1

Contents

Foreword to the Second Edition

UNDERNEATH the title on the very first page of this book you will find words from Leviticus 23:4—"These are the set times of the Eternal, the sacred occasions, which you will celebrate each at its appointed time." Our tradition (*Mishnah Rosh HaShanah*) tells of a great disagreement between sages in the second century CE in the Land of Israel. The subject of the debate was the calendar and who had the authority to fix the date of the New Year. In order to persuade his teacher Rabbi Joshua to accept an opinion that he considered to be incorrect, Rabbi Akiva offered a startling reading of our verse from Leviticus: these are the set time of the Eternal, the sacred occasions—the ones *you* human beings fix, the ones *you* human beings celebrate.

The Jewish calendar, like all great expressions of religious civilization, comprises an encounter between the sublime and the specific, the divine and the mundane. In this book, Reform Jews offer their perspectives on how we can be faithful heirs to an ancient tradition. Since in Reform thinking to be an heir is also to be a pioneer, you will find in these pages fidelity to the past, integrity in the present, and commitment to the future. The men and women brought together in this volume are in some sense the heirs of Rabbi Akiva, striving to fix and celebrate the age-old holy moments in a way that adds meaning—to the moments and to us.

"Meaning" is an important word for Reform Jews, but there is another "M" word that is even more central to this book—*mitzvah*, sacred doing. Here you will find Reform Jews looking for ways to live the drama of the Jewish year with honesty, passion, joy, curiosity, wisdom, knowledge, and openness. It offers a "thick" Jewish experience, not just marking off days in a calendar but investing them with significance and giving them resonance.

Modern religion has something in common with modern art. If classical artists tried to represent things as they seem, modern artists sometimes try to capture the essence of their subject with something other than a simple likeness. Often, Reform Jews portray the Jewish calendar impressionistically, aiming for the essence and not so caught up with the details. This book is intended for readers of different tastes and interests—from those who want to know "what Judaism says" about its great festivals all the way through to those who are looking for new ways to capture the essence of Judaism. As you read its pages, from the description of the holidays through the essays and the attached notes, you are encouraged to ask: how should we fulfill the words of Leviticus, how should we fix and celebrate the sacred occasions at their appointed times? It may be that we cannot touch the essence without grappling with the details—at least some of them.

In his foreword to the 1983 edition of *Gates of the Seasons*, Rabbi Simeon J. Maslin teaches us that it is our duty to study, to make decisions, and to find expression for our spiritual feelings. This updated edition provides many new voices and reflects some of the changes in ethical theory and Jewish practice that characterize our dynamic movement. Thirty years later, our ways of responding to the calls of tradition have changed and developed. Much, however, has stayed the same—not least, the masterful editorial hand of Rabbi Peter S. Knobel.

Whether your approach is old school or avant-garde, whether you are taking first steps on your Jewish journey or planning new adventures, this guide to the Jewish seasons will serve you well. The Eternal sets time for sanctity. May we be true partners in the *mitzvah* of bringing these sacred times to life.

—RABBI MICHAEL MARMUR, *Ph.D.*

Foreword to the First Edition, *"Gates of the Seasons"*

Wнат? Another book on Jewish practices from the Reform Movement? *A Shabbat Manual* in 1972; then the new prayer book with its constant refrain "Be mindful of all my mitzvot . . ." in 1975; *Gates of the House* with a whole variety of home rituals and services in 1977; and, of course, *Gates of Mitzvah: A Guide to the Jewish Life Cycle* in 1979. What is happening to the Reform Movement?!

There has been an undeniable trend toward the reinstitution of traditional practices in Reform Judaism during the past decade. And so, one has every right to ask where the Reform Movement is going. Is it, as many claim, returning to Orthodoxy? And is this latest publication, with its many suggestions for the celebration of Sabbaths and Festivals, symptomatic of that return?

In order to answer these questions properly, one must begin with an understanding of what Reform Judaism really is. It would be simplistic to define our movement on the basis of more or less ritual observances. It is our philosophy of Judaism that makes us Reform Jews. Particular ritual practices that, on the one hand, do not negate our philosophy and that, on the other, reinforce and enrich our Judaism are not only acceptable in Reform, they are desirable.

As Reform Jews, we are free to take upon ourselves the performance of certain customs and ceremonies and to reject others. We do not believe that revelation happened at one moment in ancient history and that we are bound today by the way that a pre-scientific civilization understood that revelation. A beautiful passage in the old *Union Prayer Book* teaches us that we should

> welcome all truth, whether shining from the annals of
> ancient revelation or reaching us through the seers of
> our own time, for Thou hidest not Thy light from any
> generation of Thy children that yearn for Thee and
> seek Thy guidance.

In this book, as in *Gates of Mitzvah*, certain ancient practices are recommended and others are not. Equally important, though, is the fact that certain new practices are also recommended as mitzvot—the bringing of female babies into the *b'rit* and the observances of Yom HaShoah and Yom HaAtzma-ut come readily to mind. Those customs of long standing that still have meaning and that add beauty and Jewish depth to our lives should be observed. But, as Reform Jews, we have every right to discard practices that have lost meaning for contemporary Jews and that lack an aesthetic dimension. It is our duty to study each and every tradition and, on the basis of that study, either to adopt it or to reject it. And it is our duty also to find new and contemporary modes for the expression of inchoate spiritual feelings.

We must never forget, though, that we are first and foremost Jews, related to four thousand years of Jewish history and related to thirteen million Jews the world over. Therefore, *the burden of proof must always be on those who want to abandon a particular tradition, not on those who want to retain it.* Without strong links to the vast body of Jewish tradition, we may be good people but we are certainly not good Jews capable of transmitting Judaism to the next generation.

This volume, *Gates of the Seasons*, is the creation of the CCAR's Committee on Reform Jewish Practice and, more particularly, of its editor, Rabbi Peter Knobel. Rabbi Knobel devoted countless hours over a three-year period to this volume and was always receptive to suggestions by members of the committee and by colleagues in the CCAR. We owe him a debt of gratitude as we do also to Rabbi W. Gunther Plaut, ל״ז, who guided the committee in its first years and originally conceived this sacred project. Thanks are due also to Rabbi Bennett Hermann, who did much of the original research on the notes to this volume, and to Rabbi Elliot Stevens, whose expert advice guided the committee from the day this book was conceived through its publication.

While *Gates of Mitzvah* covers the Jewish life cycle, this new volume—*Gates of the Seasons*—deals with the Jewish calendar. With these two volumes, however, we have by no means exhausted the possibilities for mitzvot within our Jewish tradition. We have not even touched upon the vast field of ethical mitzvot—business ethics, family ethics, medical ethics, etc. We look forward to the publication someday soon of a volume on ethics from a Reform Jewish point of view. Our purpose in these two volumes was not to include every possible mitzvah, but rather to describe and recommend those mitzvot of the Jewish life cycle and the Jewish calendar that might add depth and beauty to the lives of modern Jews.

It is our mitzvot—our traditional and particular Jewish practices— that put us in touch with Abraham, Moses, Esther, and the Jews of fifth-century Babylonia, twelfth-century Spain, eighteenth-century Poland, and twentieth-century Auschwitz. It is the study and the practice of our mitzvot that has "kept us in life, sustained us, and brought us to this moment."

—RABBI SIMEON J. MASLIN, *chairman*
Committee on Reform Jewish Practice
Elul 5743 / August 1983

Introduction

MISHKAN MOEID: *A Guide to the Jewish Seasons* is designed to
be an accessible and user-friendly guide to celebrating and commemorating the Jewish holidays. It is a revision of *Shaarei Moeid*
(*Gates of the Seasons*); *Shaarei Moeid* and *Shaarei Mitzvah* (*Gates of
Mitzvah*) were pioneering works in summarizing a comprehensive
approach to Jewish living. Rather than being works of halachah
(Jewish law), these books emphasized the doing of mitzvot. They
offered readers an opportunity to explore how Jewish practice
adds a sacred dimension to their lives at life cycle events as well as
during daily living, especially on Shabbat and holidays. They were
designed to deepen Jewish commitment and reinforce the important dedication of Jews to the mitzvot connected to *tikkun olam*
(repairing the world).

    Mishkhan Moeid is an updated and fully revised version of
the original *Shaarei Moeid*. It is designed to tap into the current
interest in Jewish spirituality in a meaningful and clear way. It
offers a useful reference guide to the many practices that constitute
Reform observance, without any attempt to limit the creativity or
diversity characteristic of contemporary Jewish life. This book is an
invitation to explore and to do. The key to observance is to begin:
to experiment and to discover which mitzvot transform the
ordinary into the sacred. Some readers may want to take a comprehensive approach, structuring observance of each sacred day
with a clear beginning and clear end. Others might sample the
mitzvot that inspire or galvanize them. Some could use *Mishkhan
Moeid* as a reference book to consult as needed. It is our hope that
in exploring the observance of sacred time, readers will be moved
to consider more deeply the ways in which they can build the
sanctification of time into their lives and become more comfortable
with the many opportunities for holiness offered by the cycle of the
Jewish year.

Mishkhan Moeid, while following the outline and structure of *Shaarei Moeid*, offers new essays that explore current thinking about how best to understand the concept of mitzvah. It includes new voices that supplement the previous work or investigate areas not addressed in *Shaarei Moeid*. In addition, readers will find changes related to shifts in current Reform practice and liturgy, as well as an updated section of "For Further Reading." It is part of the ongoing effort of the CCAR to provide important and attractive texts that enhance contemporary Jewish life.

In accepting the covenant at Mount Sinai, the Israelites respond to God with the promise *naaseh v'nishma*, "We will do and we will understand" (Exodus 24:7). It is through mitzvot that we come to find God and the sacred in human life. A deed has the power to transform beyond our ability to explain. The mitzvot associated with special days in the Jewish calendar put us in touch with our deepest values and preserve the history of the Jewish people. The Jewish calendar is our window on the mission of the Jewish people and provides the signposts on our journey toward a better world.

Acknowledgments

THIS BOOK would not have been possible without the pioneering and visionary work of Rabbi Simeon Maslin, who chaired the Committee on Reform Practice and edited *Gates of Mitzvah* after which this volume is patterned. The original version of this work would not have been possible without the support of Temple Emanu-El in New London, Connecticut, and Beth Emet the Free Synagogue in Evanston, Illinois, whose leadership valued my involvement in the Central Conference of American Rabbis and the broader Reform Movement. The current edition of *Mishkan Moeid* owes its existence to the work of Rabbi Hara Person, the publisher of the CCAR Press, who has worked assiduously to create new publications that enhance the work of the rabbinate and mission of Reform Judaism and who is updating and improving past publications.

Tremendous gratitude is due to Rabbi Steven A. Fox, CCAR Chief Executive, who was an enthusiastic supporter of this revision, and to everyone at CCAR Press who helped work on the book, including Debbie Smilow, Ortal Bensky, Rabbi Jillian Cameron, rabbinic interns Josh Beraha and Yael Rooks-Rapport, Debra Hirsch Corman, and Scott-Martin Kosofsky.

Thanks go to all the members of the CCAR Committee on Worship and Practice, who reviewed the manuscript and made helpful suggestions, including Rabbi Elaine Zecher, chair, and Rabbis David Adelson, Nicole Greninger, Rosie Haim, Tamar Malino, Joel Mosbacher, Rex Perlmeter, Beth Schwartz, Joel Sisenwine, Joseph Skloot, and Rabbi Cantor Alison Wissot.

I am deeply grateful to all of my colleagues who have contributed new essays or sections of essays to add new dimensions to the book. As always nothing I do is possible without the loving support of my wife of more than forty-six years, Elaine. My children Seth and Jeremy Knobel, their wives Dara and Alyssa, and my six grandchildren Leah, Alana, Heather, Stephen, Lily, and Oliver give meaning to my existence.

—RABBI PETER S. KNOBEL, *Ph.D.*

RELIGIOUS PRACTICE

Judaism emphasizes action rather than creed as the primary expression of a religious life, the means by which we strive to achieve universal justice and peace. Reform Judaism shares this emphasis on duty and obligation. Our founders stressed that the Jew's ethical responsibilities, personal and social, are enjoined by God. The past century has taught us that the claims made upon us may begin with our ethical obligations, but they extend to many other aspects of Jewish living, including creating a Jewish home centered on family devotion, lifelong study, private prayer and public worship, daily religious observance, keeping the Sabbath and the holy days, celebrating the major events of life, involvement with the synagogue and community, and other activities which promote the survival of the Jewish people and enhance its existence. Within each area of Jewish observance, Reform Jews are called upon to confront the claims of Jewish tradition, however differently perceived, and to exercise their individual autonomy, choosing and creating on the basis of commitment and knowledge.

—From the "Centenary Perspective" adopted by the Central Conference of American Rabbis in 1976

Mishkan Moeid

A Guide to the Jewish Seasons

The Cycle of the Jewish Year

AS THE EARTH rotates upon its axis, night becomes day, and day turns once again into night. As the earth revolves around the sun, autumn gives way to winter, winter yields to spring, spring blossoms into summer, summer once again becomes fall. The moon also exhibits cyclical changes, waxing and waning at regular intervals. The rhythmic movements of the celestial bodies divide the endless flow of time into days, months, and years. By monitoring these repetitions, we have established a calendar to measure the passage of time. The calendar rules our lives, telling us when to work and when to rest, differentiating special days from ordinary days.

As Jews living in the Diaspora, two calendars regulate our lives: the civil and the Jewish. For us the days, the months, and the years bear two dates and two distinct rhythms. This volume, *Mishkan Moeid: A Guide to the Jewish Seasons*, is designed to help Jews feel more clearly the flow of Jewish time.

Every day of the week points toward Shabbat[1]—day of rest, day of joy, day of holiness. Every month begins with Rosh Chodesh, the marking of each new month. Each year begins in the fall with Rosh HaShanah. The blast of the shofar ushers in the New Year, announcing the season of repentance. Yom Kippur follows with its daylong fast and majestic liturgy. We confess our sins and become reconciled with God so that we can begin the new year free from accumulated guilt. Then Sukkot, the joyous celebration of the harvest, reminder of the ancient journey of our people to the Land of Israel, arrives rich with agricultural symbolism.

However, soon fall becomes winter, and the dark nights are illuminated by the brightly burning lights of Chanukah, recalling for us the heroic Maccabees and our people's long struggle to remain Jewish. As winter nears its end, we read the Purim story from the *M'gilah*, and we revel in the miracle of our physical survival despite the numerous attempts to destroy us. Tu BiSh'vat arrives in the middle of winter with its promise of rebirth, reconnecting us to both the natural world, and the Land of Israel.

Spring liberates the world from the grip of winter, and we recall our liberation from Egyptian bondage. We gather at the seder table to recite the words of the Haggadah, to eat the symbolic foods, and to renew our commitment to the liberation of all humanity. From Passover we count seven weeks to Shavuot. During this period, on Yom HaShoah, we mourn the death of six million Jews slaughtered by the Nazis, and mourn again for Israel's fallen on Yom HaZikaron, but our grief gives way to rejoicing when we join in the celebration of Israel's rebirth on Yom HaAtzma-ut.
The counting ends with Shavuot, the festival that celebrates Revelation. We stand as at Mount Sinai with our ancestors, again receiving Torah and entering into the covenant with God.

Summer is soon upon us, and on Tishah B'Av we recall the tragic destructions of the Temples and two periods of sovereignty over the Land of Israel as we lament the historical suffering of our people. Then—the dark mood turns to anticipation as we enter the month of Elul and prepare again to greet the New Year, with Rosh HaShanah.

Mishkan Moeid: A Guide to the Jewish Seasons, like *Gates of Mitzvah*, proceeds from the premise that mitzvah is the key to authentic Jewish existence and to the sanctification of life. This book, too, was conceived to help Jews create Jewish responses to living and to give their lives Jewish depth and character. As Reform Jews, our philosophy is based on the twin commitments to Jewish continuity and to personal freedom of choice.

The edifice of Jewish living is constructed of mitzvot. As a building is constructed one brick at a time, so is a significant Jewish life. Our Sages recognized that the observance of one mitzvah leads to the observance of others. As Ben Azzai said, "One mitzvah brings another in its wake."[2] The secret of observing mitzvot is to begin.

THE JEWISH CALENDAR
Rabbi Alexander Guttmann

In order to appreciate fully the meaning of the Jewish holidays—their relationships to the seasons, to historical events, and to each other—it is necessary to have a basic understanding of the Jewish calendar. One often hears people remark, "The holidays are early this year" or "Reform Jews don't celebrate the second day." From where did the Jewish calendar come? How does it work? What is its significance for us?

The main purpose of the Jewish calendar is, and always has been, to set the dates of the festivals. Our present calendar has its roots in the Torah, but it has been modified by Jewish religious authorities through the ages. The principal rules were established by the Sages and Rabbis of antiquity and were supplemented by medieval scholars. In Talmudic times the regulation of the calendar was the exclusive right of the Jewish leadership in the Land of Israel, particularly that of the *nasi* (patriarch).[3] Since that time, such regulation has been regarded as a task of crucial importance for the observance of Judaism.

The Structure of the Jewish Calendar

The point of departure in regulating the Jewish calendar is the biblical law "Observe the month of Aviv and offer a passover sacrifice to the Eternal your God" (Deuteronomy 16:1). Passover, therefore, must fall every year in the spring at the time of Aviv (specifically, the appearance of the ripening ears of barley). And so, each year the ancient Jewish authorities watched for signs of the approaching spring. If these signs were late, they added an extra month of thirty days (called Adar II) to the year, before the Passover month.[4] Once the time of Passover had been established, the dates of all subsequent festivals would be determined based on whether an extra month (a second Adar) had been added.

In the Bible, the Hebrew months are lunar (i.e., each month begins with the "birth" of the new moon). However, since festivals such as Passover and Sukkot had to occur in the proper agricultural season (i.e., according to the solar year), it is obvious that the Jewish calendar must be lunar-solar. This means that the lunar year (approximately 354 days) and the solar year (approximately 365 days) had to be harmonized and adjusted to each other, a complex process that was meticulously refined by the ancient and medieval Rabbis.

The Jewish day has 24 hours and starts in the evening.[5] The length of the lunar month is traditionally calculated as 29 days, 12 hours, and 793 parts of an hour (divided into 1080 parts). This is the time span between one new moon and the next. Since it is impractical to start a new month at varying hours of the day, the Sages of antiquity ordained that the length of the month should alternate between 29 and 30 days. Since the lunar month is somewhat longer than 29 days and 12 hours, the remainder is taken care of by making the months of Cheshvan and Kislev flexible, that is, they can both have either 29 or 30 days.

The introduction of a permanent Jewish calendar became increasingly urgent after Jews began to spread throughout the world. As Jewry dispersed, regular contacts with the Jewish leadership in the Land of Israel, which had the sole privilege of regulating the calendar, became more and more difficult. The most important step in this process of permanent calendar reform was the adoption in the eighth century CE of a nineteen-year cycle of "intercalation" (i.e., harmonization of the solar and lunar calendars). The adoption of this cycle made the actual physical observation of the new moon and the signs of approaching spring unnecessary. This cycle of nineteen years adjusts the lunar year to the solar year by inserting into it seven leap years (i.e., the additional thirty-day month of Adar) in the following order: every third, sixth, eighth, eleventh, fourteenth, seventeenth, and nineteenth year.[6]

In the Bible, the months are most frequently designated by ordinal numbers. However, there are references both to such ancient names as Ziv, Eitanim, and Aviv and to some of the now customary names Kislev, Tevet, Adar, Nisan, Sivan, and Elul, which are of Babylonian origin.[7] But, it is only since the first century CE that the Hebrew calendar has employed the now traditional month names of Nisan, Iyar, Sivan, Tammuz, Av, Elul, Tishrei, Cheshvan, Kislev, Tevet, Sh'vat, and Adar.

AD, AM, BC, BCE, and CE

The Jewish tradition of counting years since the creation of the world has its roots in early Talmudic times, but it was not adopted authoritatively until several centuries later. In biblical times, dates were referred to as being "two years before the earthquake," "the year of the death of King Uzziah," and so on. In Talmudic times, we find instances of dating from the creation of the world,[8] but this was adopted as *the* Jewish method only much later, as a response to Christian dating.

It was in the eighth century that Christians began to date their documents generally as AD (*anno Domini*, "the year of the Lord"), and so it is hardly a coincidence that in the eighth and ninth centuries we find more and more Jewish documents dated "since the creation of the world" (sometimes referred to as AM, *anno mundi*, "the year of the world"). Obviously, calculating dates based on Christian theological principles was not acceptable to Jews; nevertheless, it was not until the twelfth century that dating "since the creation" was accepted by Jews universally.

Only a minority of Jews today would take the traditional Jewish date as being literally "since the creation of the world." Most of us accept the findings of science indicating that our world is billions of years old, rather than some fifty-seven hundred. But the date that changes each year with Rosh HaShanah is a convenient reference point to the beginnings of Jewish history and relates us to a venerable tradition.

Jewish texts often use the designations BCE (before the Common Era) and CE (Common Era) with the civil year to avoid any dating related to Christianity. To determine the Jewish year for a given civil year, the number 3,760 is added; conversely, to find the civil year for a given Jewish year, 3,760 is subtracted. Of course, since the Jewish year changes with Rosh HaShanah, the number to work with from Rosh HaShanah to December 31 is 3,761.

The Second Days of the Festivals

The greatest change that the Rabbis made in the festival calendar was the addition of a day to each of the holidays ordained in the Torah, except Yom Kippur. This was done in the early Talmudic period (i.e., first century CE). Compelling circumstances at that time forced the Rabbis to make this change.

Not only was the confirmation and sanctification of the new moon—and therefore the new month—the duty of the authorities in the Land of Israel, referred to historically as Palestine at that time, but theirs was also the task of communicating the dates of the new moons to every Jewish community. This was a task of vital importance, as the new moon determines the dates of the festivals. At an earlier time, the new moon (i.e., the first of the month) was communicated to all the Jews in Palestine and the Diaspora by kindling flares on hilltops. However, after the Samaritans kindled flares at the wrong time to confuse the Jews, the news about the new moon had to be communicated by messengers.[9] The change was introduced by Judah HaNasi (ca. 135–200 CE).[10]

Since it often happened that the messengers did not arrive in time at the places of their destination outside of Palestine because of road hazards, wars, or political upheavals, a second day was added to the holidays for the Jews in the Diaspora. This ensured that one of the two days on which they celebrated the festival was indeed the proper holy day. In Palestine the addition of these "second days" to the festivals was not necessary because the news about the sighting of the new moon, proclaimed in Palestine,[11] reached every part of that land in due time, that is, prior to the dates of the festivals. The exception was Rosh HaShanah, which falls on the first day of the month of Tishrei, making timely communication about this new moon, even in Palestine, impossible.[12]

During the Talmudic period, a stable, scientifically determined calendar was adopted, and so the pragmatic need for second days disappeared. But the Palestinian authorities did not abolish these extra days of observance for Diaspora Jews (nor the second day of Rosh HaShanah for Palestinian Jews) because of the Rabbinic principle that we "may not change the custom of [our] ancestors."[13]

Reform Judaism, from its very inception, abolished the second days of the festivals[14] and returned to the observance of seven one-day festivals as ordained in the Torah: the first day of Passover (Leviticus 23:7 and elsewhere), the seventh day of Passover (Leviticus 23:8), Shavuot (Leviticus 23:21), Rosh HaShanah (Leviticus 23:24), Yom Kippur (Leviticus 23:27), the first day of Sukkot (Leviticus 23:35), and Sh'mini Atzeret (Leviticus 23:36), though some Reform congregations have since returned to a two-day observance of Rosh HaShanah. However, except for the second days, Reform Judaism has always celebrated the festivals according to the traditional calendar. In effect, this means that Reform Jews today celebrate the festivals according to the religious calendar observed in the Land of Israel.

Every Day

JUDAISM PROVIDES RICH OPPORTUNITIES to transform the ordinary into the sacred. The mitzvot of Shabbat and the Festivals sanctify certain days by linking them to significant moments in Jewish history or to important Judaic concepts. The same may be said of the mitzvot that mark the various stages of the Jewish life cycle. While this volume concentrates on the mitzvot of Shabbat and the Festivals, the practice of Judaism is lived every day.

According to Jewish tradition, mitzvot may be divided into two general categories: those that define the divine-human relationship (*mitzvot bein adam laMakom*) and those that define the proper relationship between individuals and society (*mitzvot bein adam lachaveiro*). While space does not permit an adequate treatment of either of these categories, a few examples will suffice to indicate the comprehensive nature of mitzvah.

Daily prayer,[1] table blessings,[2] and Torah study[3] are an integral part of Jewish living and would be classified as belonging to the category of mitzvot that deal with the divine-human relationship. Honoring one's parents,[4] honesty in business transactions,[5] loving one's neighbor,[6] and judging impartially[7] are but a few of the mitzvot that define a person's obligations to society. The two categories are not separate; they complement and amplify each other. For example, Torah study teaches us to behave ethically and at the same time teaches us to observe the Festivals. The prophets denounce a society in which ritual takes precedence over ethics.[8] The task of joining ritual and ethics is the task of the Jew every day. Therefore, a volume on the mitzvot of Shabbat and the Festivals must begin with the concept of the sanctification of every day.

Rabbi Eliezer taught, "Repent one day before your death." But his disciples asked, "How is it possible to repent one day before death, since no one knows on what day one will die?" Therefore, taught Rabbi Eliezer, live each day as though it were your last.[9]

Shabbat
שבת

Shabbat

SHABBAT IS A UNIQUE Jewish contribution to our civilization. It is a weekly respite from endless toil and competition. Interrupting the pursuit of wealth and power, and concerns with the chores and responsibilities of every life, it turns us toward the meaning of human existence. Given a day without labor, we can concentrate on being a creature fashioned in the divine image and on our role as stewards of Creation and as instruments for justice and compassion. On Shabbat we take delight in the beauty of Creation, spending time with family, friends, and community and recharging our physical and spiritual batteries for the week ahead.

Jewish authenticity and a life of mitzvah are inexorably bound up with Shabbat observance. By celebrating Shabbat as an island of holy time in a sea of secular activity, the Jewish people have been able to survive the forces of assimilation and corruption. So crucial is Shabbat to Jewish survival that Achad Ha-am was moved to say, "More than Israel has kept Shabbat, Shabbat has kept Israel."[1] The essential themes of Jewish theology—Creation, Redemption, and Revelation—are woven into the fabric of Shabbat liturgy and practice. Words and deeds, performing certain acts and refraining from others, make Shabbat unique, significant, and joyous (see "For Further Reading").

The two different versions of the Ten Commandments in Exodus and Deuteronomy provide different reasons for the observance of Shabbat. In Exodus it is connected with Creation,[2] and in Deuteronomy with the Exodus from Egypt.[3] Shabbat is a day on which we celebrate both the emergence of the world from chaos to order and the emergence of the Jewish people from slavery to freedom. Shabbat is God's time, the God who created the world and who redeemed Israel. Every Shabbat, when we lift the *Kiddush* cup for blessing, we remember the One who created the universe[4] and blessed our people with freedom.[5]

As a reminder of Creation, Shabbat affords us a singular opportunity to reflect on the marvel of the universe and to contemplate our part in the continuing process of Creation. As sojourners in, and not owners of, the world, ours is the role of caretakers and preservers, not exploiters and destroyers. As a reminder of the Exodus from Egypt, Shabbat commits us to the ideals of freedom, justice, and compassion. Having experienced bondage and degradation as well as liberation, we become attuned to the needs of others. Thus, Shabbat becomes a model of the way the world *could* be, the ideal into which we, as God's partners, can help to transform it.

Our understanding of Shabbat can be further enhanced by recognizing another difference between the two versions of the Ten Commandments. Exodus 20:8 begins with the word *zachor*, "remember," implying cognition; Deuteronomy 5:12 opens with the word *shamor*, "observe," implying action. *Zachor* requires a spiritual response, *shamor* a physical response. The former prescribes rest as an act of sanctification, and the latter prescribes it as a refraining from labor.

An understanding of the deeper meaning of work and rest in today's society is important in thinking through the observance and enjoyment of Shabbat (see "Shabbat as Protest," by Rabbi W. Gunther Plaut, pages 124–125, below; and *Gates of Shabbat: A Guide for Observing Shabbat*, by Rabbi Mark Dov Shapiro [Central Conference of American Rabbis, 1996]. A primary aspect of Shabbat observance is the avoidance of gainful work and of all such activities that do not contribute to the celebration of Shabbat as a day of delight (*oneg*), a day of holiness (*k'dushah*), and a day of rest (*m'nuchah*). Shabbat is a day of leisure in which time is used to express our humanness. Through prayer and song, study and reflection, we celebrate the sanctity of Shabbat. The rest and delight of Shabbat provide opportunities for thoughtful reevaluation and new perspective, for defining and recognizing goals. Once a week we are called upon to cease the struggle of extracting a living from the world and are summoned to pay attention to the inner core of our existence.

On Shabbat we focus on people, not things. The cacophony of the daily struggle gives way to the symphony of life. A legend teaches that on Shabbat we acquire an extra soul[6] that enables us to appreciate more fully our families, friends, and ourselves. We experience the pleasure of being a part of the community of Israel reaching toward perfection. Shabbat is also a day that points toward the future. It is a day of hope and anticipation of the messianic fulfillment, which the Talmud describes as *yom shekulo Shabbat*, "a time of eternal Shabbat."[7]

The Mitzvah of Shabbat Observance

לִשְׁמוֹר שַׁבָּת
Lishmor Shabbat

It is a mitzvah for every Jew, single or married, young or old, to observe Shabbat. The unique status of Shabbat is demonstrated by its being the only one of the holy days to be mentioned in the Ten Commandments.[8] Its observance distinguishes the Jewish people as a covenant people.

> The Israelite people shall keep the Sabbath, observing the Sabbath throughout the ages as a covenant for all time: it shall be a sign for all time between Me and the people of Israel. (Exodus 31:16–17)

Shabbat observance involves both positive and negative mitzvot, that is, both doing and refraining from doing.

The Mitzvah of Delight

עֹנֶג
Oneg

It is a mitzvah to take delight in Shabbat observance, as Isaiah said, "You shall call Shabbat a delight" (58:13). *Oneg* implies celebration and relaxation, sharing time with loved ones, enjoying the beauty of nature, leisurely eating a delicious meal made special with conviviality and song, visiting with friends and relatives, taking a leisurely stroll, reading, and enjoying music. All of these are appropriate expressions of *oneg*. Because of the special emphasis on *oneg*, Jewish tradition also recommends sexual relations between loving partners on Shabbat.[9]

A simple list of activities is not adequate to describe *oneg*. It is a total atmosphere that is created by those activities that refresh the body and the spirit and promote serenity.

The Mitzvah of Sanctification

קְדוּשָׁה
K'dushah

It is a mitzvah to hallow Shabbat by setting it apart from the other days of the week. The Torah depicts Shabbat as the culmination of Creation and describes God as blessing it and sanctifying it (making it שַׁבָּת קֹדֶשׁ, *Shabbat Kodesh*).[10] Every Jew should partake of this day's special nature and abstain from that which lessens his or her awareness of its distinctive character. Shabbat is distinguished from the other days of the week so that those who observe it may be transformed by its holiness—*k'dushah*.

The Mitzvah of Rest

מְנוּחָה
M'nuchah

It is a mitzvah to rest on Shabbat. However, Shabbat rest (*m'nuchah*) implies much more than simply refraining from work.[11] The concept of Shabbat rest includes both physical relaxation (for example, a Shabbat afternoon nap) and tranquility of mind and spirit. On Shabbat one deliberately turns away from weekday pressures and activities. The pace of life on Shabbat should be different from the rest of the week.

Conversations might focus not on the problems of everyday existence but rather on the meaning of life and the awareness of beauty in God's creation.[12] One might choose, for example, to turn off the smartphone and e-mail, refrain from making business appointments, and concentrate on the beauty of one's surroundings and enjoy the relaxed atmosphere of Shabbat.[13]

If the week is characterized by competition, rush, and turmoil, their absence will contribute to serenity and to the rejuvenation of body and spirit. It is this unique quality of *m'nuchah* that moves our tradition to call Shabbat "a foretaste of the days of the Messiah."[14]

The Mitzvah of Refraining from Work

It is a mitzvah to refrain from work on Shabbat, as it is said: "Six days you shall labor and do all your work, but the seventh day is a Sabbath of the Eternal your God; you shall not do any work" (Exodus 20:9–10). Abstinence from work is a major expression of Shabbat observance; however, it is no simple matter to define work today.[15] Certain activities that some do to earn a living, others do for relaxation or to express their creativity. Where circumstances require individuals to perform work on Shabbat, they should nevertheless bear in mind that refraining from work is a major goal of Shabbat observance, and they can still find ways to set the day apart by engaging in some Shabbat mitzvot. Individuals who are responsible for the health and safety of the community such as doctors, nurses, and first responders are often required to perform these functions on Shabbat. Jewish law understands these activities as fitting into the category of *pikuach nefesh* (the saving of human life), which overrides the prohibitions on working on Shabbat. However, even these individuals can still find ways to acknowledge the holiness of Shabbat and perform these duties *lichvod Shabbat* (in honor of Shabbat). Clearly, though, one should avoid normal occupations or professions on Shabbat whenever possible and engage only in those types of activities that enhance the *oneg* (delight), *m'nuchah* (rest), and *k'dushah* (holiness) of the day (see *"M'nuchah* and *M'lachah*: On Observing the Sabbath in Reform Judaism" by Mark Washofsky, pages 126–129).

Public Events on Shabbat

In scheduling and participating in public events on Shabbat, the community and individuals should take into consideration whether those events contribute to the celebration of Shabbat. For example, the participation in an event that alleviates human suffering would be a reminder of the Exodus from Egypt, and an event or activity that protects the environment would be a reminder of Creation.

The Mitzvah of Avoiding Activities That Violate or Appear to Violate the Sanctity of Shabbat

It is a mitzvah to avoid all public activity that violates or gives the appearance of violating the sanctity of Shabbat.[16] The guiding principle of Shabbat activities should be the enhancing of the distinctive Shabbat qualities of *k'dushah*, *m'nuchah*, and *oneg*.

The Mitzvah of Preparation

הֲכָנָה לְשַׁבָּת
Hachanah L'Shabbat

It is a mitzvah to prepare for Shabbat. According to the Rabbis, this mitzvah is implied in the Exodus version of the Ten Commandments, "Remember the Sabbath day and keep it holy" (Exodus 20:8).[17] Preparations may begin well before Shabbat by buying special food[18] or waiting for Shabbat to wear a new garment.[19]

Jewish tradition compares the arrival of Shabbat to the arrival of an important guest.[20] Therefore, before the beginning of Shabbat special preparations are necessary. They could include cleaning the house, setting a festive table, cooking a celebratory meal, adorning the dining table with flowers, attending to personal grooming, and wearing clothing appropriate for Shabbat.

Because Shabbat is not only a day of physical rest but of spiritual rejuvenation as well, it is important to try to allow time prior to the commencement of Shabbat to disengage from weekday concerns and create an atmosphere and mood conducive to the serenity of Shabbat. Wherever possible, all members of the household should be involved in Shabbat preparations.[21]

The Mitzvah of Hospitality

הַכְנָסַת אוֹרְחִים
Hachnasat Or'chim

It is a mitzvah to invite guests to join in the celebration of Shabbat.[22] Ideally, no one should have to observe Shabbat alone. Therefore, one should pay particular attention to those who are alone. The delight of Shabbat is increased by gathering with others. The mitzvah is called *hachnasat or'chim*, and Jewish tradition includes it among those that merit eternal reward.

The Mitzvah of *Tzedakah*

צְדָקָה
Tzedakah

It is always a mitzvah to give *tzedakah*.[23] Following the example of Talmudic sages, the tradition has recognized the final moments before Shabbat as one of the regular opportunities to perform the mitzvah.[24] Placing money in a *tzedakah* box just prior to lighting the Shabbat candles is an excellent way to observe this mitzvah and to teach it to children. *Tzedakah* is often translated as "charity," but the Jewish concept of *tzedakah* is much broader. The word is derived from *tzedek*— "righteousness" or "justice"—and the implication is that righteousness and justice require the *sharing* of one's substance with others because ultimately, "the earth is Adonai's" (Psalm 24:1), and we are but stewards of whatever we possess. (See "*Tzedakah*," pages 162–164.)

The Mitzvah of Kindling Shabbat Candles

הַדְלָקַת נֵרוֹת
Hadlakat Nerot

The formal observance of Shabbat begins with the mitzvah of the kindling of Shabbat candles,[25] *hadlakat nerot*, followed by the recitation of the accompanying blessing:[26]

בָּרוּךְ אַתָּה, יְיָ אֱלֹהֵינוּ, *Baruch atah, Adonai Eloheinu,*

מֶלֶךְ הָעוֹלָם, אֲשֶׁר קִדְּשָׁנוּ *Melech haolam, asher kid'shanu,*

בְּמִצְוֹתָיו וְצִוָּנוּ *b'mitzvotav v'tzivanu,*

לְהַדְלִיק נֵר שֶׁל שַׁבָּת. *l'hadlik ner shel Shabbat.*

Blessed are You, Adonai our God, Sovereign of the universe, who hallows us with mitzvot, commanding us to kindle the light of Shabbat.

A complete ritual welcoming Shabbat can be found in *On the Doorposts of Your House*, pages 57–69, as well as in *Mishkan T'filah: A Reform Siddur*, pages 120–143. Tradition prescribes that the mitzvah of *hadlakat nerot* is the privilege of the women of the household, but where there are no women, a man may also perform it.[27]

The lighting of candles marks the formal beginning of Shabbat;[28] therefore, the candles are kindled before the Shabbat meal. The candles may be kindled eighteen minutes before sunset or when we gather to begin the observance of Shabbat.

It is customary to light at least two candles[29] corresponding to the words זָכוֹר (*zachor*), remember, and שָׁמוֹר (*shamor*), observe, in the two versions of the Decalogue.[30] However, in some homes it is the custom to light one candle for each member of the household.

The Mitzvah of *Kiddush*

קִדּוּשׁ

Kiddush

It is a mitzvah to recite *Kiddush* over wine or grape juice.[31] *Kiddush* is a blessing that proclaims the sanctity of Shabbat, thanks God for the gift of Shabbat, and emphasizes the themes of Shabbat as a commemoration of Creation (*zikaron l'maaseih v'reishit*) and a memorial to the Exodus from Egypt (*zeicher litziat Mitzrayim*). In many households a *Kiddush* cup is provided for each participant. The text of *Kiddush* can be found in *On the Doorposts of Our House*, pages 61–63, and in *Mishkan T'filah: A Reform Siddur*, pages 122–123, 604.

The Mitzvah of Blessing Children

בִּרְכַּת הַבָּנִים וְהַבָּנוֹת

Birkat haBanim v'haBanot

It is a mitzvah for a parent or parents to bless their children at the Shabbat table each week.[32] Families may establish their own ritual or use the traditional words:

FOR A BOY

יְשִׂימְךָ אֱלֹהִים   *Y'simcha Elohim*

כְּאֶפְרַיִם וְכִמְנַשֶּׁה.   *k'Efrayim v'chiM'nasheh.*

May God inspire you to live like Ephraim and Menasseh.

FOR A GIRL

יְשִׂימֵךְ אֱלֹהִים כְּשָׂרָה,   *Y'simeich Elohim k'Sarah,*

רִבְקָה, רָחֵל וְלֵאָה.   *Rivkah, Rachel v'Leah.*

May God inspire you to live like Sarah, Rebecca, Rachel and Leah.

יְבָרֶכְךָ יְיָ וְיִשְׁמְרֶךָ.   *Y'varech'cha Adonai v'yishm'recha.*

יָאֵר יְיָ פָּנָיו אֵלֶיךָ וִיחֻנֶּךָּ.   *Ya-eir Adonai panav eilecha vichuneka.*

יִשָּׂא יְיָ פָּנָיו אֵלֶיךָ   *Yisa Adonai panav eilecha*

וְיָשֵׂם לְךָ שָׁלוֹם.   *v'yaseim l'cha shalom.*

May God bless you and keep you.
May God's light shine upon you, and may God be gracious to you.
May you feel God's Presence within you always,
    and may you find peace.

Children may wish to respond to the blessing with words of their
own or with the following text:

הָרַחֲמָן הוּא יְבָרֵךְ   *Harachaman hu y'vareich*

אֶת אָבִי מוֹרִי   *et avi mori*

בַּעַל הַבַּיִת הַזֶּה   *baal habayit hazeh*

וְאֶת אִמִּי מוֹרָתִי   *v'et imi morati*

בַּעֲלַת הַבַּיִת הַזֶּה.   *baalat habayit hazeh.*

May God bless my beloved father and mother,
who guide our home and family.[33]

In addition, spouses recite mutual words of praise. They may
wish to use their own words, portions of Proverbs 31 (in praise of a
woman), or portions of Psalm 112 (in praise of a man), which can be
found in *On the Doorposts of Your House,* page 59, and in *Mishkan
T'filah: A Reform Siddur,* page 602.

The Mitzvah of *HaMotzi*

הַמּוֹצִיא   On Shabbat, this blessing is usually recited over חַלָּה
HaMotzi   (challah). It is customary to have two challot on the
Shabbat table as a reminder of the double portion of
manna that fell on Friday, as no manna would fall on Shabbat (Exodus 16:4–5). In many homes the challot are torn rather than cut so
that they are not touched by a metal object such as a knife, to symbolize the fact that Shabbat is a day of peace.

It is a mitzvah to recite *HaMotzi* (the blessing over bread):

בָּרוּךְ אַתָּה, יְיָ אֱלֹהֵינוּ,   *Baruch atah, Adonai Eloheinu,*

מֶלֶךְ הָעוֹלָם,   *Melech haolam,*

הַמּוֹצִיא לֶחֶם מִן הָאָרֶץ.   *hamotzi lechem min haaretz.*

Our praise to You, Adonai our God, Sovereign of the universe, who brings forth bread from the earth.

When the pieces of challah are distributed, some sprinkle them with salt as a reminder that the table is a מִזְבֵּחַ מְעַט (*mizbei-ach m'at*), a miniature altar.[34] After the destruction of the Temple, many of the priestly practices were transferred to the home. The home was understood to be a sacred place a *mikdash m'at* (Temple writ small). The family table, then, was understood as being a *mizbei-ach m'at* (altar writ small). Meals were then part of religious observance and, properly conceived, were part of the worship of God.

The Shabbat Table

סְעוּדַת שַׁבָּת   The mitzvah of taking delight in Shabbat can

S'udat Shabbat   be expressed by making the Shabbat meal special.[35] One may choose to serve favorite foods at the Shabbat table. The custom of singing זְמִירוֹת (*z'mirot*), Shabbat songs, brings even greater joy to the Shabbat meal.

According to the Talmud, our conversation on Shabbat should be different from that of the rest of the week.[36] In keeping with the spirit of Shabbat, we might discuss the weekly Torah portion or matters concerning the human condition. By focusing on those matters that increase our awareness and sensitivity to general human and Jewish values, our shared humanity as well as our Jewishness is heightened.

The Mitzvah of *Birkat HaMazon*

בִּרְכַּת הַמָּזוֹן   At the conclusion of all meals, and of course

Birkat HaMazon   on Shabbat, it is a mitzvah to recite the Blessing after Eating (*Birkat HaMazon*).[37] The text can be found in *Blessings for the Table*, pages 18–22 or 23–31; in *On*

the Doorposts of Your House, pages 23–35 or 36–40; or in *Mishkan T'filah: A Reform Siddur*, pages 606–609.

The Mitzvah of Congregational Worship

עֲבוֹדָה

Avodah

It is a mitzvah to join the congregation in worship on Shabbat.[38] As members of the Jewish people, we have personal and communal responsibilities. Participation in the congregational worship service is one such communal obligation, but our attendance at services goes beyond obligation. The public celebration of Shabbat through prayer, song, and Torah study is the heart of the Shabbat experience. Regular Shabbat worship draws us into the circle of community, strengthening our ties to one another and to the historical values that we as Jews hold dear. If illness prevents attendance at services, Shabbat prayers may be recited at home. Many synagogues also offer services through the Internet or over the telephone to allow one to participate from home in the case of illness or other inability to be physically present at synagogue. *Mishkan T'filah*, the Reform prayerbook, is also available in digital format for those who are prevented from attending communal worship.

The Shabbat Noon Meal

סְעוּדַת שַׁבָּת

Se'udat Shabbat

The noon meal provides additional opportunities for making Shabbat special. The mitzvot of *Kiddush*,[39] *HaMotzi*, and *Birkat HaMazon* are observed, as well as the singing of *z'mirot*, as on Friday evening (see above). The texts can be found in *Blessings for the Table* (pp. 15, 18), *On the Doorposts of Your House* (pp. 21, 23), and *Mishkan T'filah: A Reform Siddur* (p. 606). At the noon meal also, conversation should be in keeping with the spirit of Shabbat (see above).

The Mitzvah of Study

תַּלְמוּד תּוֹרָה

Talmud Torah

Torah study is a daily mitzvah,[40] which is even more meaningful on Shabbat.[41] The reading of the סִדְרָה (*sidrah*), the weekly Torah selection, during the synagogue service should lead to further appropriate reading and related study.[42] By joining with family or friends to study on Shabbat, the joy of learning is increased and the observance of Shabbat is enriched through intellectual and spiritual stimulation and companionship. On Shabbat afternoon, it is the custom to study the weekly *sidrah* as well as some other work of Jewish significance—traditional texts such as *Pirkei Avot* or contemporary works that increase one's Jewish knowledge.

The Mitzvah of Visiting the Sick

בִּיקוּר חוֹלִים

Bikur Cholim

It is a mitzvah to visit the ill and shut-ins at any time.[43] By performing this mitzvah on Shabbat, one brings them a measure of Shabbat joy.

Weddings and Wedding Preparations

Weddings should not take place on Shabbat.[44] When making unavoidable final preparations for a Saturday evening wedding, care should be taken to preserve the spirit of Shabbat preceding the wedding.

Mourning on Shabbat

שִׁבְעָה

Shivah

Since Shabbat is meant to be a day of joy, formal mourning (i.e., the observance of shivah) is interrupted for the observance of Shabbat. On Shabbat and the Festivals mourners should attend synagogue services and observe the mitzvot of that day[45] (see *Gates of Mitzvah*, page 60, D-3). Funerals are not held on Shabbat, nor do people visit the cemetery[46] (see *Gates of Mitzvah*, page 55, C-4).

Maintaining the Special Quality of Shabbat

One should maintain and enjoy the special quality of Shabbat throughout the entire day, from the lighting of Shabbat candles until the recitation of *Havdalah*. This may be done by choosing those activities that will complement and enrich one's spiritual life. Special care should be taken to conduct oneself in such a manner and to participate in such activities as will promote the distinctive Shabbat qualities of *k'dushah*, *m'nuchah*, and *oneg*.

The Mitzvah of *Havdalah*

הַבְדָּלָה
Havdalah

At the conclusion of Shabbat, it is a mitzvah to recite *Havdalah*,[47] separating the holy from the ordinary and Shabbat from the other days of the week. The *Havdalah* service includes four blessings:

OVER WINE

בָּרוּךְ אַתָּה, יְיָ אֱלֹהֵינוּ,   *Baruch atah, Adonai Eloheinu,*
מֶלֶךְ הָעוֹלָם,   *Melech haolam,*
בּוֹרֵא פְּרִי הַגָּפֶן.   *borei p'ri hagafen.*

Praise to You, Adonai our God, Sovereign of the universe, Creator of the fruit of the vine.

OVER SPICES

בָּרוּךְ אַתָּה, יְיָ אֱלֹהֵינוּ,   *Baruch atah, Adonai Eloheinu,*
מֶלֶךְ הָעוֹלָם,   *Melech haolam,*
בּוֹרֵא מִינֵי בְשָׂמִים.   *borei minei v'samim.*

Praise to You, Adonai our God, Sovereign of the universe, Creator of varied spices.

OVER LIGHT

בָּרוּךְ אַתָּה, יְיָ אֱלֹהֵינוּ,   *Baruch atah, Adonai Eloheinu,*
מֶלֶךְ הָעוֹלָם,   *Melech haolam,*
בּוֹרֵא מְאוֹרֵי הָאֵשׁ.   *borei m'orei ha-eish.*

Praise to You, Adonai our God, Sovereign of the universe, Creator of the lights of fire.

בָּרוּךְ אַתָּה, יְיָ אֱלֹהֵינוּ, *Baruch atah, Adonai Eloheinu,*

מֶלֶךְ הָעוֹלָם, *Melech haolam,*

הַמַּבְדִּיל בֵּין קֹדֶשׁ לְחוֹל, *hamavdil bein kodesh l'chol,*

בֵּין אוֹר לְחֹשֶׁךְ, *bein or l'choshech,*

בֵּין יִשְׂרָאֵל לָעַמִּים, *bein Yisrael laamim,*

בֵּין יוֹם הַשְּׁבִיעִי *bein yom hash'vi-i*

לְשֵׁשֶׁת יְמֵי הַמַּעֲשֶׂה. *l'sheishet y'mei hamaaseh.*

בָּרוּךְ אַתָּה, יְיָ, *Baruch atah, Adonai.*

הַמַּבְדִּיל בֵּין קֹדֶשׁ לְחוֹל. *hamavdil bein kodesh l'chol.*

Praise to You, Adonai our God, Sovereign of the universe, who distinguishes between the holy and ordinary, between light and dark, between Israel and the nations, between the seventh day and the six days of work. Praise to You, Adonai, who distinguishes between the holy and ordinary.

A special multi-wicked braided candle is used,[48] which is customarily held by the youngest person present. At the conclusion of the service, the participants wish each other, *Shavua tov* (A good week).

The Days of Awe
ימים נוראים

The Days of Awe (Yamim Noraim)

Rosh HaShanah

> *In the seventh month, on the first day of the month, you shall observe complete rest, a sacred occasion commemorated with loud blasts.* —LEVITICUS 23:24

> *In the seventh month, on the first day of the month, you shall observe a sacred occasion: you shall not work at your occupations. You shall observe it as a day when the horn is sounded.* —NUMBERS 29:1

> *On the first day of the seventh month, Ezra the priest brought the Teaching before the congregation, men and women and all who could listen with understanding. He read from it, facing the square before the Water Gate, from the first light until midday.* —NEHEMIAH 8:2–3

ROSH HASHANAH, which falls on the first of the Hebrew month of Tishrei, marks the beginning of the new year.[1] It is, however, far more than the first day of the calendar year. It is the beginning of a ten-day period of rigorous introspection and self-examination that continues through Yom Kippur.[2] So important did the Rabbis consider this period, that they proclaimed the whole of the preceding month of Elul as a period of preparation.[3]

The Torah designates the first of Tishrei as "a sacred occasion commemorated with loud blasts" (Leviticus 23:24; see also Numbers 29:1). For Jews the sound of the shofar became a multifaceted symbol recalling past events, looking to the messianic future—a time of universal peace and prosperity, proclaiming divine sovereignty—and much more.[4] The sound of the shofar is a call to hearken to the divine summons, to examine our hearts, and to plead our case before the Eternal Judge.

Rabbinic tradition identifies Rosh HaShanah as Yom HaDin, "Judgment Day." In this spirit, a Talmudic parable pictures God as sitting in judgment of the world as a whole, as well as each individual on Rosh HaShanah.[5] The image of God as Judge, about to inscribe human beings according to their deeds in the appropriate Book of Life, underscores the Jewish concept of human beings as moral free agents responsible for the choices that they make. We are further encouraged to believe that our fate, and indeed the fate of the entire world, depend upon our every act.[6]

Following from the theme of divine judgment is the concept of making amends for the past and beginning the year with a clean slate. According to Jewish tradition, "repentance, prayer, and charity [*t'shuvah*, *t'filah*, and *tzedakah*] temper judgment's severe decree."[7] Through these mitzvot, Jews seek to reestablish their relationship with God and with other human beings and accomplish reconciliation with both. This is also the opportunity to forgive ourselves for wrongdoings committed during the past year. While we cannot determine our fate, how we respond to the exigencies of life is under our control, and these three mitzvot help us to persevere in spite of the inevitable vicissitudes of life.

The theme of Rosh HaShanah is that in spite of human weakness, "the gates of repentance are always open."[8] The struggle for righteousness never ceases. The mitzvot and customs of Rosh HaShanah are designed to help Jews enter into the new year with a new spirit so that they might be inscribed in the Book of Life and Blessing.

The Month of Elul

אֱלוּל
Elul

סְלִיחוֹת
S'lichot

שׁוֹפָר
Shofar

It is a mitzvah to prepare for the Days of Awe during the preceding month of Elul.[9] Special penitential prayers called *S'lichot* are added to the daily liturgy,[10] and many congregations have a late-night *S'lichot* service, usually on the Saturday night before Rosh HaShanah.[11] The text of the service can be found in *Gates of Forgiveness*. Some congregations follow the custom of blowing the shofar each weekday during the month of Elul as a reminder of the approaching season of atonement.[12]

Since proper preparation includes serious reflection and self-examination, it is important to set aside regular periods of time for contemplation and study. The High Holy Day liturgy of *Gates of Repentance* and other appropriate texts for study are listed in the section "For Further Reading."

It is customary to visit the graves of relatives during the month of Elul and during the Ten Days of Repentance.[13] Through these visits, links to preceding generations are reinforced, and by contemplating the virtues of the deceased and their devotion to faith and people, we find strength and inspiration. (An appropriate prayer to recite at the grave can be found in *On the Doorposts of Your House*, page 209.)

The Mitzvah of Observing Rosh HaShanah

It is a mitzvah to observe Rosh HaShanah on the first of Tishrei. As the Torah teaches, "In the seventh month, on the first day of the month, you shall observe a sacred occasion: you shall not work at your occupations. You shall observe it as a day when the horn is sounded" (Numbers 29:1).

The Mitzvah of Repentance

תְּשׁוּבָה
T'shuvah

It is a mitzvah to express one's personal repentance (*t'shuvah*) on Rosh HaShanah.[14] Through repentance (*t'shuvah*), prayer (*t'filah*), and charity (*tzedakah*), one begins moving toward reconciliation with God, other human beings, and oneself. This process reaches its climax on Yom Kippur.

Repentance begins with the recognition of one's faults, failures, and weaknesses and the commitment to change and sincere efforts to rectify impaired relationships. Through discussion with friends and family, one seeks understanding and forgiveness and, where appropriate, to offer compensation to right the wrong that one has inflicted. The reciting of confessional prayers opens the heart to repentance. The goal of repentance is to turn (לָשׁוּב, *lashuv*) the individual and the community toward each other and toward God and for the individual to become a new person.

Tashlich (literally, "you shall cast off") is an annual ceremony of symbolically casting off the sins of the past year. The Hebrew root *shin-lamed-kaf* means "to throw away." It takes place on Rosh Ha-Shanah afternoon, unless the first day is Shabbat, in which case it takes place on the second day in congregations that observe two days of Rosh HaShanah. This ceremony became popular among Ashkenazic Jews in the Middle Ages and has become a beloved portion of the High Holy Day cycle in many communities.

The custom seems to be derived from the following verses from the Book of Micah:

> *Who is a God like You, pardoning iniquity and passing over the transgression of the remnant of Your posses-sion? God does not retain anger forever, because God delights in showing clemency. God will again have com-passion upon us; our iniquities will be tread underfoot. You will cast all our sins into the depths of the sea.*
> —MICAH 7:18–20

The custom of *Tashlich* involves going to a body of water and symbolically casting off one's sins by throwing small pieces of bread into the water while reciting a very brief liturgy. Its meaningful symbolism is explained by Rabbi Moses Isserles, who added glosses to Joseph Caro's work, the *Shulchan Aruch* (the "code of Jewish law"), who wrote: "The depths of the sea saw the genesis of Creation; therefore to throw bread into the sea on New Year's Day, the anniversary of Creation, is an appropriate tribute to the Creator" (*Torat HaOlah* 3:56).

The Mitzvah of *Tzedakah*

צְדָקָה
Tzedakah

It is always a mitzvah to give *tzedakah*, but on Rosh HaShanah, this mitzvah takes on added signifi-cance.[15] *Tzedakah* is one of the mitzvot that tempers judgment's "severe decree." Through direct aid to the needy and to the institutions that serve those in need, and through aid to synagogues and other institutions that support the spiritual and cultural life of the Jewish community, we exemplify our obligation as human beings to share the bounty of the earth with others. The period immediately before Rosh HaShanah is an especially appropriate time to fulfill this mitzvah.

In many homes, it is the custom to deposit money in the *tzedakah* box as one comes to the table for the lighting of the candles before the festive meal.

The Mitzvot of the Holy Day

Shabbat observance is the model for the observance of Rosh Ha-Shanah and all other major festivals.[16] The following mitzvot are common to both Shabbat and Rosh HaShanah:

1. preparation (see page 17, "The Mitzvah of Preparation [*Hachanat L'Shabbat*]");
2. including guests at the festive table (see page 17, "The Mitzvah of Hospitality [*Hachnasat Or'chim*]");
3. lighting candles (see page 18, "The Mitzvah of Kindling Shabbat Candles [*Hadlakat Nerot*]");
4. *Kiddush* (see page 19, "The Mitzvah of *Kiddush*");
5. blessing children (see page 20, "The Mitzvah of Blessing Children [*Birkat haBanim v'haBanot*]");
6. *HaMotzi* (see page 20, "The Mitzvah of *HaMotzi*");[17]
7. Blessing after Eating (see page 21, "The Mitzvah of *Birkat HaMazon*").

Some of the blessings and prayers differ from those on Shabbat. The texts can be found in *On the Doorposts of Your House.*

Apples and Honey

It is customary to dip a piece of apple in honey and to eat it after reciting the appropriate blessing. The apple and honey symbolize hope for a good and sweet year. The text of the prayer is as follows:

בָּרוּךְ אַתָּה, יְיָ אֱלֹהֵינוּ,   *Baruch atah, Adonai Eloheinu,*

מֶלֶךְ הָעוֹלָם,   *Melech haolam,*

בּוֹרֵא פְּרִי הָעֵץ.   *borei p'ri ha-eitz.*

Praise to You, Adonai our God, Sovereign of the universe, Creator of the fruit of the tree.

יְהִי רָצוֹן מִלְּפָנֶיךָ,   *Y'hi ratzon milfanecha,*

יְיָ אֱלֹהֵינוּ   *Adonai Eloheinu*

וֵאלֹהֵי אֲבוֹתֵינוּ וְאִמּוֹתֵינוּ,   *velohei avoteinu v'imoteinu,*

שֶׁתְּחַדֵּשׁ עָלֵינוּ   *shet'chadeish aleinu*

שָׁנָה טוֹבָה וּמְתוּקָה.   *shanah tovah um'tukah.*

Our God and God of our people, may the new year be good for us, and sweet.

The Mitzvah of Congregational Worship

עֲבוֹדָה
Avodah

It is a mitzvah to join the congregation in worship on Rosh HaShanah.[18] As members of the Jewish people, we have personal and communal responsibilities. Participation in the congregational worship service is one such communal obligation, but our attendance at services is more than a matter of obligation. The public celebration of Rosh HaShanah through prayer, song, and Torah study is the heart of the Rosh HaShanah experience. Rosh HaShanah worship draws us into the circle of the community, strengthening our ties to one another and to our historical values. If illness prevents attendance at services, Rosh HaShanah prayers should be recited at home. Some synagogues offer live streaming of their services as well, for those who are not able to leave the house.

For a discussion of the special features of the services and the Torah and haftarah selections, see "Approaching the High Holy Days" by Elaine Zecher, page 110, and "The Festival and Holy Day Liturgy of *Mishkan T'filah*" by Joel Sisenwine, page 115.

The Mitzvah of Hearing the Shofar

שׁוֹפָר
Shofar

Hearing the sound of the shofar on Rosh HaShanah is a mitzvah, as the Torah teaches, "You shall observe it as a day when the horn is sounded" (Numbers 29:1).[19] Jewish tradition is rich with explanations for the meaning of the shofar.[20] The liturgy of the Shofar Service emphasizes the themes of God's sovereignty (מַלְכֻיּוֹת, *Malchuyot*), reminiscences of encounters between God and Israel (זִכְרוֹנוֹת, *Zichronot*), and God's promise of redemption (שׁוֹפָרוֹת, *Shofarot*). As the shofar is sounded, we are invited to concentrate on its meaning and hearken to its call.[21] Provisions should be made so that those unable to attend the synagogue because of illness or infirmity may hear the sound of the shofar.

The Mitzvah of Refraining from Work on Rosh HaShanah

It is a mitzvah to refrain from work on Rosh HaShanah. As the Torah teaches, "In the seventh month, on the first day of the month, you shall observe complete rest" (Leviticus 23:24). (See also page 15, "The Mitzvah of Rest [*M'nuchah*].") For the purpose of observing the holiday, children and university students are encouraged to refrain from attending classes, and all who are able should attend synagogue services.

Greetings on Rosh HaShanah

It is a time-honored tradition to greet friends and neighbors during the Days of Awe, especially on Rosh HaShanah, by expressing the wish that they be blessed with a good year. The traditional words of blessing, whether uttered personally or sent through the mail or the internet, are לְשָׁנָה טוֹבָה תִּכָּתֵבוּ (*L'shanah tovah tikateivu*), May you be inscribed [in the Book of Life] for a good year. After Rosh HaShanah one might say, גְּמַר חֲתִימָה טוֹבָה (*G'mar chatimah tovah*), May the final decree be good; or לְשָׁנָה טוֹבָה תֵּחָתֵמוּ (*L'shanah tovah teichateimu*), May you be sealed [in the Book of Life] for a good year.

Visiting with Friends and Relatives

שִׂמְחָה
Simchah

On Rosh HaShanah it is customary to visit with friends and relatives, to wish them well. Such visits are part of *simchah,* the joy of the festival.

The Second Day of Rosh HaShanah

Although early Reform Judaism adopted the biblical practice of observing Rosh HaShanah for only one day, as is specified in the Torah (Leviticus 23:21; Numbers 29:1), currently Reform Judaism follows the calendar of the Land of Israel, with increasing numbers of congregations observing two days. (See "The Jewish Calendar" by Alexander Guttmann, page 5–7.)

Mourning on Rosh HaShanah

שִׁבְעָה
Shivah

Formal mourning (i.e., the observance of shivah) is suspended for the observance of Rosh HaShanah, at which time the mourners attend services and observe the customs of the day (see page 23, "Mourning on Shabbat"). The Talmud prescribes the complete termination of formal mourning when a festival intervenes.[22] Although Reform Judaism agrees to the suspension of formal mourning for the holy day itself, it is left to the family and their rabbi to decide whether or not to resume shivah after a festival, particularly when the festival falls within a day or two of the death (*Gates of Mitzvah*, page 60, D-3).

The Mitzvah of *Havdalah*

הַבְדָּלָה
Havdalah

At the conclusion of Rosh HaShanah, it is a mitzvah to recite *Havdalah* prayers separating the holy from the ordinary—Rosh HaShanah from the other days of the year.[23]

The text of *Havdalah* can be found in *On the Doorposts of Your House*, pages 108–111.

Aseret Y'mei T'shuvah
(The Ten Days of Repentance)

עֲשֶׂרֶת יְמֵי
תְּשׁוּבָה

*Aseret Y'mei
T'shuvah*

The ten-day period from Rosh HaShanah through Yom Kippur is known as *Aseret Y'mei T'shuvah*, the Ten Days of Repentance.[24] On Rosh HaShanah we take the first steps toward atonement. But this initial recognition of wrongdoing with its accompanying remorse requires further steps to complete the process of repentance.[25]

Activities during this period should be directed toward the sacred goal of reconciliation with both God and other human beings. Jewish tradition teaches that Yom Kippur makes atonement only for those sins that we commit against God, but it does not atone for those sins that we commit against other human beings unless we first attempt to make amends and seek their forgiveness.[26]

The mood of Rosh HaShanah and Yom Kippur permeates these days. A high point during this period is Shabbat Shuvah, the "Sabbath of Return." Turning toward God and toward other people is the purpose of these days.

The Mitzvah of Self-Examination

חֶשְׁבּוֹן
הַנֶּפֶשׁ

*Cheshbon
Hanefesh*

It is a mitzvah to reflect upon our behavior during the ten-day period beginning with Rosh HaShanah and concluding with Yom Kippur and to determine how to improve ourselves in the new year.[27] This process of self-examination is known as *cheshbon hanefesh*. During these intervening days we are encouraged to set aside a period each day for reflection and self-examination.

The Mitzvah of Reconciliation

It is a mitzvah to seek reconciliation during the Ten Days of Repentance with those whom we may have hurt or harmed during the past year. Our tradition teaches, "For transgressions against God, the Day of Atonement atones; but for transgressions of one human being against another, the Day of Atonement does not atone until they have made peace with one another."[28] It is appropriate to approach any person whom we might have offended in order to bring about reconciliation.

The Mitzvah of Forgiveness

סְלִיחָה
S'lichah

It is a mitzvah to forgive a person who has wronged you during the past year and who seeks your forgiveness.[29] The Talmud states, "A person should be as pliant as a reed and not hard like a cedar in granting forgiveness."[30] Bearing a grudge is destructive to both parties and subverts the purpose of the Ten Days of Repentance.

Visiting Graves of Relatives

Many observe the custom of visiting the graves of relatives during this period and reciting prayers in their memory.[31] Texts of appropriate prayers can be found in *On the Doorposts of Your House* on page 209.

Shabbat Shuvah

שַׁבָּת שׁוּבָה
Shabbat Shuvah

The Shabbat between Rosh HaShanah and Yom Kippur is known as Shabbat Shuvah. Its name is derived from the first word of the haftarah, Hosea 14:2–10, which begins with the words שׁוּבָה יִשְׂרָאֵל, (*Shuvah Yisrael*), Return, O Israel. Attending Shabbat Shuvah services to hear the reading of this haftarah provides an important introspective prelude to Yom Kippur.

Yom Kippur

For on this day atonement shall be made for you to puri-
fy you of all your sins; you shall be pure before the Eter-
nal. It shall be a sabbath of complete rest for you and you
shall practice self-denial; it is a law for all time.
                                        —LEVITICUS 16:30–31

Mark, the tenth day of this seventh month is the Day of
Atonement. . . . For it is a Day of Atonement, on which
expiation is made on your behalf before the Eternal your
God. . . . Do no work whatever; it is a law for all time,
throughout the ages in all your settlements. It shall be a
sabbath of complete rest for you, and you shall practice
self-denial; on the ninth day of the month at evening,
from evening to evening, you shall observe this your
sabbath.
                                    —LEVITICUS 23:27–28, 31–32

On the tenth day of the same seventh month you shall
observe a sacred occasion when you shall practice self-
denial.
                                            —NUMBERS 29:7

YOM KIPPUR, the Day of Atonement, occurs on the tenth of Tishrei (Leviticus 23:27). It is the culmination of the Ten Days of Repentance. It alone of all the Jewish holidays is the equivalent of
Shabbat in sanctity.[32] Its mood is reflective and introspective—a
day devoted totally to personal and communal self-examination,
confession, and atonement. Yom Kippur provides us with the opportunity to alter our conduct, readjust our values, and set things
right in our lives. The day demands absolute honesty as we confess
our wrongdoings: "We have gone astray, we have sinned, we have
transgressed."[33] The grandeur of the liturgy and music adds to the

drama and seriousness of the day. From *Kol Nidrei*, the eve of Yom Kippur, to the last triumphant note of the shofar at the conclusion of the *N'ilah* service, its purpose is to move us toward reconciliation with God and our fellow human beings and to aid us to do better in the coming year.

Primary among the Yom Kippur mitzvot is fasting. The Torah says three times, "And this shall be to you a law for all time: In the seventh month, on the tenth day of the month, you shall practice self-denial" (Leviticus 16:29, 23:27; Numbers 29:7). The Mishnah interprets "self-denial" to include not eating, drinking, engaging in sexual activity, bathing for pleasure, anointing, and the wearing of leather shoes.

The threefold repetition of this mitzvah in the Torah has suggested three reasons for fasting, as described in our prayer book:

> Judaism calls for self-discipline. When we control our appetites on Yom Kippur, we remember that on other days, too, we can be masters, not slaves, of our desires.
>
> Judaism calls for empathy. When we consciously experience hunger, we are more likely to consider the millions who need no Yom Kippur in order to suffer hunger. For some, most days are days without food enough for themselves and their children.
>
> Judaism calls for penitence. The confession we make with our lips is a beginning. The penance we inflict upon our bodies through fasting leads us along further still toward the acknowledgment that we have sinned against ourselves and others. (*Gates of Repentance*, page 229)

Yom Kippur is a day of concentration on the past so that the future may be better for us as individuals, as a community, and as part of the human family. Despite its solemnity, Yom Kippur is also a day of joy, when the truly penitent person begins gradually to feel at one with God and humankind. Reconciliation and change are the goals of the day's prayers and fast. When the final blast of the shofar is heard at the end of *N'ilah*, those who have observed the day with sincerity should feel that they have been inscribed and sealed in the Book of Life.

The Mitzvah of Observing Yom Kippur

It is a mitzvah to observe Yom Kippur on the tenth of the Hebrew month of Tishrei. As the Torah says, "Mark, the tenth day of this seventh month is the Day of Atonement. It shall be a sacred occasion for you. . . . For it is a Day of Atonement, on which expiation is made on your behalf before the Eternal your God" (Leviticus 23:27–28).

The Mitzvah of Repentance

תְּשׁוּבָה
T'shuvah

It is a mitzvah to repent on Yom Kippur.[34] As the intense ten-day period of self-examination, reflection, and reconciliation initiated on Rosh HaShanah reaches its climax, the recitation of confessional prayers brings into sharp focus our shortcomings and failures and initiates a process of change and transformation.

It is through repentance (*t'shuvah*) that we return to God and find God returning to us.[35]

The Mitzvah of Reconciliation

It is a mitzvah for each of us to seek reconciliation with members of our family and with all those we might have offended before the onset of Yom Kippur.[36] We should enter into the sacred day having made sincere efforts at personal reconciliation.

The Mitzvah of *Tzedakah*

צְדָקָה
Tzedakah

It is always a mitzvah to give *tzedakah*.[37] However, *tzedakah* (charity)—along with *t'filah* (prayer) and *t'shuvah* (repentance)—is an integral part of Yom Kippur observance.

There is an old custom of setting aside money (referred to as *kaparah*, atonement money) before sunset on the eve of Yom

Kippur. Implicit in this act of *kaparah* is the idea that this charity money serves as an atonement for one's sins.[38]

Therefore, it is especially appropriate before the onset of the day to perform specific acts of *tzedakah* that will improve the spiritual and material well-being of the community.

The Meal on Erev Yom Kippur

סְעוּדָה
מַפְסֶקֶת

S'udah Mafseket

Unlike the meal held on the eves of Shabbat and other festivals, there are no special rituals connected with the Erev Yom Kippur meal, because it is eaten before the sacred day begins. The mitzvot of *Ha-Motzi* and *Birkat HaMazon* are observed, as at any meal. This meal, which is called *s'udah mafseket* (the concluding meal before a fast), should begin early so that it is completed before the onset of the holy day.[39]

It should be noted that *Kiddush* is not recited at this meal, which must be completed before the onset of Yom Kippur. Since the *Kiddush* usually sets aside the festival as holy and may not be recited before the beginning of the festival, and since the *Kiddush* is normally recited over either wine or bread (neither of which may be consumed on Yom Kippur), *Kiddush* is not recited at the *s'udah mafseket*.

The Mitzvah of Kindling Yom Kippur Lights

הַדְלָקַת נֵרוֹת
Hadlakat Nerot

Unlike on Shabbat and the other festivals, Yom Kippur candles are lit *after* the meal, because the lighting of the candles marks the formal beginning of Yom Kippur and therefore the beginning of the fast. Before lighting the Yom Kippur candles, it is customary to light a memorial candle, which will burn throughout the holy day. A single candle may be used for all who are to be remembered.

It is a mitzvah to light and recite the appropriate blessing over the Yom Kippur lights after the meal and before leaving for the synagogue:[40]

בָּרוּךְ אַתָּה, יְיָ אֱלֹהֵינוּ,   *Baruch atah, Adonai Eloheinu,*
מֶלֶךְ הָעוֹלָם, אֲשֶׁר קִדְּשָׁנוּ   *Melech haolam, asher kid'shanu,*
בְּמִצְוֹתָיו וְצִוָּנוּ   *b'mitzvotav v'tzivanu,*
לְהַדְלִיק נֵר שֶׁל   *l'hadlik ner shel*
יוֹם הַכִּפּוּרִים.   *Yom HaKippurim.*

Blessed are You, Adonai our God, Sovereign of the universe, who hallows us with mitzvot, commanding us to kindle the lights of the Day of Atonement.

The Mitzvah of Blessing Children

בִּרְכַּת הַבָּנִים וְהַבָּנוֹת

Birkat haBanim v'haBanot

It is a mitzvah for parents to bless their children before leaving for the synagogue. Families may establish their own ritual or use the traditional words (see pages 19–20, "The Mitzvah of Blessing Children"; or *On the Doorposts of Your House*, page 107).

The Mitzvah of Fasting

צוֹם

Tzom

It is a mitzvah to fast (*tzom*) throughout Yom Kippur.[41] The Torah (Leviticus 16:29, 23:27) designates Yom Kippur as a day of self-denial or, more literally, affliction of the soul. Fasting requires self-discipline and is an attempt to control one's physical needs in order to concentrate on the spiritual. By symbolically denying the most basic biological necessity that humans share with all animals, we focus on that aspect of human nature that we share with God (see "Fasting on Yom Kippur," page 123).

Children below the age of bar/bat mitzvah should be taught to fast by beginning with a few hours' fast and increasing the number of hours each year until at thirteen they fast throughout Yom Kippur.[42] A person who is ill or pregnant should follow the advice of a physician on fasting.[43]

The fast begins with the kindling of Yom Kippur candles and concludes with the sounding of the shofar at the end of *N'ilah* and *Havdalah*.

The Mitzvah of Congregational Worship

עֲבוֹדָה
Avodah

It is a mitzvah to join the congregation in worship by attending the *Kol Nidrei* service on Yom Kippur night and the several services on Yom Kippur day until the sounding of the shofar at the end of *N'ilah* and recitation of *Havdalah*.[44] As members of the Jewish people, we have personal and communal responsibilities. Participation in the congregational worship service is one such communal obligation, but our attendance at services goes beyond obligation. The public celebration of Yom Kippur through prayer, song, and Torah study is the heart of the Yom Kippur experience. Yom Kippur worship draws us into the circle of the community, strengthening our ties to one another and to the historical values that we Jews hold dear. If illness prevents attendance at services, Yom Kippur prayers should be recited at home.

The Mitzvah of *Yizkor* (Memorial Service)

יִזְכּוֹר
Yizkor

It is a mitzvah to recite *Yizkor* on Yom Kippur.[45] In some communities, it is a custom that everyone remains for *Yizkor* even if one's parents are alive since *Yizkor* is a service of remembrance for the martyrs of our people as well as for our own relatives and friends (see "Yizkor," pages 120–122; and *Gates of Mitzvah*, page 63, D-10).

The Mitzvah of Refraining from Work

It is a mitzvah to refrain from work on Yom Kippur. As the Torah states, "You shall do no work throughout that day. . . . It shall be a sabbath of complete rest for you" (Leviticus 23:28, 32). The same concepts that apply to Shabbat apply to Yom Kippur, known as the Sabbath of Sabbaths (see page 16, "The Mitzvah of Refraining from Work").

The Mitzvah of *Havdalah*

הַבְדָּלָה
Havdalah

At the conclusion of Yom Kippur it is a mitzvah to recite *Havdalah*, separating the holy from the ordinary, and Yom Kippur from the other days of the year.[46]

The text of *Havdalah* can be found in *Gates of Repentance*, pages 526–528, and in *On the Doorposts of Your House*, pages 108–111.

Beginning the Sukkah after Yom Kippur

סֻכָּה
Sukkah

Immediately after *Havdalah*, it is customary to make a symbolic start on the sukkah—by putting up one board or driving one nail.[47] In this manner we conclude the Ten Days of Repentance and turn at once to the performance of a mitzvah.

Breaking the Fast

The meal following Yom Kippur should be a particularly joyous one. There is a feeling of exhilaration and relief that comes from having experienced a day of introspection and prayer in addition to a sense of divine forgiveness. "Go your way, and eat your food with joy, and drink your wine, for God has already accepted your deeds."[48] It is especially appropriate to seek out those in the synagogue who are alone and invite them to join in breaking the fast.

The Pilgrimage Festivals
שָׁלֹשׁ רְגָלִים

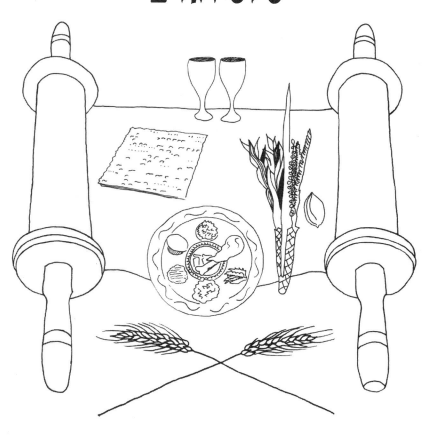

The Pilgrimage Festivals (*Shalosh R'galim*)

Three times a year you shall hold a festival for Me. You shall observe the Feast of Unleavened Bread—eating unleavened bread for seven days as I have commanded you—at the set time in the month of Aviv, for in it you went forth from Egypt; and none shall appear before Me empty-handed; and the Feast of the Harvest, of the first fruits of your work, of what you sow in the field; and the Feast of Ingathering at the end of the year when you gather in the results of your work from the field.

—EXODUS 23:14–16

Three times a year—on the Feast of Unleavened Bread, on the Feast of Weeks, and on the Feast of Booths—all your males shall appear before the Eternal your God in the place that [God] will choose.

—DEUTERONOMY 16:16

Then Solomon offered up burnt offerings to the Eternal upon the altar . . . as the duty of each day required . . . and the annual feasts—the Feast of Unleavened Bread, the Feast of Weeks, and the Feast of Booths.

—II CHRONICLES 8:12–13

PESACH, SHAVUOT, and SUKKOT are collectively known as the *Shalosh R'galim*, the Three Pilgrimage Festivals.[1] During the existence of the Temple, they were the three annual occasions for pilgrimage to Jerusalem with offerings of thanksgiving for the bountiful harvest (Exodus 23:14). The day following Sukkot, Sh'mini Atzeret–Simchat Torah, although a separate festival,[2] is considered part of the Sukkot holiday. Although the origins of the Festivals are bound up with the seasonal changes and the agricultural cycle of ancient Israel, each also commemorates an important event in the history of the Jewish people: Pesach—the Exodus from Egypt; Shavuot—the giving of the Torah at Mount Sinai; and Sukkot—the forty-year journey through the wilderness. Through these historical associations, the Festivals have remained significant in the life of the Jewish people even when they lived in the Diaspora, far from the Land of Israel and its natural rhythms. Wherever Jews live they are able to celebrate liberation, Revelation, and the journey toward the promised future.

The dates for celebrating the Festivals depend on the seasons as they occur in the Land of Israel. Thus, through the celebration of the Festivals, Jews, no matter where they live, feel a connection to the Land of Israel. The reestablishment of the State of Israel has helped renew the original agricultural significance of the Festivals for Jews throughout the world.

Rejoicing is characteristic of the Festivals, for they are opportunities to enrich our lives by renewing our commitment to the Jewish ideals of redemption, responsibility, and hope. Through the performance of the unique mitzvot of the Festivals, we participate in the continuing drama of sacred history, and through our celebration, we reaffirm our identity as part of the Jewish people.

The festivals have certain mitzvot in common, and others that are unique to each festival. For the sake of clarity, the mitzvot common to all festivals are listed first in a preliminary section, followed by the mitzvot of the particular festivals.

The Mitzvah of Observing the Festivals

It is a mitzvah to observe the Festivals, as the Torah says, "Three times a year you shall hold a festival for Me" (Exodus 23:14). The Festivals are Pesach, Shavuot, and Sukkot (including Sh'mini Atzeret–Simchat Torah).

The Mitzvah of Rejoicing (*Simchah*) on the Festivals

שִׂמְחָה

Simchah

It is a mitzvah to rejoice on the Festivals. The Torah teaches, "You shall rejoice in your festival" (Deuteronomy 16:14). This mitzvah sets the tone and mood of the Festivals.[3]

Special liturgy, special ceremonial objects, and special foods make each celebration distinctive. Our joy is also derived from our recalling the decisive moments in the history of the Jewish people that helped shape the ideals of Judaism. Through the reaffirmation of our commitment to those ideals and by joining together with other Jews in the ongoing task of working to repair the world תִּקּוּן עוֹלָם (*tikkun olam*), our lives take on renewed significance.

The Mitzvot of the Festivals

Shabbat observance provides the paradigm for the observance of the Festivals.[4] The following mitzvot are common to both Shabbat and the Festivals: (1) preparation (see page 17, "The Mitzvah of Preparation"); (2) including guests at the festive table (see page 17, "The Mitzvah of Hospitality [*Hachnasat Or'chim*]); (3) lighting candles (see pages 18–19, "The Mitzvah of Kindling Shabbat Candles [*Hadlakat HaNerot*]); (4) *Kiddush* (see page 19, "The Mitzvah of *Kiddush*"); (5) blessing of children (see pages 19–20, "The Mitzvah of Blessing Children"); (6) *HaMotzi* (see pages 20–21, "The Mitzvah of *HaMotzi*"); and (7) concluding the meal with *Birkat HaMazon* (see pages 21–22, "The Mitzvah of *Birkat HaMazon*"). Several of the blessings for the Festivals differ from those for Shabbat. The text of these prayers can be found in *On the Doorposts of Your House*, pages 23–35, 36–40, 83–98, and in *Mishkan T'filah: A Reform Siddur*, pages 384–387, 605–609.

It is customary for the mealtime conversation to reflect the joy and holiness of the occasion and talk can be interspersed with *z'mirot* (table songs). The festival table is a particularly appropriate place to discuss the meaning of the festival.

The Mitzvah of Resting and Avoiding Work on the Festivals
It is a mitzvah to rest and abstain from work on the Festivals:[5] on
the first and seventh day of Pesach (Leviticus 23:7–8), on Shavuot
(Leviticus 23:21), on the first day of Sukkot (Leviticus 23:35), and
on Sh'mini Atzeret–Simchat Torah (Leviticus 23:36). (See also page
16, "The Mitzvah of Refraining from Work"). Since the Festivals are
set aside for sanctification, we make an effort to refrain from those
activities that do not contribute to the spirit of holiness.

The Mitzvah of Congregational Worship

עֲבוֹדָה
Avodah

It is a mitzvah to join the congregation in worship on
the Festivals:[6] on the first and seventh day of Pesach,
on Shavuot, on the first day of Sukkot, and on Sh'mini
Atzeret–Simchat Torah. Through being part of the worship service,
we are able to share the concerns of the community, strengthening
it through our participation. Each service has unique features that
emphasize the special themes of the Festivals.

Mourning on the Festivals

שִׁבְעָה
Shivah

Formal mourning (i.e., the observance of shivah)
is suspended for the observance of the Festivals, at
which time the mourners are encouraged to attend
services and observe the customs of the day (see page 23, "Mourning on Shabbat").[7] The Talmud (*Moeid Katan* 19a-b ff) and *Shulchan
Aruch* (*Orach Hayyim Hilchot Yom Tov* 548:4) prescribe the complete termination of shivah when a festival intervenes, as the mitzvah to be joyful on the holiday overrides mourning. While Reform
Judaism agrees to the suspension of formal mourning for the holy
day itself, it is left to the family to decide whether or not to resume
shivah after a Festival, particularly when it falls within a day or
two of the death. If death occurs during the intermediate days of a
festival (i.e., *chol hamoeid* of Pesach or Sukkot), the rabbi should be
consulted about the mourning period (see *Gates of Mitzvah*, page
60, D-3).

Weddings on the Festivals

Jewish tradition holds that Shabbat and the Festivals are days on which weddings may not be held (see page 23, "Weddings and Wedding Preparations"; *Gates of Mitzvah*, pages 31–32, B-2).[8] The reason is twofold: first, the signing of the *ketubah* and the exchange of rings are derived from contract law and fall into the category of a business transaction; second, since Shabbat and the Festivals are already days of joy and holiness, prohibiting weddings on Shabbat and the Festivals emphasizes the special joy and holiness of the wedding, according to the concept *ein m'ar'vin simchah b'simchah*, not to mix two happy occasions together.[9]

The Mitzvah of *Havdalah*

הַבְדָּלָה

Havdalah

It is a mitzvah to recite *Havdalah* at the conclusion of the Festivals.[10] The blessing of separation is recited over wine and marks the end of the Festivals. The text can be found in *On the Doorposts of Your House*, page 98. As the formal beginning of a festival is marked by blessings and the festival set apart and distinguished from ordinary days, the departure of the festival is similarly marked. Having both a formal beginning and formal conclusion helps us to hallow the festival and to savor the experience of the festival even after it is concluded.

PESACH

> You shall observe the [Feast of] Unleavened Bread, for on this very day I brought your ranks out of the land of Egypt; you shall observe this day throughout the ages as an institution for all time. In the first month, from the fourteenth day of the month at evening, you shall eat un-leavened bread until the twenty-first day of the month at evening. —EXODUS 12:17–18

You shall observe this as an institution for all time, for you and your descendants. . . . And when your children ask you, "What do you mean by this rite?" you shall say, "It is the passover sacrifice to the Eternal, who passed over the houses of the Israelites in Egypt when smiting the Egyptians, but saved our houses."

—EXODUS 12:24, 26–2 7

You shall observe the Feast of Unleavened Bread—eating unleavened bread for seven days, as I have commanded you—at the set time of the month of Aviv, for in the month of Aviv you went forth from Egypt.

—EXODUS 34:18

Pesach, which begins on the fifteenth of the Hebrew month of Nisan and lasts for seven days, commemorates the Exodus from Egypt.[11] In the Torah, it is designated by several names: Chag HaAviv (based on Deuteronomy 16:1), the Spring Festival; Chag Ha-Matzot (based on Exodus 12:20), the Festival of Unleavened Bread; and Chag HaPesach (based on Exodus 12:21), the Festival of the Paschal Lamb.

While current Pesach observance draws some of its symbolism from the agricultural and pastoral origins of the festival, it is primarily a celebration of the Exodus from Egypt.[12]

The liberation of the Jewish people from Egyptian bondage has become a powerful symbol of redemption—not only the redemption of the Jewish people, but the redemption of the entire world. The Haggadah, reflecting the historical experience of the Jewish people, recognizes that slavery is not limited to physical bondage, but that spiritual slavery and social degradation are no less potent methods of depriving human beings of liberty.[13]

The highlight of Pesach observance is the seder, with its many symbolic foods and its elaborate liturgy, the Haggadah. The seder is designed to re-create the events of redemption:

In every generation, each of us should feel as though we ourselves had gone forth from Egypt, as it is written: "And you shall explain to your child on that day, it is because of what the Eternal did for me when I, *myself*, went forth from Egypt."[14]

As *z'man cheiruteinu*, "the season of our freedom," Pesach is a constant reminder of our responsibility to those who are oppressed or enslaved physically, intellectually, or ideologically. On Pesach we express our solidarity with other members of the Jewish community who are unable to celebrate Passover in freedom. The experience of redemption in the Passover celebration inspires us all to assist in the future redemption of humanity. As the midrash teaches, just as the Sea of Reeds did not split until the Israelites stepped into it, so redemption cannot come unless we take the first step.[15]

The Mitzvah of Observing Pesach

פֶּסַח

Pesach

It is a mitzvah to observe Pesach for seven days, beginning on the eve of the fifteenth of Nisan, as the Torah says, "In the first month, from the fourteenth day of the month at evening,[16] you shall eat unleavened bread until the twenty-first day of the month at evening" (Exodus 12:18).

The Mitzvah of Removing Leaven

בְּדִיקַת חָמֵץ

B'dikat Chameitz

It is a mitzvah to remove leaven from our homes prior to the beginning of Pesach. Leaven refers to products made from wheat, barley, rye, oats, and spelt that have been permitted to leaven.[17] Ashkenazi custom adds rice, millet, corn, and legumes (e.g., peas, beans), referred to as *kitniyot*. [18] The removal of leaven is based on the biblical injunction found in Exodus 12:15: "On the very first day you shall remove leaven from your houses." Some will choose to remove all leaven from their homes. Others may choose to put all the leaven in a specially marked cabinet or closet that is appropriately marked, as a constant reminder of the special dietary elements of Pesach.[19] Still others use this as an opportunity to donate food to a local food bank or soup kitchen.

Searching for leaven, *b'dikat chameitz*, on the night before the first seder is a Pesach custom that adds a wonderful dimension to Pesach preparation.[20] After the house has been cleaned for Pesach, a symbolic search for the last remains of leaven is made. At various places in the home, pieces of leaven are hidden. Then children and adults, with flashlights or other illumination, search them out in the dark. Often a wooden spoon and a candle are used. When the leaven is found, it is scooped onto the wooden spoon with a feather. The leaven is gathered in a bag and burned or disposed of the next morning at which time we recite the following blessing:

בָּרוּךְ אַתָּה, יְיָ אֱלֹהֵינוּ,   *Baruch atah, Adonai Eloheinu,*

מֶלֶךְ הָעוֹלָם, אֲשֶׁר קִדְּשָׁנוּ   *Melech haolam, asher kid'shanu*

בְּמִצְוֹתָיו וְצִוָּנוּ   *b'mitzvotav v'tzivanu,*

עַל בִּעוּר חָמֵץ.   *al biur chameitz.*

Blessed are You, Eternal our God, Sovereign of the universe, who sanctifies us with Your commandments and calls upon us to remove leaven.

Since leaven has been removed, refraining from eating bread after breakfast on the day before the seder is part of the preparation for the observance of Pesach. To heighten the appetite for matzah at the seder itself, it is a custom not to eat matzah at least a full day before the seder.[21]

The Mitzvah of Abstaining from Eating Leaven

חָמֵץ

Chameitz

It is a mitzvah to abstain from eating leaven during the entire seven days of Pesach, as the Torah states, "You shall eat nothing leavened" (Exodus 12:20). Abstaining from leaven may take many forms—from not eating those foods that obviously contain leaven, such as bread or cake, to avoidance and examination of all ingredients in a particular food-stuff. By consciously making a choice to abstain during the whole week of Pesach, we are constantly aware of the festival and of our Jewish identity. (See the essay "Passover Kashrut: A Reform Approach" by Mary L. Zamore, pages 153–156.)

The Mitzvah of Preparing a Seder

סֵדֶר
Seder

The word *seder* means "order." The seder is an or-dered table service, using a Haggadah, of fourteen (or in some interpretations, fifteen) steps that lead from slavery to freedom. It is a mitzvah for everyone to participate in the preparation for the seder—cooking, cleaning, and setting the festive table.[22] The leader of the seder has the special obligation to review the Haggadah in advance and decide which passages will be included. The experience of the seder is enhanced when all the participants are provided with the same Haggadah.

The Central Conference of American Rabbis offers several differ-ent Haggadot. The well-known classic is *A Passover Haggadah*, ed-ited by Rabbi Herbert Bronstein and illustrated by Leonard Baskin, with essays by Rabbis Lawrence A. Hoffman and W. Gunther Plaut. An innovative Haggadah with many readings and songs from around the Jewish world is *The Open Door*, edited by Rabbi Sue Levi Elwell and drawings by Ruth Weisberg. Another wonderful option is *Sharing the Journey: The Haggadah for the Contemporary Jewish Family*, written by Alan Yoffie and illustrated by Mark Pod-wal, with an inclusive, welcoming text that is a great introduction for first-time seder participants. This Haggadah offers a track list of seder songs for download, as well as a step-by-step leader's guide. CCAR also publishes a Haggadah for children, *A Children's Hag-gadah*, with text by Rabbis Howard Bogot and Robert Orkand and illustrated by Devis Grebu.

In addition, the tradition encourages the use of beautiful ritual items to increase our enjoyment of the mitzvot (see *"Hidur Mitz-vah*: The Aesthetics of Mitzvot," pages 107–109).

Although Reform Jews do not officially celebrate the second day of Pesach as a holiday, many people have a second seder. Sometimes they join in a congregational seder or gather with relatives and friends who attended other first-night sedarim. The second seder may follow the same pattern as the first or may have another focus. A second seder may provide the opportunity for additional reflection that was omitted on the first night.

The Mitzvah of Hospitality (*Hachnasat Or'chim*)

הַכְנָסַת אוֹרְחִים
Hachnasat Or'chim

It is a mitzvah to invite guests to join in the seder. So important is it that the invitation is included in the text of the Haggadah, "Let all who are hungry come and eat. Let all who are in want share the hope of Passover."[23] Arrangements should be made to see that no one has to celebrate Passover alone. Many communities make special arrangements for those who are alone, including the elderly and college students who are away from home. One might also invite non-Jewish friends and family to join in this important celebration of human freedom. It is an excellent way for people to learn about Judaism in an engaging and enjoyable manner.

It is a mitzvah to give *tzedakah* before the beginning of Passover.[24] Tradition encourages the solicitation of מָעוֹת חִטִּין (*ma-ot chitin*), special funds, to provide a proper seder for the poor.[25]

The Mitzvah of Participating in the Seder and Reciting the Haggadah

הַגָּדָה
Haggadah

It is a mitzvah for every Jew to participate in the recitation of the Haggadah, which recalls the Exodus from Egypt.[26] The text of the Haggadah teaches that we should look upon ourselves as having personally experienced the Exodus. "In every generation, each of us should feel as though we ourselves had gone forth from Egypt, as it is written: 'And you shall explain to your child on that day, it is because of what the Eternal did for me when I, *myself*, went forth from Egypt.'"[27]

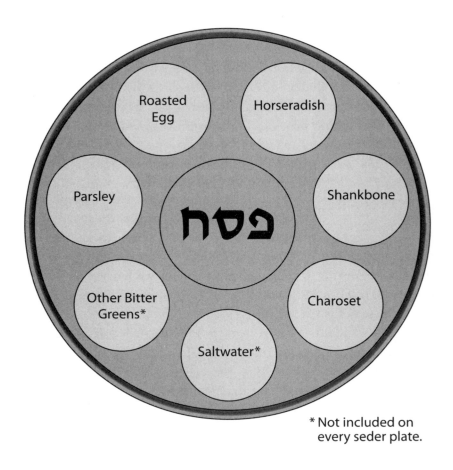

Roasted
Egg

Horseradish

Parsley

פסח

Shankbone

Other Bitter
Greens*

Charoset

Saltwater*

* Not included on
every seder plate.

The Seder Plate

In front of the leader or in front of each participant, a special seder plate is set.[28] The following are arranged on it: three separate pieces of מַצָּה matzah—two pieces represent the two traditional loaves לֶחֶם מִשְׁנֶה (lechem mishneh) set out in the ancient Temple during Sabbaths and festivals, and the third matzah is symbolic of Passover; a roasted shank bone זְרוֹעַ (z'roa), burned or scorched, representing the ancient Passover sacrifice; parsley or green herbs כַּרְפַּס (karpas), symbolizing the growth of springtime, the green of hope and renewal; the top part of horseradish root מָרוֹר (maror) or other bitter herbs, symbolic of the bitterness that our ancestors experienced in Egypt and, in a contemporary sense, the lot of all who are enslaved; חֲרוֹסֶת (charoset), representing the mortar that our ancestors used for Pharaoh's labor; a roasted egg בֵּיצָה (beitzah), representing the חֲגִיגָה (chagigah), or festival offering, a symbol of life itself, the triumph of life over death. Some seder plates also include a place for additional bitter greens like romaine lettuce חֲזֶרֶת (chazeret), and some also include salt water. In recent years, a new tradition has developed of placing an orange on the seder plate, as a symbol of gay and lesbian inclusion. This is meant to represent the additional fruitfulness of a society that welcomes and includes all people.

The Cup of Elijah

כּוֹס אֵלִיָּהוּ
Kos Eliyahu

A special cup filled with wine is placed prominently on the table. In popular legend the prophet Elijah (herald of redemption) visits every Jewish home at some time during the seder. Therefore, one cup of wine is set aside for him.[29] After the meal, one of the participants, usually a young child, opens the door for Elijah. This is a moment filled with hope and anticipation.

The Cup of Miriam

כּוֹס מִרְיָם
Kos Miriam

A recent addition to the seder table is a ceremonial cup for the prophetess Miriam, who led the Jewish people in song and dance after the crossing of the Reed Sea (Exodus 15:20–21). According to legend, a special well called Miriam's well traveled with the Israelites as they journeyed through the desert. Miriam's cup represents the life-giving waters.[30]

The Mitzvah of Eating Unleavened Bread

מַצָּה
Matzah

By eating matzah we recall that the dough prepared by our people had no time to rise before the final act of redemption: "And they baked unleavened cakes of the dough since they had been driven out of Egypt and could not delay, nor had they prepared provisions for themselves."[31]

It is a mitzvah to eat matzah during the seder and to recite the appropriate blessings.[32]

בָּרוּךְ אַתָּה, יְיָ אֱלֹהֵינוּ,
Baruch atah, Adonai Eloheinu,

מֶלֶךְ הָעוֹלָם,
Melech haolam,

הַמּוֹצִיא לֶחֶם מִן הָאָרֶץ.
hamotzi lechem min haaretz.

Blessed are You, Eternal our God, Sovereign of the universe, who brings forth bread from the earth.

בָּרוּךְ אַתָּה, יְיָ אֱלֹהֵינוּ,
Baruch atah, Adonai Eloheinu,

מֶלֶךְ הָעוֹלָם, אֲשֶׁר קִדְּשָׁנוּ
Melech haolam, asher kid'shanu

בְּמִצְוֹתָיו וְצִוָּנוּ
b'mitzvotav v'tzivanu

עַל אֲכִילַת מַצָּה.
al achilat matzah.

Blessed are You, Eternal our God, Sovereign of the universe, who has sanctified us with Your commandments and has commanded us concerning the eating of unleavened bread.

The Mitzvah of Eating Bitter Herbs

מָרוֹר
Maror

Maror is eaten to remind us that the Egyptians embittered the lives of our people, as it is written: "With hard labor at mortar and brick and in all sorts of work in the field, with all the tasks ruthlessly imposed upon them."[33]

It is a mitzvah to eat maror, the bitter herbs, with the appropriate blessing.[34]

בָּרוּךְ אַתָּה, יְיָ אֱלֹהֵינוּ,
Baruch atah, Adonai Eloheinu,

מֶלֶךְ הָעוֹלָם, אֲשֶׁר קִדְּשָׁנוּ
Melech haolam, asher kid'shanu

בְּמִצְוֹתָיו וְצִוָּנוּ
b'mitzvotav v'tzivanu

עַל אֲכִילַת מָרוֹר.
al achilat maror.

Blessed are You, Eternal our God, Sovereign of the universe, who has sanctified us with Your commandments and has commanded us concerning the eating of bitter herbs.

The Mitzvah of Four Cups

אַרְבַּע כּוֹסוֹת *Arba Kosot* It is a mitzvah to drink four cups of wine or grape juice during the seder.[35]

The Four Questions

אַרְבַּע קֻשְׁיוֹת *Arba Kushyot* It is customary for the youngest participant or participants to recite the Four Questions.[36] These questions point to the unusual features of the seder meal and provide an opportunity to teach the lesson of Passover. The text can be found in *A Passover Haggadah*, page 29; *The Open Door*, pages 30–31; and *Sharing the Journey*, pages 29–31.

Reclining

הֲסַבָּה *Hasabah* It is the custom to simulate a reclining position while eating by propping oneself up with cushions.[37] Reclining at the seder is symbolic of being free people who are able to eat wth leisure.

Afikoman

אֲפִקוֹמָן *Afikoman* The *afikoman* is the half matzah that is set aside during the breaking of the matzah early in the seder. An old tradition held that the group could not leave the seder table unless all had tasted of the *afikoman*.[38] In connection with this, and in order to arouse and maintain the interest of the children and to provide some entertainment for them, a practice developed of hiding and searching for the *afikoman*. Sometime during the meal, the leader hides the *afikoman*, trying to elude the watchful observance of the children, whose endeavor it is to search out its hiding place. Prizes might be awarded to all who participated, with a special gift to the one who actually finds it. In some households, it is the custom for children to "steal" the *afikoman* in order to hide it and hold it for "ransom," since the meal cannot conclude without it.

Chol HaMoeid

חוֹל הַמּוֹעֵד
Chol Hamoeid

The intermediate days, between the first and the seventh days, are known as *chol hamoeid*. During this period no leaven is eaten, but many people enjoy cooking and eating special Passover foods.[39] Every effort is made to preserve the holiday mood.

The Song of Songs

שִׁיר הַשִּׁירִים
Shir HaShirim

On the Shabbat during Pesach, the Song of Songs (*Shir HaShirim*) is read.[40] The Song of Songs refers to springtime and thus befits the Festival. In addition, Jewish tradition has interpreted Song of Songs as an allegory of the love of God for Israel. The experiences of hope and redemption, which characterize Pesach, make the Song of Songs particularly appropriate to this season.

The Mitzvah of *Yizkor*

יִזְכֹּר
Yizkor

It is a mitzvah to recite *Yizkor* on the seventh day of Pesach.[41] It memorializes our relatives and our friends, as well as the martyrs of our generation and previous generations. (See "*Yizkor*," pages 120–122; and *Gates of Mitzvah*, page 63, D-10. The text for the *Yizkor* service can be found in *Mishkan T'filah: A Reform Siddur*, pages 574–583.)

The Study of *Pirkei Avot*

פִּרְקֵי אָבוֹת
Pirkei Avot

Beginning with the first Shabbat after Pesach, it is customary to study one of the chapters of *Pirkei Avot* (Ethics of the Ancestors) each Shabbat afternoon until Shavuot. *Pirkei Avot* is devoted to the ethical-religious maxims of the Rabbis. The study of this material is part of the preparation for Shavuot. As we complete each weekly study session, we are one week closer to Shavuot and the recollection of מַתַּן תּוֹרָה (*matan Torah*), the giving of the Torah at Sinai.

Counting the Omer

סְפִירַת הָעֹמֶר

Counting the Omer

The period between Pesach and Shavuot is known as *s'firah*, "counting," or *S'firat HaOmer*, "counting the wave offering." The mitzvah of counting the Omer begins on the second day of Pesach and continues until Shavuot (Leviticus 23:15). Although the wave offering is no longer practiced because of the destruction of the Temple in Jerusalem (70 CE), the tradition of counting the days from Pesach to Shavuot still continues. For some, this period that moves thematically from the slavery of Pesach to the revelation of the Torah at Sinai on Shavuot is a period of spiritual uplift and renewal, often accompanied by the study of texts. The following blessing is recited from the second night of Pesach until the eve of Shavuot at the end of the evening service *(maariv)*:

בָּרוּךְ אַתָּה, יְיָ אֱלֹהֵינוּ,   *Baruch atah, Adonai Eloheinu,*

מֶלֶךְ הָעוֹלָם, אֲשֶׁר קִדְּשָׁנוּ   *Melech haolam, asher kid'shanu*

בְּמִצְוֹתָיו וְצִוָּנוּ   *b'mitzvotav v'tzivanu*

עַל סְפִירַת הָעֹמֶר.   *al s'firat haomer.*

Praise to You, Adonai, Sovereign of all, who hallows us with mitzvot, commanding us to count the Omer.

This blessing is followed by the actual counting; for example: "This is the eighth day, making one week and one day of counting the Omer."[42]

SHAVUOT

> *You shall observe the Feast of Weeks, of the first fruits of the wheat harvest.* —EXODUS 34:22

> *On the day of the first fruits, your Feast of Weeks, when you bring an offering of new grain to the Eternal, you shall observe a sacred occasion.* —NUMBERS 28:26

*You shall count off seven weeks; start to count the seven
weeks when the sickle is first put to the standing grain.
Then you shall observe the Feast of Weeks for the
Eternal your God, offering your freewill contribution
according as the Eternal your God has blessed you.*
—DEUTERONOMY 16:9–10

Shavuot occurs on the sixth of the Hebrew month of Sivan. The
name Shavuot (meaning "weeks") derives from its celebration
seven weeks (a week of weeks) after Pesach.[43] In the Torah it is also
designated by the names Chag HaKatzir, the Harvest Festival
(Exodus 23:16), and Chag HaBikurim, the Festival of First Fruits
(Exodus 34:22). It is also know as *z'man matan torateinu*, the time
of the giving of the Torah.

Current observance is based on the Talmudic identification of
Shavuot with the events at Sinai.[44] Therefore it is called *z'man
matan Torateinu*, "the season of the giving of the Torah." On
Shavuot, we celebrate our covenantal relationship with God and
reaffirm our commitment to a Jewish life of study (*talmud Torah*)
and practice (mitzvah). The significance of the events at Sinai derives not only from the receiving of mitzvot but also from their acceptance, as is illustrated in Israel's response, *Naaseh v'nishma*, "We
will faithfully do" (Exodus 24:7). Sinai represents a constant effort
to confront life and history in light of this covenantal relationship.
The ceremony of confirmation (*Kabbalat Torah*) is a Reform inno-
vation and has added a new dimension to the meaning of the festival. It provides an opportunity for students of post–bar/bat mitzvah
age to affirm their relationship to Judaism and the Jewish people.

The Mitzvah of Observing Shavuot

שָׁבוּעוֹת
Shavuot

It is a mitzvah to observe Shavuot seven weeks after
Passover, on the sixth of Sivan, as it is said, "From
the day on which you bring the sheaf of elevation
offering—the day after the Sabbath [understood by the Rabbis to
mean the first day of Passover][45]—you shall count off seven weeks.

They must be complete: you must count until the day after the seventh week—fifty days. . . . On that same day you shall hold a celebration; it shall be a sacred occasion for you" (Leviticus 23:15–16, 23:21).

Decorating the Home and Synagogue

בִּכּוּרִים
Bikurim

It is customary to decorate one's home and the synagogue with greens and fresh flowers on Shavuot.[46] The greenery is a reminder of the ancient practice of bringing first fruits (*bikurim*) to the Temple in Jerusalem. It also calls to mind our hopes for an abundant harvest.

The Mitzvah of Reaffirming the Covenant

בְּרִית
B'rit

It is a mitzvah to reaffirm the covenant on Shavuot. Through the reading of the Ten Commandments at services, which recalls the establishment of the covenant and the contemplation of the importance of Torah and its lifelong study, תַּלְמוּד תּוֹרָה (*talmud Torah*), we renew our commitment to being part of the covenant people, עַם בְּרִית (*am b'rit*).[47] As part of the celebration of Shavuot, many congregations practice the custom of studying Torah late into Shavuot night.[48] This Torah vigil is called תִּקּוּן לֵיל שָׁבוּעוֹת (*Tikkun Leil Shavuot*).

Attending Confirmation Service

The ceremony of confirmation is one of the highlights of Shavuot observance in many synagogues.[49] When the Temple stood, Jews brought offerings of first fruits, *bikurim*, to the Temple on Shavuot. Today, parents bring their children to participate in confirmation. These young people are the first fruits of each year's harvest. They represent the hope and promise of tomorrow. During the service, the confirmands reaffirm their commitment to the covenant. "[The confirmation's] purpose is to encourage the intellectual and spiritual growth of young people, to strengthen the bonds between them and the Israelites who received the Torah at Sinai (Exodus 19:3–8 and Deuteronomy 29:9–14), and to stimulate their love for God and the Jewish people" (*Gates of Mitzvah*, page 22, E-8).

Reading of the Book of Ruth

מְגִילַת רוּת

M'gilat Rut

The Book of Ruth (*M'gilat Rut*) is read on Shavuot.[50] The story of Ruth takes place during the barley harvest at the Shavuot season. More important, Rabbinic tradition sees a parallel between Ruth's willing acceptance of Judaism and the Jewish people's acceptance of Torah.[51]

Special Foods

It is customary to eat dairy dishes on Shavuot. Rabbinic tradition draws an analogy between the sweetness and physical nourishment the Jew receives from milk and honey and the sweetness and spiritual nourishment of the words of Torah.[52]

Yizkor on Shavuot

יִזְכֹּר

Yizkor

Yizkor is recited on Shavuot. It is a mitzvah to join with the congregation in reciting *Yizkor*. It memorializes our deceased relatives and friends as well as the martyrs of our generation and previous generations. (See "*Yizkor*," pages 120–122; and *Gates of Mitzvah*, page 63, D-10. The text for the *Yizkor* service can be found in *Mishkan T'filah: A Reform Siddur*, pages 574–583.)

SUKKOT
(Including Sh'mini Atzeret–Simchat Torah)

On the fifteenth day of this seventh month there shall be the Feast of Booths to the Eternal, [to last] seven days.
—LEVITICUS 23:34

After the ingathering from your threshing floor and your vat, you shall hold the Feast of Booths for seven days.
—DEUTERONOMY 16:13

On the eighth day you shall observe a sacred occasion.
                                    —LEVITICUS 23:36

Sukkot begins on the fifteenth of the Hebrew month of Tishrei and concludes on the twenty-second with Sh'mini Atzeret–Simchat Torah. Sukkot is the fall harvest festival.[53] The eighth day, Sh'mini Atzeret, functions as the conclusion of Sukkot but is also a separate festival.[54] Since Reform Jews follow the calendar of the Land of Israel and do not add a ninth day to the festival, we celebrate Simchat Torah and Sh'mini Atzeret on the same day.

More than any other of the Pilgrimage Festivals, Sukkot, also known as *HeChag,* has retained its agricultural character. However, Sukkot is also the commemoration of a significant event in the life of the Jewish people: the journey through the wilderness toward the Land of Israel. The Torah identifies the sukkah (booth) with the temporary dwellings in which the Israelites lived during that journey (Leviticus 23:42).

The mood of Sukkot is particularly joyous. Its beautiful symbolism of the successful harvest provides a welcome change of religious pace from the solemn days of prayer and introspection of Rosh HaShanah and Yom Kippur. While all of the Three Pilgrimage Festivals are times of rejoicing, Sukkot is specifically designated as *z'man simchateinu,* "the season of our rejoicing."[55] Even while we rejoice, the sukkah's temporary and fragile structure reminds us how precarious life can be.

Through the use of the *lulav* and *etrog,*[56] we acknowledge our dependence on God for the food we eat. Living in an urban environment, it is easy to forget that both human labor and divine blessing make the world fruitful. On Sukkot our thoughts turn to the wonder and beauty of the world, to our responsibilities as its caretakers, and to our obligation to share, for God is the true owner of the land and its produce.

Sh'mini Atzeret–Simchat Torah is the day on which we finish reading the last verses of Deuteronomy and immediately begin again with the first verses of Genesis. The Torah scrolls are removed from the ark and carried around the synagogue. The celebration is one of unbridled joy as we express our happiness at having lived to complete the reading of the Torah yet another time and to begin reading it again.

The Mitzvah of Observing Sukkot

It is a mitzvah to observe Sukkot for seven days, from the fifteenth of the Hebrew month of Tishrei, and to conclude on the twenty-second (the eighth day) with the observance of Sh'mini Atzeret–Simchat Torah, as the Torah says, "On the fifteenth day of the seventh month there shall be the Feast of Booths to the Eternal, [to last] seven days. . . . On the eighth day you shall observe a sacred occasion" (Leviticus 23:34, 36).

The Mitzvah of Rejoicing

זְמַן שִׂמְחָתֵנוּ
Z'man Simchateinu

It is a mitzvah to rejoice on Sukkot, as the Torah teaches, "You shall rejoice on your festival . . . for the Eternal your God will bless all your crops and all your undertakings, and you shall have nothing but joy" (Deuteronomy 16:14–15). While rejoicing is a mitzvah on all of the Three Pilgrimage Festivals, it is characteristic of the observance of Sukkot—so much so that the tradition has designated it as *z'man simchateinu*, "the season of our rejoicing."

The Mitzvah of *Tzedakah*

צְדָקָה
Tzedakah

It is always a mitzvah to give *tzedakah*.[57] However, since on Sukkot we give thanks for the harvest, all the more should we feel obliged to share with those who are less fortunate.

The Mitzvah of Building a Sukkah

סוּכָּה
Sukkah

It is a mitzvah for every Jew to dwell in the sukkah, though today that generally means spending time in the sukkah rather than actually living in it.[58] It is a custom to begin the construction of the sukkah immediately after the conclusion of Yom Kippur services (see page 44, "Beginning the Sukkah after Yom Kippur,") followed by decorating it. The sukkah may be built in a yard or on a roof or balcony. Those who live in apartments or other locations where the construction of a sukkah is not feasible can help in the building or decorating of the sukkah at the synagogue, the community center, or the home of friends—and spend time within it.

The Mitzvah of *Lulav* and *Etrog*

לוּלָב / אֶתְרוֹג
Lulav/Etrog

It is a mitzvah to take up the *lulav* and *etrog* and recite the appropriate blessing at any time during the whole day of Sukkot.[59]

בָּרוּךְ אַתָּה, יְיָ אֱלֹהֵינוּ,
מֶלֶךְ הָעוֹלָם, אֲשֶׁר קִדְּשָׁנוּ
בְּמִצְוֹתָיו וְצִוָּנוּ
עַל נְטִילַת לוּלָב.

Baruch atah, Adonai Eloheinu,
Melech haolam, asher kid'shanu
b'mitzvotav v'tzivanu
al n'tilat lulav.

Praise to You, Adonai, Sovereign of all, who hallows us with mitzvot, commanding us to take up the *lulav*.

The text of the blessing and additional prayers can be found in *On the Doorposts of Your House*, page 97, and in *Mishakn T'filah: A Reform Siddur*, page 571. By taking up the לוּלָב (*lulav*) and אֶתְרוֹג (*etrog*) and waving them in all directions, we symbolically acknowledge the sovereignty of God over all nature.[60]

The *lulav* and *etrog* are two of the four species, אַרְבָּעָה מִינִים (*arbaah minim*). They consist of *etrog* (citron), *lulav* (palm), הֲדַס *hadas* (myrtle), and עֲרָבָה *aravah* (willow). The identification of the four species is based on the interpretation of Leviticus 23:40, "On the first day you shall take the product of the *hadar* trees, branches of palm trees, boughs of leafy trees, and willows of the brook."[61]

The *etrog* has maintained a separate identity. Two willow branches and three myrtle branches are bound together around one palm branch and are called the *lulav*.[62]

It is desirable to acquire a *lulav* and *etrog,* and it is preferable, where possible, to select one's own set.[63] By selecting a beautiful *lulav* and *etrog,* we enhance the performance of the mitzvah (see *"Hidur Mitzvah:* The Aesthetics of Mitzvot," pages 107–109). The palm, myrtle, and willow should be fresh and green. It is customary to take special care in selecting the *etrog.* It should be yellow, with no discoloration on its skin. The tip (*pitom*) should not be broken.

The Mitzvah of Celebrating in the Sukkah
It is a mitzvah to celebrate in the sukkah. The Torah says, "You shall live in booths seven days; all citizens of Israel shall live in booths, in order that the future generations may know that I made the Israelite people live in booths when I brought them out of the land of Egypt" (Leviticus 23:42–43).

The Torah speaks of living in the sukkah for seven days. Where climate and circumstances permit, some will want to do so. However, others will prefer to fulfill this mitzvah by eating in the sukkah (either a whole meal or a symbolic meal or by making *Kiddush* there). When eating or reciting *Kiddush* in the sukkah, an additional blessing is recited:

בָּרוּךְ אַתָּה, יְיָ אֱלֹהֵינוּ,

מֶלֶךְ הָעוֹלָם, אֲשֶׁר קִדְּשָׁנוּ

בְּמִצְוֹתָיו וְצִוָּנוּ

לֵישֵׁב בַּסֻּכָּה.

Baruch atah, Adonai Eloheinu,
Melech haolam, asher kid'shanu
b'mitzvotav v'tzivanu
leisheiv basukkah.

Praise to You, Adonai our God, Sovereign of the universe, who hallows us with Your mitzvot, commanding us to dwell in the sukkah.

When circumstances do not permit one to fulfill this mitzvah in one's own sukkah, one should seek out the sukkah at the synagogue, at the community center, or at the home of friends.

The Mitzvah of Hospitality

הַכְנָסַת
אוֹרְחִים
*Hachnasat
Or'chim*

As part of the mitzvah of hospitality, we are urged to share our meals in gratitude for God's gifts.[64] There is a ceremony of welcoming guests known as אֻשְׁפִּיזִין (*ushpizin*), which evokes the presence of the Patriarchs and Matriarchs as our spiritual companions in the sukkah. (The text can be found in *On the Doorposts of Your House*, pages 94–96.)

Reading of *Kohelet*

קֹהֶלֶת
Kohelet

The Book of *Kohelet* (Ecclesiastes) is read on the Shabbat during Sukkot.[65] Like the sukkah, it reminds us of the transitory nature of life.

Chol HaMoeid

חוֹל הַמּוֹעֵד
Chol Hamoeid

The intermediate days of Sukkot are known as *chol hamoeid*. The mitzvot of celebrating in the sukkah and blessing the *lulav* can be performed during this time. Each day can be an opportunity for rejoicing and for preserving the festival atmosphere.[66]

Sh'mini Atzeret–Simchat Torah

שְׁמִינִי עֲצֶרֶת
Sh'mini Atzeret

שִׂמְחַת תּוֹרָה
Simchat Torah

Sh'mini Atzeret–Simchat Torah follows the seventh day of Sukkot[67] and is celebrated as a day of rejoicing. The mitzvot that are common to all the other festivals are observed on Sh'mini Atzeret–Simchat Torah (see page 48, "The Mitzvah of the Festivals").

The Mitzvah of Completing and Beginning the Torah Cycle on Sh'mini Atzeret–Simchat Torah

קְרִיאַת הַתּוֹרָה
K'riat HaTorah

It is a mitzvah to participate in the *hakafah* (Torah procession) honoring the completion and beginning of the Torah-reading cycle and to hear the reading of the end of Deuteronomy and the beginning of Genesis.[68] The Torah is divided into weekly portions that are read throughout the entire year, from beginning to end. The completion of the reading of the Torah is a time of rejoicing and an opportunity to express love for Torah. Immediately after completing the reading of the last verses of Deuteronomy, the first verses of Genesis are read to indicate that the study of Torah never ends. It symbolizes our obligation to observe the mitzvah of *talmud Torah* constantly.

The Mitzvah of *Yizkor*

יִזְכֹּר
Yizkor

Yizkor services take place on Sh'mini Atzeret–Simchat Torah.[69] It is a mitzvah to join with the congregation in reciting *Yizkor*. It memorializes our deceased relatives and friends as well as the martyrs of our generation and previous generations. (See "*Yizkor*," pages 120–122 and *Gates of Mitzvah*, page 63, D-10. The text for the *Yizkor* service can be found in *Mishkan T'filah: A Reform Siddur*, pages 574–583.)

Consecration

Since Simchat Torah is a joyful affirmation of the mitzvah of Torah study, some congregations hold a special ceremony for children entering religious school for the first time. The ceremony, called consecration, emphasizes the importance and joy of *talmud Torah* in Jewish tradition. It is also the custom at consecration to give the children something sweet so that they may look upon the learning of Torah as sweet.[70] In addition, many congregations present the children with miniature Torah scrolls, which the children then keep in a special place.

Chanukah and Purim

חנוכה ופורים

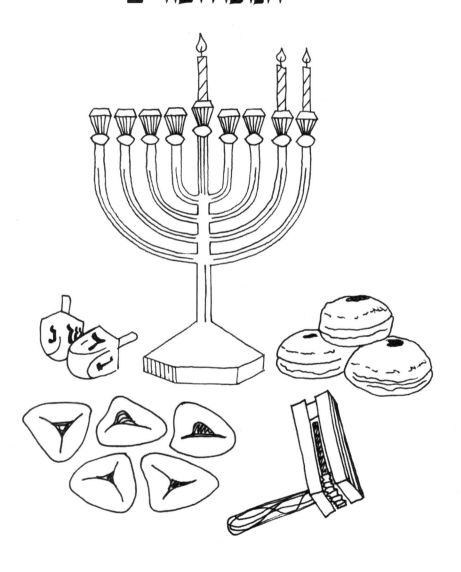

Chanukah and Purim

CHANUKAH

> *Now on the twenty-fifth day of the ninth month, which
> is called the month of Kislev, in the 148th year, they rose
> up in the morning and offered sacrifice according to the
> law upon the new altar of burnt offerings, which they
> had made. At the very season and on the very day that
> the gentiles had profaned it, it was dedicated with songs,
> citterns, harps, and cymbals. . . . And so they kept the
> dedication of the altar eight days. . . . Moreover Judah
> and his brethren, with the whole congregation of Israel,
> ordained that the days of the dedication of the altar
> should be kept in their season from year to year for eight
> days, from the twenty-fifth day of the month Kislev, with
> mirth and gladness.*
>
> —I MACCABEES 4:52–59

> *What is Chanukah? For the Rabbis have taught: Com-
> mencing with the twenty-fifth day of the month of Kislev,
> there are eight days upon which there shall be neither
> mourning nor fasting. For when the Hellenists entered
> the Temple, they defiled all the oil that was there. It was
> when the might of the Hasmonean dynasty overcame
> and vanquished them that, upon search, only a single
> cruse of undefiled oil, sealed by the High Priest, was
> found. In it was oil enough for the needs of a single day.
> A miracle was wrought and it burned eight days. The
> next year they ordained these days a holiday with songs
> and praises.*
>
> —BABYLONIAN TALMUD, SHABBAT 21b

CHANUKAH BEGINS on the twenty-fifth day of the Hebrew month of Kislev and lasts for eight days. It commemorates the victory of Judah Maccabee and his followers over the forces of the Greco-Syrian tyrant Antiochus Ephiphanes and the rededication of the Temple in Jerusalem, which the Syrians had profaned. Chanukah celebrates more than the end of an unsuccessful attempt by an outside power to destroy Judaism. The threat to Judaism was both internal and external. The assimilation to Hellenistic culture was so great that certain elements within Jewish society sought to become fully assimilated, to be accepted as Greek citizens, and to participate in Greek culture at the expense of their own unique Judaic culture. The resistance of the Maccabees and their allies to the blandishments of assimilation preserved Judaism. The story of Chanukah is the age-old struggle of the Jewish people to remain Jewish in a non-Jewish world.

To celebrate their victory and to rededicate the Temple, the Maccabees proclaimed an eight-day festival, which was to be observed annually.[1] According to the Talmudic legend, when the Hasmoneans recaptured and cleansed the Temple, they were able to find only a single cruse of oil with the seal of the High Priest, sufficient for one day's lighting of the menorah. But, as the story goes, a miracle occurred, and it burned for eight days.[2]

The nightly kindling of the menorah with its increasingly brighter light has become a symbol for both our physical and spiritual resistance to tyranny and assimilation.[3] Jewish tradition has preserved this twofold concept of resistance. The heroic Maccabean triumph is counterbalanced by the words of the prophet Zechariah: "Not by might, nor by power, but by My Spirit, says the God of heaven's hosts" (Zechariah 4:6).[4]

The Mitzvah of Observing Chanukah
It is a mitzvah to observe Chanukah for eight days. The Rabbis taught, "Commencing with the twenty-fifth of Kislev, there are eight days upon which there shall be neither mourning nor fasting."[5]

The Mitzvah of Kindling Chanukah Lights

It is a mitzvah to kindle the Chanukah lights at home with the appropriate blessing. Some people choose to use oil lamps instead of candles to strengthen the connection to the rekindling of the menorah in the Temple:[6]

בָּרוּךְ אַתָּה, יְיָ אֱלֹהֵינוּ, *Baruch atah, Adonai Eloheinu,*

מֶלֶךְ הָעוֹלָם, אֲשֶׁר קִדְּשָׁנוּ *Melech haolam, asher kid'shanu*

בְּמִצְוֹתָיו וְצִוָּנוּ *b'mitzvotav v'tzivanu*

לְהַדְלִיק נֵר שֶׁל חֲנֻכָּה. *l'hadlik ner shel Chanukah.*

Blessed are You, Adonai our God, Sovereign of all, who hallows us with mitzvot, commanding us to kindle the Chanukah lights.

בָּרוּךְ אַתָּה, יְיָ אֱלֹהֵינוּ, *Baruch atah, Adonai Eloheinu,*

מֶלֶךְ הָעוֹלָם, שֶׁעָשָׂה נִסִּים *Melech haolam, she-asah nisim*

לַאֲבוֹתֵינוּ וְאִמּוֹתֵינוּ *laavoteinu v'imoteinu*

בַּיָּמִים הָהֵם *bayamim haheim*

בַּזְּמַן הַזֶּה. *baz'man hazeh.*

Blessed are You, Adonai our God, Sovereign of all, who performed wondrous deeds for our ancestors in days of old at this season.

FOR FIRST NIGHT ONLY:

בָּרוּךְ אַתָּה, יְיָ אֱלֹהֵינוּ, *Baruch atah, Adonai Eloheinu,*

מֶלֶךְ הָעוֹלָם, שֶׁהֶחֱיָנוּ *Melech haolam, shehecheyanu*

וְקִיְּמָנוּ וְהִגִּיעָנוּ *v'kiy'manu v'higianu*

לַזְּמַן הַזֶּה. *laz'man hazeh.*

Blessed are You, Adonai our God, Sovereign of all, for giving us life, for sustaining us, and for enabling us to reach this season.

Appropriate readings for each night can be found in *On the Doorposts of Your House*, pages 113–119, and in *Mishkan T'filah: A Reform Siddur*, page 572.

One candle is lit for each night. The candle for the first night is placed on the right side of the special eight-branched מְנוֹרָה (menorah) (or חֲנֻכִּיָּה, *chanukiyah*). On each subsequent night, an additional candle is placed to the left of the preceding night's candle.

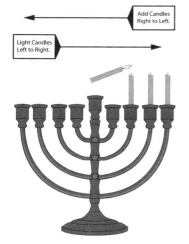

The lighting proceeds from left to right so that the new candle is kindled first. No practical use may be made of the Chanukah lights, such as illuminating the room. Therefore, according to Jewish tradition, a special candle known as the שַׁמָּשׁ (*shamash*) is used to light the others and to provide light.[7]

On Friday night the Chanukah lights are lit before Shabbat candles, and on Saturday night they are lit after *Havdalah*.[8]

Displaying the חֲנֻכִּיָּה (*Chanukiyah*)
(*Persumei HaNeis*—Publicizing the Miracle)

It is an old custom to place the *chanukiyah* where its lights will be visible from the outside.[9] The public proclamation of the miracle of Chanukah (of the cruse of oil and of our survival against the external enemy Antiochus and the internal threat of assimilation) is part of the observance of the holiday. Displaying the *chanukiyah* is a demonstration of Jewish pride and an affirmation of Jewish identity.

Special Foods

The food customs of Chanukah include eating dairy dishes, as well as foods cooked in oil.[10] Among Ashkenazi Jews, the most frequently served dish is potato latkes. Some communities also make sweet cheese latkes. The Israeli custom of serving *sufganiyot* (jelly doughnuts) has been adopted around the Jewish world. The eating of special foods adds to the enjoyment of the holiday. (See "The People of the Food," by Tina Wasserman, pages 141–144.)

Dreidel

Playing games has long been associated with Chanukah. The most popular is the game of dreidel (or *s'vivon.*)[11] A dreidel is a four-sided top with the Hebrew letters *nun, gimel, hei,* and *shin* inscribed on its sides. The letters have been popularly identified as a mnemonic for *Neis gadol hayah sham,* "A great miracle happened there." Dreidels in Israel use the letters נ (*nun*), ג (*gimel*), ה (*hei*), and פ (*pei*), standing for *Neis gadol hayah po,* "A great miracle happened *here.*"

Chanukah Gifts

Many people exchange gifts during Chanukah or give small sums of money to children. These practices are part of Chanukah's special appeal during what has become a time of almost universal gift giving. While this practice can add to the enjoyment of the holiday, undue emphasis should not be placed upon the giving and receiving of gifts. When money is given, children can be encouraged to use some of it for *tzedakah.* In any case, it is important to stress the real message of Chanukah—the struggle of the Jewish people to remain distinctive in a non-Jewish world.

PURIM

> *The rest of the Jews, those in the king's provinces, likewise mustered and fought for their lives. . . . That was on the thirteenth day of the month of Adar; and they rested on the fourteenth day and made it a day of feasting and merrymaking. (But the Jews in Shushan mustered on both the thirteenth and fourteenth days, and so rested on the fifteenth, and made it a day of feasting and merrymaking.) That is why village Jews, who live in unwalled towns, observe the fourteenth day of the month of Adar and make it a day of merrymaking and feasting, and as a holiday and an occasion for sending gifts to one another.*
>
> —ESTHER 9:16–19

Purim, which occurs on the fourteenth of the Hebrew month of Adar (or in Jerusalem, on the fifteenth),[12] is a celebration of the events described in the Scroll of Esther (*M'gilat Esther*). The holiday, with its joyous carnival-like atmosphere, focuses on one of the main themes in Jewish history—the survival of the Jewish people despite the attempts of their enemies to destroy them. According to the Scroll of Esther, the name Purim is derived from the lot (*pur*) cast by Haman to determine the day on which the Jews would be exterminated (Esther 3:7).

The story of Purim is about hunger for power and about hatred born of the Jews' refusal to assimilate and their unwillingness to compromise religious principles by bowing before the secular authority. It is an old story. However, it has been repeated many times, making it both an ancient and modern tale.[13]

In the story, it is related that Mordecai, Esther's cousin, refuses to prostrate himself before Haman, the vizier of King Ahasuerus. So infuriated is Haman that he seeks the annihilation of the Jewish people. Haman's accusation against the Jewish people has become the paradigm for all anti-Semites: "There is a certain people, scattered abroad and dispersed among the peoples . . . their laws are different from those of other people, they do not obey the king's law, and the king should not tolerate them" (Esther 3:8). The prudent actions of Mordecai and the courage of Esther avert tragedy.

Purim recalls the dangers of minority status. Hatred of the foreigner and the stranger is still prevalent throughout the world. Anti-Semitism has not disappeared, but despite everything, the Jewish people has survived. Purim, however, is most of all a happy story—a story of survival and triumph over evil.

The Mitzvah of Observing Purim

It is a mitzvah to observe Purim on the fourteenth of Adar.[14] This is based on the statement "Village Jews, who live in unwalled towns, observe the fourteenth day of the month of Adar and make it a day of merrymaking and feasting, and as a holiday and an occasion for sending gifts to one another" (Esther 9:19). However, in walled cities like Shushan, Purim was observed on the fifteenth day (Esther 9:18). Even though the walls of Jerusalem had been destroyed at this time, the Rabbis designated Jerusalem the status of a walled city.

The Mitzvah of Reading the Scroll of Esther (*M'gilat Esther*)

מְגִלַּת אֶסְתֵּר
M'gillat Esther

It is a mitzvah to read the biblical Scroll of Esther (*M'gilat Esther*; commonly, the *M'gilah*) and to celebrate the holiday with the congregation.[15] As part of the *M'gilah* reading, it is customary for the listeners to attempt to drown out the sound of Haman's name by shouting or using *gragers* (*raashanim*—special noisemakers).[16] Purim blessings can be found in *On the Doorposts of Your House*, page 120, and in *Mishkan T'filah: A Reform Siddur*, page 573.

Rejoicing and Feasting

מִשְׁתֶּה
Mishteh

The almost unrestrained merriment that pervades the celebration of Purim makes it unique among the Jewish holidays.[17] Adults and children are encouraged to wear costumes.[18] Synagogues and communities stage Purim plays, hold carnivals, and serve festive communal meals. All these activities are an expression of great joy at having survived Haman and countless other enemies.

Special Foods

אָזְנֵי הָמָן
Oznei Haman

Hamantaschen (Haman's pockets), or *oznei Haman* in Hebrew (Haman's ears), are three-cornered cookies filled with poppy seeds or other fruits served on Purim.

The Sending of Portions (*Mishlo-ach Manot*)

מִשְׁלוֹחַ מָנוֹת
Mishlo-ach Manot

Traditionally Purim is a time for exchanging gifts. It is customary to send gifts of food or pastries to friends and family. The sending of these gifts is called *mishlo-ach manot*, "the sending of portions" (Esther 9:22). (This custom is often called *shalachmanos*.)

The Mitzvah of Sending Gifts to the Poor

מַתָּנוֹת לָאֶבְיוֹנִים
Matanot La-evyonim

It is a mitzvah to send gifts to the poor on Purim.[19] The sending of gifts to the poor is an act of *tzedakah* that is especially connected with Purim.

Other Special Days

ימים מיוחדים

ROSH CHODESH (New Month)

The months of the Hebrew calendar are determined by the recurring phases of the moon; the new month begins when the new moon appears (see "The Jewish Calendar," pages 5–9).

From the earliest times, the lunar month was far more than a measuring device for Jews. The cycles of *hama-or hakatan*, "the lesser light" (Genesis 1:16), served as a reminder of God's work of Creation and led naturally to the celebration of the new moon as an important festival in biblical times.[20] The major festivals, with the exception of Shabbat, in turn, were dated by the new moon's occurrence.

The Mishnah describes in detail the procedure by which the new month was fixed in the days before the destruction of the Temple.[21] That catastrophe, combined with the development of a scientifically calculated calendar in the Talmudic period, served to diminish the significance of Rosh Chodesh, reducing it to a minor festival. Its observance today is generally limited to its proclamation in certain synagogues on the preceding Shabbat and to some liturgical changes in the service on the day of Rosh Chodesh.[22] (See *Mishkan T'filah: A Reform Siddur*, page 379.)

The one unusual feature of Rosh Chodesh is that, while it remained an ordinary workday for men, an ancient tradition declares it a women's holiday. Jewish women were to refrain from all work, or at least heavy work, on that day.[23] According to legend, God rewarded them with a special day of rest for refusing to join with the Israelite men in the sin of the Golden Calf.[24] Today, many Jewish women are reviving and reinterpreting this Rosh Chodesh tradition.[25] But Rosh Chodesh stands as a reminder to all Jews—women and men—of a special and distinct rhythm in our lives: the rhythm of Jewish time. Today many synagogues and other Jewish organizations have established special women-only Rosh Chodesh groups and experiences. Women gather together for study, ritual and celebration. There are also Rosh Chodesh groups for girls that are meant to strengthen self-esteem and Jewish identity.

YOM HASHOAH (Holocaust Remembrance Day)

The 27th of the Hebrew month of Nisan, called Yom HaShoah, was set aside in 1951 as a day of remembrance for the victims of the Holocaust by the Knesset (the Israeli Parliament). The Central Conference of American Rabbis in June 1977 called for the annual commemoration of Yom HaShoah on this date.[26]

Anti-Semitism and Nazism did not die with the end of World War II. The Shoah is a constant reminder of the potential for evil that lies below the veneer of civilization. The seeds of the Holocaust must not be allowed to find fertile soil again.

It is a mitzvah to remember the six million Jews who were murdered in the Shoah by attending special memorial services or programs at synagogues. Also, we should remember all of those who were singled out for death by the Nazis, such as Gypsies, handicapped people, and gays and lesbians. In addition we should remember and pay tribute to *chasidei umot haolam*, the righteous non-Jews who gave their lives in attempts to save members of the Jewish people.

To fulfill the mitzvah of remembrance, it is suggested that a memorial candle, often yellow, be lit, and relevant passages be read. Either as preparation or as part of the observance, one should spend time reviewing the events that led to the Shoah and discussing ways of preventing its recurrence. A service for Yom HaShoah can be found in *Mishkan T'filah: A Reform Siddur*, pages 521–533.

In keeping with the spirit of Yom HaShoah as a day of mourning, weddings should not be scheduled. It is further suggested that one eat a very simple meal on the eve of Yom HaShoah as an act of identification and solidarity with those who were in the concentration camps and slowly starved to death. It is particularly important to provide a permanent memorial to the *K'doshim*, the holy ones who perished. Therefore, our *tzedakah* on Yom HaShoah should be directed to institutions that preserve their memory.

YOM HAZIKARON (Israel Memorial Day)

The Israeli Knesset established the day before Yom HaAtzma-ut, Independence Day, as Memorial Day for soldiers who lost their lives fighting in the War of Independence and subsequent battles. Yom HaZikaron begins with an official ceremony at the Western Wall, as the flag of Israel is lowered to half-staff. Places of entertainment are closed by law. Radio and television stations play programs about Israel's military history and show programming that conveys the somber mood of the day.

As on Yom HaShoah, an air-raid siren is sounded twice during Yom HaZikaron. When the siren is heard, all activity, including traffic, immediately stops. People get out of their cars, freeze where they are, and stand at attention in memory of those who died defending Israel. The first siren marks the beginning of Memorial Day, and the second is sounded immediately prior to the public recitation of prayers in military cemeteries.

Numerous public ceremonies are held throughout Israel. There is a national ceremony at the military cemetery on Mount Herzl, where many of Israel's leaders and soldiers are buried. Many schools and public buildings have created memorials for those from their community who died in Israel's wars.

The day formally draws to a close at sundown with the official opening ceremony of Israel Independence Day on Mount Herzl, when the flag of Israel is returned to full staff. Scheduling Yom HaZikaron right before Yom HaAtzma-ut is intended to remind people of the sacrifice soldiers and their families and friends have made for Israel's independence and security. This transition shows the importance of this day among Israelis, most of whom have served in the armed forces or have a connection with people who were killed during military service.

Outside of Israel some congregations commemorate Yom HaZikaron by reciting a memorial prayer like the one found in *Mishkan T'filah,* page 534, or by observing a moment of silence at the time when it is observed in Israel. Some hold their own public ceremonies in solidarity with the State of Israel and create their own memorials to the fallen.

YOM HAATZMA-UT (Israel Independence Day)

On the fifth day of the Hebrew month of Iyar 5708 (May 14, 1948), Israel was reborn as a modern, independent state. Since that time Jews throughout the world have celebrated the day in commemoration and rejoicing. In response to the widespread observance of Yom HaAtzma-ut among Reform Jews, the Central Conference of American Rabbis, at its convention on Mount Scopus in 1970, proclaimed Israel Independence Day "a permanent annual festival in the religious calendar of Reform Judaism."[27] In addition, the Reform Movement has provided special Torah and haftarah readings for the day.[28]

The celebration of Yom HaAtzma-ut recognizes that a new era has dawned in the life of the Jewish people. It attests to the essential unity of the whole household of Israel and marks the cultural and spiritual renaissance that draws strength from the symbiotic relationship between Israel and world Jewry. The rebirth of Israel from the ashes of the Shoah is a symbol of hope against despair, of redemption against devastation.

It is a mitzvah for every Jew to mark Yom HaAtzma-ut by participation in public worship services or celebrations that affirm the bond between the Jews living in the Land of Israel and those living outside. A service for Yom HaAztma-ut can be found in *Mishkan T'filah: A Reform Siddur*, pages 538–553. Furthermore, a special act of *tzedakah* to an organization or institution that helps to strengthen the State of Israel is a significant way of affirming the unity of the Jewish people. Preparing a festive meal on Yom HaAtzma-ut that includes foods from Israel and Israeli songs is also an appropriate way to mark the day.

These three new commemorations, Yom HaShoah, Yom HaZikaron, and Yom HaAtzma-ut represent the effect of modern culture on the lengthy history of the Jewish people, being the first additions to the Jewish holiday calendar since antiquity. Together they function as a vital part of Israel's "civil religion," Yom Ha-Zikaron being a perfect example of a holiday whose commemoration and practice are uniquely Israeli while still being universally Jewish.

TISHAH B'AV (Ninth of Av)

Tishah B'Av (the Ninth of Av) has been the traditional day of mourning that commemorates major tragic events of the past—the destruction of the First Temple by the Babylonians in 587 BCE and of the Second Temple by the Romans in 70 CE,[29] and the expulsion from Spain in 1492. Tradition has assigned additional subsequent major tragedies to the ninth of Av.[30] The special liturgy of the day, which has developed from the biblical Book of Lamentations, recalls the pain and suffering of the Jewish people.

Although many Jews have abandoned Tishah B'Av, in part because of the reestablishment of the State of Israel, others continue to observe it by attending special services or by fasting, or both. (See "*Tzom*: Fasting as a Religious/Spiritual Practice" by Rabbi Sue Levi Elwell, in *The Sacred Table: Creating a Jewish Food Ethic*, edited by Rabbi Mary Zamore, pages 445–455.)

It is suggested that weddings not be scheduled for Tishah B'Av. Many Reform Jews do not, however, observe the traditional strictures of avoiding weddings during certain periods before Tishah B'Av.

TU BISH'VAT (Fifteenth of Sh'vat)

The fifteenth day of Sh'vat (Chamishah-Asar BiSh'vat or Tu BiSh'vat)[31] is designated by the Mishnah as the New Year for Trees. While it is a minor holiday without many prescribed observances, it is customary to eat fruits grown in Israel, especially the fruit of the carob tree (*bokser*). Among the kabbalists, a seder modeled on

Pesach developed that highlighted the seven biblical species found in the Land of Israel.[32] These are wheat, barley, olives, pomegranate, honey (most likely from dates), figs, and grapes.

Two options for Tu Bish'vat seders can be found in *Seder Tu Bishevat,* by Adam Fisher (CCAR Press, 1989).

Since the resettling of Israel, the day has been observed as a time for planting trees as a part of the reclamation of the land. Many Reform religious schools arrange special programs aimed at raising funds for the Jewish National Fund and celebrating the gradual awakening of the land from the grip of winter. Because there are no special mitzvot associated with Tu BiSh'vat, its observances vary from place to place, and new celebrations are emerging.

Essays

What Is a Mitzvah?

THE WORD mitzvah is used many times throughout this volume. Mitzvah is a complicated concept, one with which Jews have long wrestled. As you notice, we have made a deliberate choice to not translate mitzvah. The word mitzvah derives from the Hebrew root *tzadi-vav-hei*, which means "to command," and is used throughout the Torah. The simplest way to translate the word mitzvah would then be "commandment," but that the leads to a number of important questions. What is the source of the commandments? God? If so, how did God communicate the commandments? And as Reform Jews we have to ask: If God is not the sole author of the material in the Torah, then how do we understand the meaning of mitzvah? Perhaps the source of the commandments is the historical experience of the Jewish people. Perhaps the source of the commandments is the lived interaction with our environment and the wisdom we have gained to create a better world. Or perhaps the only thing we can truly call a commandment is ethical behavior, where we treat others with the respect and dignity that is implied in the concept that each human being is created in the image of God.

Rather than defining this complex term mitzvah, we share with you the thoughts of prominent Jewish thinkers from past and current generations. Perhaps in reading their thoughts on the meaning of mitzvah, you will be able to shape your own sense of what it means to live in relationship with the commandments as a Jew. In *Gates of Mitzvah*, a companion volume to this publication, there are four essays by leading rabbinic scholars of the past generation who explored each of these possibilities from their own perspective. Each essay, excerpted here, provides a different perspective on mitzvah. Following these are excerpts from more contemporary rabbis.

Rabbi Herman E. Schaalman affirms the divine authority of the mitzvah. He writes:

A mitzvah—commandment—comes from a *M'tzaveh*, a Commander. In our case, indisputably, that Commander was God, first by way of Moses and then by way of prophets and rabbis, the spiritual descendants of Moses. . . .

What do we mean by stating that God is Commander, *M'tzaveh*? How does God command? Does God "speak"? How did Moses or others "hear"? Why these commandments as found in Torah and later tradition and not others?

Revelation, for that is what we are talking about, is a mystery. The character of a mystery, its very essence, precludes our ability to describe and analyze it with precision, in clearly stated detail. If we could so understand and describe it, it would no longer be a mystery. There is something impenetrable about a mystery, something that ultimately defies our human efforts at understanding in ordinary, day-to-day terms. . . .

Language is the problem here. We use terms such as "speaks" and "hears" when talking of God in the same manner as we do when talking of humans. We apply them to the mystery of encounter with God, to the unique and rare moments when a given person and the Divine Presence "meet," without making due allowance for the essentially different use and meaning of these words when they are applied to the mystery of revelation.

God becomes the "Speaker," the "Commander," the *M'tzaveh*, because Moses, in his extraordinary nearness to God, thus understood, thus interpreted, thus "heard," the impact and meaning of God's Presence. God is *M'tzaveh*—Commander—because Moses experienced himself as *m'tzuveh* —commanded, summoned, directed. And this is why Moses transmitted what he "heard," why he expressed the meaning of God's Presence in the mitzvot, the commandments to the people at Sinai and to their descendants ever after. This is why the Torah is both *Torat Adonai*, God's Torah, and *Torat Mosheh*, Moses's Torah.

This is why the Talmud can say, *Dibra Torah bilshon b'nei adam*, "Torah speaks human language." . . .

Why do we do mitzvot? Why should we do mitzvot? Because we are the descendants of those ancestors, the children of those parents who said at Sinai, *Naaseh v'nishma*, "We shall do and we shall hear" (Exodus 24:7). All authentic Judaism until now has so understood itself, has so acted, and so handed it on to hitherto faithful new generations. Thus the Divine Presence waits for us, and we for It. Thus the commandment comes to us in our time, asking to be heard, understood, and done. . . .

It is built into the very definition and basic assumption of a mitzvah that it is the human response to the "Commanding Presence of God." That response is not, and cannot be, invariably the same. It depends on circumstances. It is not automatic. That response to the commanding God should never be altogether unthinking, routine. To be a genuine response of the person to God, it needs to take account of the condition, capacity, responsiveness, of the commanded one, that is, me.

Rabbi David Polish (*z"l*) asserts that the historical experience of the Jewish people is the source of the mitzvot. He writes:

The observance of mitzvot reflects a Jewish conception of history. This conception is composed of two elements. The first consists of historical events of which we are reminded by specific practices. The second consists of an outlook upon human events and the world that is embodied in a system of conduct and discipline, individual as well as corporate.

Mitzvot are related to historic experiences in which the Jewish people sought to apprehend God's nature and God's will. They are to be observed not because they are divine fiats, but because something happened between God and Israel, and the same something continues to happen in every age and land. Note the words of blessing preceding the performance of a mitzvah: *asher kid'shanu b'mitzvotav, v'tzivanu* . . . , "who has sanctified us through mitzvot and has commanded us. . . ." Mitzvot sanctify the Jewish people because they mark points of encounter by the Jewish people with God. They are enjoined upon us, because through them we perpetuate memories of the encounters and are sustained by those memories. Since they are so indigenous to us, they are incumbent primarily upon us, the Jewish people, and they constitute the singularity of the Jewish religion. . . .

Mitzvot are "signs" of the covenant, affirmed and reaffirmed through the ages at various turning points in which Jewish existence stood in the balance. Out of these turning points came hallowed insights, pointing to the pivotal moment and fashioning the mitzvah marking it. Thus, the Chanukah lights, marking Israel's rededication after near extinction. Thus, *milah* (circumcision), which began with Abraham and which was invoked with special intensity during critical periods in Jewish history. . . . Moments in the life of the individual Jew are intimately related to Israel's historic career. . . .

It cannot be stressed too strongly that the observance of any particular mitzvah is a symbol of, and points to, a higher truth. Some symbols, because of their overpowering hold on us, endure; others change. Some fall into desuetude; new ones come into being. . . .

Finally, the mitzvah enabled the Jewish people to live creatively.

Rabbi Roland B. Gittelsohn (*z"l*) was a religious naturalist. He writes:

What is a religious naturalist? Briefly, he or she is a person who believes in God, but asserts that God inheres within nature and operates through natural law. A religious naturalist perceives God to be the Spiritual Energy, Essence, Core, or Thrust of the universe, not a discrete Supernatural Being. . . .

Mitzvah, by its very definition, must be cosmically grounded; it must possess empyreal significance. For the religious naturalist, as for all believing, practicing Jews, in

order to have mitzvah—that which has been commanded—
there must be a *m'tzaveh*, a commander. That commander,
moreover, needs to be more than human ingenuity or
convenience. . . .

But how can an Energy or Essence, a Core or a Thrust,
command? For the religious naturalist, who is the *m'tzaveh*?
Answer: reality itself. Or, more precisely, the physical and
spiritual laws that govern reality. Mitzvot must be observed
because only by recognizing and conforming to the nature
of their environment can human beings increase the prob-
ability of their survival in any meaningful way. Mitzvot are
not human-made; they inhere within the universe. . . .

Most of the mitzvot spelled out in this guide, however,
deal with ritual observance rather than physical law or ethics. Are they, too, related to cosmic reality? In a less obvious
but equally binding sense than the physical or moral im-
peratives suggested above, yes. Human nature is such that
we need to express our emotions and ideals with our whole
bodies, not just our tongues. We need also to be visually and
kinetically reminded of our noblest values and stimulated to
pursue them. As otherwise lonely and frightened individuals, we need common practices and observances that bind
us into meaningful and supportive groups. All of which adds
up to the fact that we need ritual as something more than
social luxury or convenience. For us as Reform Jews, a particular ritual may not be mitzvah. But the need for a pattern
of such rituals, this—because it grows out of and satisfies
our very basic nature as human beings—is mitzvah. And this
we desperately need. . . .

The seder means no less, however, to the religiously natu-
ralistic Jew, who rejects miracles. Plugging into centuries of
our people's tradition as well as its unique pursuit of freedom, we visually, audibly, and dramatically commemorate
that pursuit and rededicate ourself to it. Our *m'tzaveh* is tri-
une: our very special human need to be free, both as a person and a Jew; our equally human need to augment speech
with memory and motion in reinforcement of our highest

values; and our specifically Jewish need to identify with our people's destiny.

Rabbi Arthur J. Lelyveld (*z"l*) reminds us that as Reform Jews we are deeply committed to ethics and social justice. He writes:

> We liberal Jews read Scripture not as the literal word of God, but as the work of members of the people of Israel seeking to understand the demand of God. Once we approach our Bible within that frame of reference, we necessarily become selective, for there are points in Scripture at which humans have broken through to an understanding of the highest, while there are also points that preserve primitive practices, anachronisms, or injunctions that long ago became obsolete.
>
> The solution of our difficulty lies in the very fact that we use the word mitzvah in two distinct ways. We talk about specific mitzvot, and we also speak of mitzvah in a more generalized sense, as enjoining upon us a certain attitude toward our fellows. . . .
>
> "Small-m" mitzvot—the performance of ritual acts—have an aesthetic and affective function. They both beautify and enhance by religious drama the moral values and the ideals of our heritage. They become a structure on which the preservation of our people's tradition and its continuity may rest. We select the mitzvot we will perform, we shape our folkways, change our music, revise our prayers, eliminate customs, and add other and new customs. But mitzvah is not the product of our human social engineering. Mitzvah is God's demand issuing in moral and spiritual values. Ceremonial mitzvot with their folk associations, their customs, and their symbolic objects and actions are the carrier of the values, the structural framework for the people's task of transmission. But "large-M" Mitzvah is the enduring essence to which the structure of small-m testifies and pays obeisance. . . .
>
> In the last analysis, liberalism cannot escape its commitment to the supreme right and obligation of decision that is

reserved to the individual soul. It is true that this makes the individual the ultimate authority as to what is Mitzvah and what is not Mitzvah.

Contemporary Reform Jews continue to study and think about the meaning of mitzvah in our lives. The following statements represent further ideas on this subject, both from some of today's Reform rabbinic leaders and from the up-and-coming next generation of rabbinic leadership.

Rabbi Herbert Bronstein writes about mitzvah as part of the relationship to the Divine Other outside the self:

> No one knowledgeable about Judaism will deny that these terms, Torah and mitzvah, are central to its lexicon. They are integral with the overreaching metaphor of the relationship between God and the community of Israel: the covenant (*b'rit*). No metaphor for the relationship between God and the people of Israel has been more pervasive in the Jewish religious outlook. This has been the case from the stories of the ancestors, through the prophetic literature, the later codes of law, and rabbinic discourse, to the theological expositions of our own day. The covenant relationship, whether conceived of as a partnership, alliance, or bond with God, or as engagement with God, can be actualized on the human side only through mitzvot, that is, deeds, actions, observances, and practices.
>
> This interrelated cluster of terms (Torah, mitzvah, *b'rit*) implies a spiritual mind-set that assumes an authority that transcends the individual ego, a sense of obligation, an "ought" to the Other beyond the individual self. Furthermore, after Sinai, the covenant with God is with the entire community of Israel as a group. All of these constructs—Torah, mitzvah, *b'rit*— therefore imply not only a strong sense of obligation

to God but also a communal consciousness, a sense of "we" that transcends the "me" or ego. This is clearly manifest in the communal stance of Jewish worship, of communal Jewish confession, of communal moral obligation, all of which have long been recognized as characteristics of historic Jewish identity.[1]

Rabbi Elaine Zecher offers the idea of mitzvah as the quintessential Jewish action:

Our tradition guides us with this teaching: *"Eilu d'varim she-ein lahem shiur:* These are things that are limitless, of which a person enjoys the fruit of this world, while the principal remains in the world to come. They are: honoring one's father and mother; engaging in deeds of compassion; arriving early for study, morning and evening; dealing graciously with guests; visiting the sick; providing for the wedding couple; accompanying the dead for burial; being devoted in prayer; and making peace among people."

These are mitzvot, deeds that have the potential to bring enhanced meaning to our lives and to those of others through conscious, mindful choices. Being present in our choices, being conscious in our decisions, draws us nearer to Judaism.

What does it mean to "to do a mitzvah" for us as liberal Jews? For one thing, mitzvot teach us how to regard our lives, how to "measure our days."

Tradition has it that 613 mitzvot exist in the Torah. There are 248 positive ones, like "honor your father and mother" (Exodus 20:12) and "remember the Sabbath day and keep it holy" (Exodus 20:8). There are 365 negative mitzvot, such as "do not murder" (Exodus 20:13) or "do not boil a calf in its mother's milk" (Exodus 23:19). A poetic interpretation of the numerical value of the division provides us with a great metaphor for the purpose of mitzvot. What if the 365 represented the number of days in the solar year, and what if 248 corresponded to the number of parts of the human body, modern scientific knowledge notwithstanding? Couldn't these numbers remind us that our tradition provides us with a way to live our lives every day with our whole being?

A mitzvah is a quintessential Jewish action, whether it is ethical or ritual, rational or irrational. Infused with a mindfulness of action, it has the potential to take on a variety of meanings. Consider the mitzvot related to keeping kosher, for example. We could spend hours analyzing them anthropologically, sociologically, or even politically. No matter how hard we try, however, we will never truly understand why some animals are kosher and others aren't. Understanding the essence of the mitzvah is another story. Could keeping kosher help to raise our consciousness about the food we eat? Could it help teach us how precious food is and how others might be hungry while we feast? The mitzvah of kashrut may raise our awareness about the issues of this world, like hunger or pollution or the sanctity of our own tables.

The divisions of ethical mitzvot and ritual mitzvot, or rational and irrational, are modem interpretations. All are inextricably intertwined. Abraham Joshua Heschel, one of the greatest modern-day theologians, saw no difference between different kinds of mitzvot. When he marched in Selma, Alabama, beside Dr. Martin Luther King, in the fight for civil rights, he returned home and described what he did. He said, "I felt my legs were praying" (*Moral Grandeur and Spiritual Audacity* by Abraham Joshua Heschel, p. viii). Heschel took the daily obligation of prayer and transformed it. The action spoke for itself. Heschel never wavered in his sense of purpose and mission. Mitzvot motivated him. They can motivate us as well, even when we are not sure we are able to take action.

Rabbi Elyse Frishman sees mitzvah as a way that we can find meaning and seek a connection with God:

Covenant can be understood in two ways: as obligation and as relationship. If one has little sense of relationship, covenant feels like a burdensome obligation. When one is embraced in relationship, the responsibilities of upholding it seem reasonable and necessary.

Reform Judaism is based on voluntary covenant: We choose to live Jewishly. It is crucial to base our theology in Torah. Torah is the starting point of all things Jewish. No matter what an individual believes, if it's not rooted in Torah, it's not Jewish; it is merely personal opinion. Torah has been commented upon, interpreted, even challenged; but all Judaism grows from it.

When we listen to Torah, we are listening to God's voice. But this is not necessarily what God speaks; it reflects what we hear. Dialogue between two people grows not from what is said but from what is heard. . . .

Tradition holds that God gave us mitzvot, that God commands certain behaviors. These commands were given to us in Torah. We consider the dialogue of Torah as God speaking to us. But, what if, instead, we consider that the language of Torah is not necessarily God's; it's a record of how we heard God. . . .

So why follow God's directions? Because they are compelling and infuse our lives with meaning. This is why liberal Jews observe and uphold the ritual and ethical guidelines. . . .

Perhaps the extensive comfort and security possessed by American Jewry frees us to hear God's voice differently from the way a persecuted community might. Indeed, freedom is our reality. The current trend toward spiritual life reflects the desire for more than personal fulfillment. We want to be of something greater than our individual selves. We yearn for true community. We seek God. And God's voice need not be heard as stern and commanding. God is the blessed Holy One: loving, caring, and seeking relationship with us.[2]

Rabbi Richard Levy writes about mitzvah as an act of love:

Mitzvah means "command." But to understand Torah as a call suggests that the call comes in a manner befitting the relationship we have with God. Two of the important ways in which Jews have traditionally related to God are as a child to a parent and as a lover with a spouse. . . . From human relationships we know that a child relates most closely with a parent and a lover relates most closely with the beloved, in hearing not a demand, but a request: As my wife puts it, "This is something I want you to do that is very important to me." One may say "No" to such requests—but the act of saying "No," or as Rosenzweig put it, "Not yet," also is a response.

In all these cases, heeding the call of a mitzvah becomes an act of love, responding to the call *V'ahavta et Adonai Elohecha*, "You shall love Adonai your God," just as, two prayers earlier, *Ahavah rabbah ahavtanu*, "A great love has God loved us."

How is that love most profoundly manifest? The *Ahavah Rabbah* asks that the God who taught our ancestors the laws of life might also show how much God loves us, however unworthy we may be, by teaching us Torah, as well (*t'choneinu ut'lamdeinu*). We are encouraged, when we study Torah, to feel ourselves invited to sit at God's study table, while the Author of the universe says, in a tone pitched differently for each of us, "This is a law that will help you live out more fully the direction of your life. This is a mitzvah by which you can further the harmony of the universe. I would like you very much to do it."

Mitzvah as loving request reminds us again of Franz Rosenzweig's distinction between the two kinds of Torah—the entire tradition that has a claim on us all and the individual mitzvah that speaks to each of us differently, at different times, out of the darkness. But it is not we who choose—it is the text, and the God behind it, who chooses us. This is a text study that asks, "What do you hear in this mitzvah?" This is an encounter with a text that says, "Listen to the self in you that stood at Sinai when you first heard this mitzvah: What do you hear that self saying to you? What does your self today hear in it?"[3]

Rabbi Evan Moffic defines mitzvah as that which creates the boundaries of a community, understood through studying and living in an ongoing encounter with God:

> In a seminal essay, my late mentor and teacher Arnold Jacob Wolf argued that "there is no Judaism but Orthodoxy and all Jews are Reform." For Rabbi Wolf, and for me, Judaism cannot be understood outside of a system of commandments, of mitzvot, given by God. Yet, neither can it be understood without recognizing that the nature of those mitzvot changes over time, and that we have a choice as to the way we follow them. There is no Judaism without mitzvah, and there is no Judaism without autonomy. Mitzvot are what create the boundaries that define our community. Yet, the boundaries are different for every synagogue, every community, every individual. This core tension may seem to lead to anarchy and confusion. Yet, it is a tension that has stood at the heart of Jewish life since the onset of modernity and that is not inconsistent with building communities of study, worship, and action. The tension is resolved only when we, as Franz Rosenzweig put it, "enter into life."
>
> In my life, God is the partner in the covenant with Israel established in the Torah and explicated through Torah. We discover what God demands of us by studying Torah and by living within communities dedicated to living by its teachings. That is what it means to be part of the covenant. We do not discover God's will by hearing a voice from on high or by memorizing a book of laws. Each of us learns it by studying and living. We discover what God demands of us only by studying the texts that reflect our people's ongoing encounter with God.[4]

Rabbi Rachel Timoner envisions mitzvah as an opportunity to create a set of values by which to live:

> The question of whether liberal Jews should live by a halachah (a set of mitzvot) is not whether we should have rules. We already follow many norms and expectations absorbed from our surrounding culture. The question is whether the rules by which we are already living will get us where we need to go. Will they make us who we want to be? Do they allow us to respond effectively to the moral and existential crises of our times? If the answer to these questions is no, then what rules would enable us to be who we are meant to be in the world?
>
> One might say that Judaism is a three-thousand-year-old yearning on this very question: given the commanding presence of God, how should we live? The halachic conversation, as preserved in Rabbinic texts, demonstrates a creative and courageous approach to the question of how Jews ought to live. Halachah was originally designed to respond to the changing circumstances of the changing world, to be reinterpreted and adapted by each generation. Unfortunately, halachah became constricted to a narrow range of topics and ideas over the centuries, leaving important areas of Jewish life and significant portions of the Jewish people unaddressed. Even with the responsa system, halachah has not expanded or adapted enough to speak to the changing demands of our world, the changing challenges facing Jewish life, and the changing consciousness and values of the Jewish people.
>
> Increasing numbers of Reform and liberal Jews are seeking a Jewish path by which to live spiritually and responsibly in this time. Perhaps this is the time to shape a liberal halachah. Perhaps this is the time for liberal Jews to collectively live out our values through our actions, to commit to a set of mitzvot that would bridge the world we live in to the world as it should be. (Inspired by "Here Comes Skotsl: Renewing Halakhah" from *Engendering Judaism: An Inclusive Theology and Ethics* by Rabbi Dr. Rachel Adler.)

Rabbi Jeff Goldwasser proposes that mitzvot are part of our heritage, to be studied and argued with and reinterpreted, and to ultimately be woven into who we are as Jews:

> In 1885, Reform Judaism declared, "We accept as binding only [Torah's] moral laws." The Pittsburg Platform stated that Reform Jews would accept the parts of Torah that conformed with "modern civilization" and reject the rituals and superstitions that did not.
>
> The division, to me, seems arrogant. I do not believe that I have the authority to run an editor's red pen through Torah. It is the transcendent teaching that guides us toward sanctity. How can the preferences of "modern civilization" overrule it?
>
> The problem, I think, is the way we fundamentally understand Torah and the mitzvot. If you think of mitzvot as rules of behavior—what to do and what not to do—then it makes sense to pick and choose. We choose to observe "love your neighbor," but not putting people to death for insulting their parents. That makes sense.
>
> However, Jewish tradition has never viewed Torah as just a checklist of dos and don'ts. To do so is to see only the external garment and ignore what lies beneath. The Rabbis of the Talmud did not kill people for insulting their parents any more than we do. They read the Torah as they saw it—a wedding present from God given on the day we were married at Mount Sinai. It is not to be accepted or rejected; it is to be loved.
>
> Reform Judaism today should recapture that relationship. The work of the ancient Rabbis is not complete; it is our job to continue to search Torah for its timeless truths. We do not need to reject anything in Torah to make it live within us.
>
> Reform Jews today probe the dietary laws to find ways to dignify our lives by eating ethical food. We rediscover tallit and *t'fillin*, not to tie ourselves to empty obligation, but to brighten our spiritual dimension. Yes, we should argue and struggle with Torah, but we should never ignore or reject it.

The challenge for our times, as it has been for all times, is to read Torah actively so as to interpret it. We linger over the words to find treasures, even in the difficult parts.

Rabbi Jason Rosenberg approaches a definition of mitzvah by describing the relationship between mitzvah and habit:

Franz Rosenzweig teaches that performing an act can, over time, lead to that act becoming a mitzvah—a commandment. For me, it's easiest to explain with an example.

I started keeping kosher almost by accident. I was living with some more observant Jews in Jerusalem for a semester, and keeping kosher was an almost default behavior; I did it because that's how we ate. I was deeply surprised when, a few months into the semester, someone offered me some pork and I turned it down. I couldn't say why, exactly. I just realized, suddenly, that keeping kosher had become something—a habit, maybe, or maybe more than that. I wasn't ready to commit to it, but I wasn't ready to stop, either. So, I committed to trying it and—this was the key— learning more about it.

And so, learn I did. I learned theories of the origins of kashrut. I learned modern interpretations. And, I learned through the practice, as well. I learned what it felt like to have Judaism be a regular part of my day, not something with which I engaged only sporadically. I learned about taking a mundane part of my life and treating it like a sacred one instead.

And, I learned that the more I kept kosher, and the more that I learned about and thought about it, the more it meant to me.

Somewhere along the way, I had a realization—I couldn't stop keeping kosher. Not without a penalty. Not a penalty in the form of divine punishment, of course. But, I had spent so much time engaged with this one set of mitzvot that, if I *did* stop, it would hurt me. I would lose something. My regular, thoughtful practice had turned into something that I loved to do and needed to keep doing. My habit had become a mitzvah.

Rabbi Ariana Silverman suggests that a commandment is divine unless proved otherwise:

> The easiest answer for why one should observe the commandments is that they come from God. But in the Reform Movement we do not have the luxury of such certainty. Many of us are unsure what we believe about God and God's role in the writing of the Torah. So I start from the premise that there is a God, and that the Torah's commandments reflect God's divinity, unless and until a commandment is inconsistent with a central tenet of our faith. Many commandments fall into the latter category. But many remain, and we do not get to discard them simply because they are inconvenient or complicated.
>
> Sometimes, we need to observe them precisely *because* they are inconvenient or complicated. Part of living a life of holiness is feeling obligated and feeling limited. Observing some kind of dietary restriction reminds us that we cannot have an insatiable appetite for the earth's resources. Developing a Shabbat practice keeps our obsession with productivity in check. We do not get to do whatever we want.
>
> And we cannot simply choose to observe the "ethical" commandments. As Rabbi Arnold Jacob Wolf (*z"l*) taught us, "Distinctions between 'ethical' and 'ritual' commandments are invariably premature if not downright useless" (Arnold Jacob Wolf, *Unfinished Rabbi* [Chicago: Ivan R. Dee, 1998], page 21). The commandments cited above are technically ritual commandments, but they have clear ethical implications.
>
> When asked if I observe a particular commandment, I often reply, "Not yet." If I believe that it violates a major tenet of my life as a Jew, I say no. But if not, I presume the positive. My Jewish practice is evolving, and I am constantly prioritizing which obligations I wish to assume—not based on whether they are convenient, but based on serious study and reflection.

The question remains: do we really need to know the source of a mitzvah to determine whether to perform it? While belief and theology are important, Judaism teaches us that theology and belief are derived from doing, not the other way around. There is a famous quotation from the Talmud where God says, "Would that my people would abandon Me and observe My Torah, for then they would find Me." One other way to think about mitzvah is as a sacred opportunity. By observing a mitzvah, we have the potential to enhance the spiritual quality of our lives, connect to the Jewish people, perform acts of *tikkun olam*, and encounter the Divine.

While in this volume we sketch out what we believe are the key mitzvot to sanctifying time, *Mishkan Moeid* is not a recipe book where if one ingredient is omitted the whole dish is spoiled. Reform Jewish observance is not an all-or-nothing approach. It is about entering into observance as a dialogue between oneself and the traditions of the Jewish people. Our approach to observance is pluralistic, as is demonstrated in *The Sacred Table* (2011), our publication on ethical eating. The goal is to make good choices about how best to incorporate Jewish observance into our lives. Some will decide to take a comprehensive approach and observe many or all of the mitzvot in this book. Others will decide just to stick their toe into the fountain of observance. During the course of our lives, depending on many factors, our pattern of observance may change. That which was most important may become less important, and that which seemed insignificant can take on new meaning. As one explores the mitzvot that create sacred time and enhance the Jewish cycle of the year, it is helpful to find an empathetic and wise teacher and a supportive community. Each day is an opportunity to add another mitzvah. The real key to observance is to begin.

Hidur Mitzvah:
The Aesthetics of Mitzvot

THE SOURCES delineate the minimum requirements of the mitzvot. A sukkah must have certain dimensions and must be constructed in a particular manner. The cup for *Kiddush* must be large enough to hold a specified minimum amount of wine. While some may be satisfied with minimum standards, the Jewish tradition recognizes and encourages the addition of an aesthetic dimension. Beauty enhances the mitzvot by appealing to the senses. Beautiful sounds and agreeable fragrances, tastes, textures, colors, and artistry contribute to human enjoyment of religious acts, and beauty itself takes on a religious dimension. The principle of enhancing a mitzvah through aesthetics is called *hidur mitzvah.*

The concept of *hidur mitzvah* is derived from Rabbi Ishmael's comment on the verse "This is my God and I will enshrine Him" (Exodus 15:2):

> Is it possible for a human being to add glory to the Creator? What this really means is: I shall glorify [God] in the way I perform mitzvot. I shall prepare before [God] a beautiful *lulav*, a beautiful sukkah, beautiful fringes (*tzitzit*), and beautiful phylacteries (*t'fillin*).[1]

The Talmud adds to this list a beautiful shofar and a beautiful Torah scroll that has been written by a skilled scribe with fine ink and fine pen and wrapped in beautiful silks.[2]

"In keeping with the principle of *hidur mitzvah,*" Rabbi Zera taught, "one should be willing to pay even one-third more [than the normal price]."[3] Jewish folklore is replete with stories about Jews of modest circumstances paying more than they could afford for the most beautiful *etrog* to enhance their observance of Sukkot or for the most delectable foods to enhance their observance of Shabbat. The midrash suggests that not only are mitzvot enhanced by an aesthetic dimension, but so is the Jew who observes it: *"You are beautiful, my love, you are beautiful,* through mitzvot . . . beautiful through mitzvot, beautiful through deeds of loving-kindness, . . . through prayer, through reciting the *Sh'ma,* through the *mezuzah,* through phylacteries, through sukkah and *lulav* and *etrog."*[4] There seems to be reciprocity of beauty through the agency of mitzvot: the Jew becomes beautiful while performing a mitzvah. "But, conversely, Israel 'beautifies' God by performing the commandments in the most 'beautiful' manner."[5]

There are many ways to apply the principle of *hidur mitzvah.* For example, one might choose to observe the mitzvah of kindling Chanukah lights with an inexpensive tin *chanukiyah,* or one might make an effort to build one by hand or to buy a beautiful one. Some families might prefer an oil-burning *chanukiyah* rather than one that uses the standard candles, in order to relate their observance of the mitzvah more closely to the times of the Maccabees. Certainly the mitzvah of lighting Chanukah candles is fulfilled with any kind of *chanukiyah,* but by applying the principle of *hidur mitzvah,* one enriches both the mitzvah and oneself.

Another example of *hidur mitzvah* relates to the choice of a Haggadah to use at the Passover seder. There are many beautiful options available, including the CCAR's *A Passover Haggadah,* edited by Rabbi Herbert Bronstein and illustrated by Leonard Baskin; *The Open Door,* edited by Rabbi Sue Levi Elwell and illustrated by Ruth Weisberg; and the newest one, *Sharing the Journey: The Haggadah for the Contemporary Family,* by Alan S. Yoffie with art by Mark Podwal. Alternatively, a family or group of families may wish to edit and illustrate their own Haggadah. Similarly, beautiful matzah covers, seder plates, and *Kiddush* cups could be used. These may be family heirlooms, items created by contemporary artists, or ones designed and executed by the children in religious school. The whole celebration is enriched when care is taken in the selection or creation of ceremonial objects.

The same sense of care and joy relates to the choosing of ritual garments to wear in a prayer setting. There are many different kinds of *kippot* and tallitot available, made from an enormous range of colors, designs, and fabrics. Choosing something beautiful, special, and meaningful to wear when praying is another way of expressing *hidur mitzvah*.

Affixing a mezuzah to the doorpost of a Jewish house is a mitzvah (see *Gates of Mitzvah*, page 38, E-4). The concept of *hidur mitzvah* suggests that the mezuzah be artistically fashioned. If one's eye is attracted by the beauty of the mezuzah, one will be more likely to consider its significance (i.e., that as you enter, you pause to think of God). Some might even study the traditions relating to the writing of a mezuzah scroll and then lovingly create their own mezuzah. *Hidur mitzvah* means taking the time and making an effort to create or acquire the most beautiful ceremonial objects possible in order to enrich the religious observance with an aesthetic dimension.

Approaching the High Holy Days
RABBI ELAINE ZECHER

THE WORLD can be a very scary place. The uncertainty—over there, around the corner, under here, somewhere, everywhere—has created a dis-ease, a disequilibrium, a dissatisfaction, a disintegration in every direction. Where should we turn?

Fortunately, Judaism provides us with a sanctuary within the sanctuary of the synagogue, a moment of repose to collect ourselves, to turn in so that we might turn out, not to escape but to contemplate and prepare ourselves to face the world. That refuge comes in the form of the High Holy Days. Judaism invites us to engage and to use these days for introspection, evaluation, and motivation. As we make our way from the first days of the Hebrew month of Elul to the prayers of *S'lichot* on the Saturday night before the first of Tishrei, to the sound of the shofar on Rosh HaShanah, to the path of the intervening days leading up to Yom Kippur eve with the *Kol Nidrei* melody, to the final, long blast of the shofar to mark the end of *N'ilah*, Jewish tradition offers us a great gift.

These days afford us the opportunity to reflect on our past, to discover our authentic selves again, to be present in this moment, and then to look forward and toward the future. As we experience these days, we visit, revisit, transfix, and transform what has happened, how it is happening, and what will happen.

Our lives spiral and circle back again. We open ourselves to creating a vision of our own future based on our understanding of the past and the present. Not all of our past is perfect. Some of it is even traumatic. We also know the future will arrive no matter what we do. How we regard it all and what we do with it, however, is in our control.

In Judaism, we move in a circular motion. Defining *t'shuvah* as "repentance" does not do it justice. Moses Maimonides called *t'shuvah* a positive commandment. It means the act of turning.[1] It means coming around again in a constant state of remembering, applying wisdom and experience, to transform our behavior, our outlook, our lives. *T'shuvah* enables us to perceive the way we view the world differently. *T'shuvah*, the act of turning, returning, reviewing, re-collecting, recasting, and reframing our understanding has the power to transform the way we respond now and the way we will construct our respective futures.

Have you ever played back a conversation in your head, interacting as if you could push the replay button? You are not acting in that previous moment. You are using the present with its transformed understanding to inform your reaction to that situation. You have already processed the past and integrated it into the present. Hindsight is 20/20.

So is looking forward, potentially. The Talmud (BT *M'nachot* 29b) has multiple tales that are not factual but reveal truths nonetheless. In one story, when Moses went up on high to receive the Torah, he found the Holy One sitting and embellishing each letter with calligraphic marks. He said to the Holy One, "Ruler of the universe, why do You need to add these marks?" The Holy One answered, "There is a man who will appear at the end of several generations and Akiva the son of Joseph is his name, and he will need these crowns, because from each and every calligraphic mark above the letter he will derive scores and scores of laws." Moses implored, "Ruler of the universe, show this man to me." The Holy One said, "Turn around!"

So, Moses went and sat in the back of Rabbi Akiva's class, the very Rabbi Akiva who lived in the first century CE, in other words, several millennia after Moses lived. Moses had no idea what they were saying with regard to Torah passages. It sounded nothing like what he was receiving from Sinai. He did not understand their interpretation and became weak and disoriented. Soon the class reached an issue and a student asked, "Rabbi Akiva, what's your source for this ruling?" He said, "It's a law of Moses from Sinai." Ah, the past recalled in order to inform a moment in the future. Moses was relieved.

At the precise moment when Moses went up on the mountain for those forty days and forty nights, he "went back to the future." The story is wildly imaginative. God surely did not take pen to parchment and literally serve as calligrapher—scribe, but the message is clear. Embedded in the Torah scroll itself, these crowns, as they are called, adorn the letters as a sacred reminder that the Torah contains not only the past and the present but the future as well.

Why should this be important? As Alan Lew teaches, "when we reach the point of awareness, everything in time—everything in the year, everything in our life—conspires to help us. Everything becomes the instrument of our redemption," our own promise for the potential of what is to come.[2] This is the essence of these Days of Awe. They inspire us to aspire to our better, higher selves. As time circles around us, we can acknowledge the truth of our own lives in the fullness of our individual and collective past, present, and future.

Hashiveinu v'nashuvah k'kedem are the words that conclude the Book of Lamentations, "Return to us and we will return to You, as in the beginning" (Lamentations 5:21).

On these High Holy Days, we can go back to the beginning—like a fresh place, a time to contemplate what paths our lives will take from these days forth, not simply a reflection of all the days that have passed behind us. How will we plot a future course? How might we open our hearts, search our soul to turn around and look ahead with greater clarity and purpose?

Every single one of us was once a child. There is no escaping it. You can't be here if you weren't there, and yet does that experience need to remain solely in the past? From a child's point of view, the world is a great wonder. The fascination is unspoiled. Our minds were facile, elastic, plastic, and open to the new and different (except food with weird texture or that was green or that touched anything else on the plate). We were not yet tainted by so many disappointments, hesitant to the potential of failure, frightened by all that is wrong or by the fact that unexpected tragedies happen to good people all the time, even people we know and love. Think of a picture of yourself as a child. Her face is sweet. His expression sparkles. What do you want to tell that little human being? Watch out? Be careful? No, we want to share hope and potential. Rather than limit them, we express excitement for the future. Their future! We want them to know that there are many paths that they may choose. It is not about perfection but possibility. Failure and disappointment are also their teachers. You can't warn that child. You can only celebrate him. You can only rejoice for her. Remember her. Remember him. Let that memory inspire you, in the sanctuary of the High Holy Days, even now to go forward.

On these holy days of the year, we invoke our communal memory for God, taking note of our ancestors, of God remembering the covenant, of God paying attention. And though we may not feel we are direct recipients of God's focus, we are. This day tells each of us, "You matter!" The Talmud (BT *Rosh HaShanah* 16a) states that on this day we pass before God like sheep passing before a shepherd who wants to make sure each one is counted. The ancient metaphor makes its point. You can't blend into the crowd. We are not alone in our own isolated universe. Like the voice on the phone that tells us that our call is being monitored for training purposes, here, in a "meta-spiritual" way, we are noticed.

The whole universe is paying attention to us. Our tradition conveys this idea in the Torah. When Moses makes his final poetic speech to the Israelites as they stand perched preparing to enter into their future, into the Land, he uses the following image: "Give ear, O heavens, let me speak; let the earth hear the words I utter!" (Deuteronomy 32:1). Heaven and earth are aware of our presence. On Yom Kippur when we hear the words from Deuteronomy 30:19, "I call heaven and earth to witness," we are reminded again. Heaven and earth are watching. We matter. By mattering, we connect to a larger purpose with meaning. Not only *who* we are and *that* we are matters, but what we do has unmatched significance.

Rabbi Bernard Bamberger, a prominent Reform rabbi of the

twentieth century, takes this idea to an even higher level. He says: It matters what each of us does with our lives, our talents and powers, our resources and opportunities. No person's behavior is just private enterprise. What we do, what we try to do and to be makes a difference not only to ourselves and to those around us but to humanity, to the universe, and to God.[3]

And this impacts the future at every moment.

Bachya ibn Pakuda taught: Your life is like a scroll; write on it what you want remembered. We project into the future what will become our past.

On the High Holy Days we ask God, *Zochreinu l'chayim*, "Remember us toward life." It is all we have. Life and living it.

Yes, the world is a scary place. Uncertainty pervades. But this we know: from the first moments of Elul to the longest blast of the shofar ending Yom Kippur, these holy days provide the opening to ponder what we can do to harness all of the positive, creative, compassionate, and sacred obligations we are capable of. We can choose a more optimistic future for ourselves, for those who come after us, and yes, for the world, too. Let us use these days and this sacred time and the swirling, rotational pull of the life that surrounds us to harvest hope for a broken world waiting to be redeemed.

The Festival and Holy Day Liturgy of Mishkan T'filah

RABBI JOEL SISENWINE

The Three Pilgrimage Festivals

In Exodus 23:14, God says, "Three times a year you shall hold a festival for Me." And ever since, so the Jewish people has done, gathering together to rejoice in God's presence. Early in our history, the festivals of Pesach, Shavuot, and Sukkot were largely agricultural in nature, revolving around the harvest and God's role within it. Later, as Jews moved away from the farms and into the cities, historical meanings prevailed, linking each festival with the biblical narrative of the Israelites' journey. Passover was no longer solely Chag HaAviv, the holiday celebrating the onset of spring, but now emphasized the Exodus from Egypt. Shavuot was no longer solely the Festival of First Fruits (Chag HaBikurim), or the Harvest Festival (Chag HaKatzir), but now *z'man matan Torateinu*, the day that the Jewish people received the Torah. Sukkot was no longer solely Chag HaAsif, the time to rejoice in the harvest and sleep in agricultural huts (sukkot), but also a time that reminded us of our desert wanderings.

"None shall appear before Me empty-handed," the Torah continues, exhorting the people to bring an offering to God (Exodus 23:15). In Temple times, these offerings came in the form of animal sacrifices and agricultural sacrifices, carefully described in the biblical text. Jews would travel from far and wide, making pilgrimage to the Temple, giving the festivals the collective name *Shalosh R'galim*, "the Three Pilgrimage Festivals" (*shalosh* for "three"—the three times of Passover, Shavuot, and Sukkot; and *r'galim* for "feet," a reference to the necessary walking that pilgrimage requires). But soon another type of sacrifice came to dominate Jewish observance, the sacrifice of the heart, *avodah shebalev*, otherwise known as prayer.

In *Mishkan T'filah*, you will find these prayers specifically dedicated to the festival liturgy. In the words of prayer, we bring our hopes, our dreams, and our thanks to God. On the left side of each page in the festival liturgy, you will find creative readings that reflect the agricultural and historical themes of the holidays. On the right side, you will find the rubrics of the daily service, along with insertions for each festival.

Each festival evening, we begin with the lighting of the festival candles, marking the day as a *Yom Tov*, literally a "good day" dedicated to God's service. On this day, we refrain from work and praise God for the opportunity to celebrate together. The candle lighting is then followed by the *Shehecheyanu*, a special prayer acknowledging the unique blessing of the season: "Praise to You, Adonai our God, Sovereign of the universe, for giving us life, sustaining us, and enabling us to reach this season."

The daily liturgy continues, following the traditional rubrics of the service, until the *T'filah*, when the paragraph *Atah v'chartanu* (page 478) is added. It is in this insertion that we thank God for these holidays. It is in love that we have been provided with these days, and we respond to God's love with gratitude and a pledge for goodness.

We also add the paragraph *Yaaleh v'yavo* (page 480) stating that just as we remember the festival, we ask that God remember us for goodness, blessing, and life. After all, we human beings are small. We are surrounded by the intricate beauty of the world's creation and reminded of our fragility within it. And so we pray that God may remember us and care for us. And in response, we remember to make a place for God in our lives, ensuring that meaning takes a central role in our days and that we dedicate ourselves to God's purpose.

Following the *T'filah* and its final prayer for peace, *Birkat Shalom*, we continue with the special festival insertion of *Hallel*, a collection of psalms first recited in the Temple centuries ago. The psalms, attributed to King David, but most likely written over a period of hundreds of years, are words of praise to God.

"Praise Adonai, all you nations; extol God, all you peoples" (Psalm 117, page 558), and so we do, thanking God for our freedom on Passover, for Torah on Shavuot, and for the natural world that surrounds us on Sukkot. "Praise Adonai for God is good, God's steadfast love is eternal" (Psalm 118, page 558).

On page 571, there is the blessing for the sukkah and the *lulav*, to be recited on the Festival of Sukkot. Upon entering the sukkah, the temporary hut that is constructed following Yom Kippur, we recite the blessing. It is customary to welcome guests to the sukkah, share a meal, and thank God for all that is eternal: love, values, and God's caring for the world. This is in contrast to all that is temporary, the material elements, like the sukkah, that too often receive our attention, even though they are short-lived. While in the sukkah, we then take the four species, the palm branch, myrtle, willow, known collectively as the *lulav*, and *etrog*, as first described in Leviticus 23:40, and recite the blessing. We then shake the *lulav* in all six directions—up, down, right, left, forward, and back—reminding us of God's presence.

The Counting of the Omer

In *Mishkan T'filah*, page 570 is dedicated to the counting of the Omer, a practice that takes place between Passover and Shavuot. During this seven-week period, which leads up to Shavuot (literally, "weeks"), we literally count each day, as first instructed in biblical times (Leviticus 23:11, 23:15). When the Temple stood in Jerusalem, the Israelites would take an omer, a measure of barley, marking the beginning of the wheat harvest. Today, we mark this period with a blessing, followed by a Talmudic formulation for counting. Each day, we mark the days between Passover and Shavuot by carefully mentioning the number of weeks and days that have gone by, thereby preparing ourselves to receive the Torah.

You will notice that there is no *Shehecheyanu* when we count the Omer. This is traditionally a time of restraint in the Jewish year, as the Israelites had exited Egypt but had yet to receive the Torah.

Also, in the biblical period, the results of the crop season were unknown, and it was considered a time of judgment. In some communities, the omer is also a period of semi-mourning, commemorating the various tragedies that have occurred to the Jewish people at this time in years past, including the twenty-four thousand students of Rabbi Akiva who died in a plague or the thousands who died during the Crusades. Of course, the trepidation of the Omer period does end. Ultimately, the Israelites arrive at Mount Sinai, the crops prove bountiful, and Moses receives the Torah, a gift from God. The Omer period ends with the beginning of Shavuot, the celebration of the giving of the Torah.

Mishkan T'filah continues the Reform practice of following the Israeli calendar for festival observance and omitting the observance of *yom tov sheini*, a holiday's "second day." Thus, Passover is a seven-day festival as stated in the Torah; Sukkot is seven days as well, culminating in a one-day celebration of Sh'mini Atzeret–Simchat Torah. Shavuot is a one-day festival. While this is consistent with the biblical mandate, it is in contrast to the traditional Diaspora calendar, when the Rabbis added a day to the holiday observance to compensate for poor communications between communities. *Mishkan T'filah* continues the Reform practice of remaining consistent with the biblical decree.

Yizkor

Memory is an important theme in Judaism. In the Bible, we are told 169 times "to remember." Learn from the past, we are told. Through the act of remembering, we are inspired and strengthened.

The *Yizkor* (remembrance) prayers were first included in the prayer book in the eleventh century and are recited on all three festivals, as well as on Yom Kippur. With these prayers, we remember our loved ones who have gone before us and helped shape us and led us to this day.

We recite psalms asking for God's comfort. "Though I walk through a valley of deepest darkness, I fear no harm, for You are with me," we read from Psalm 23, words that are familiar also from the funeral service.

The *Yizkor* prayers conclude with the words of *El Malei Rachamim*, in which we ask that God continue to grant peace to our loved ones who have departed.

Yom HaShoah

On April 12, 1951, Knesset member Mordecai Nurok approached the podium of the Knesset and exclaimed, "The heavens cry forth, the earth cries forth, and Israel is crying." With these words, Nurok introduced an impassioned plea to develop a common Holocaust observance. Until that time, there had been no common observance, because of the unique pain of the Holocaust and the diverse needs of the community. In order to balance secular Zionist and religious concerns, Nurok proposed the 27th of Nisan as "Holocaust and Ghetto Rebellion Memorial Day." Today, this date is most often referred to as Yom HaShoah. The 27th of Nisan represented a compromise date, acknowledging that the date could not be on the anniversary of the Warsaw Ghetto rebellion, April 19, as this fell on the eve of Passover, a time of celebration. Thus Nurok proposed 27 Nisan, as it was close enough to the rebellion date but fell within the period of the Omer, a traditional time of mourning.

Unlike *Gates of Prayer*, the prior Reform Movement prayer book, *Mishkan T'filah* includes its own service for Yom HaShoah. No longer grouped with Tishah B'Av (and the Rabbinic notion that the destruction of the Temples was caused by the sins of the Jewish people), the Yom HaShoah liturgy is one of remembrance. A modern observance, the Yom HaShoah liturgy does not maintain the prayer book structure of having the traditional liturgy on the right page and creative texts on the left. Rather, the Yom HaShoah liturgy is a collection of poetry and readings that call upon the reader to remember. It also provides the community for a way to say *Kaddish* for the many Jews who were killed in mass killings and whose dates of death are unknown.

Yizkor

ONE OF the most moving portions of the Yom Kippur and Festival worship services is the Memorial Service (*Hazkarat N'shamot*). Popularly known as *Yizkor*, after the opening words of the silent devotion *Yizkor Elohim* ("May God remember [the soul of] . . ."), this service is generally recited in Reform synagogues on Yom Kippur and on the last day of Pesach, on Shavuot, and on Sh'mini Atzeret–Simchat Torah. *Yizkor* emphasizes the transience of life, our yearning for eternity, and the inspiration provided by the memory of the deceased. The service reminds us that time moves swiftly forward and bids us "to number our days that we may grow wise in heart" (Psalm 90:12).

Memory is a precious gift, for it transforms the discrete moments of our lives and events in history into an unfolding narrative. We become acutely aware of being a part of an eternal people that began a spiritual journey in the distant past with its goal to be realized in the remote future. Through the words and music of the service, we become conscious not only of our own mortality, but also of the sacred opportunity that we have in our brief lives to perform acts of sanctification that may improve our lot and the lot of humanity generally.

The life of the Jewish people is composed of sacred moments that, when recalled, inspire us to live our lives according to certain Jewish values. For example, the bitter experience of slavery is tasted in the eating of *maror* on Pesach. By re-creating the sense of physical and spiritual bondage, we commit ourselves to an ethical system that teaches us that freedom is essential for human development. How we act toward others must be judged in the light of the verse "We were slaves to Pharaoh in Egypt" (Deuteronomy 6:21).

On Shavuot, when we hear the Ten Commandments read, we are transported backward to Mount Sinai and utter in our hearts the ancient formula of commitment *Naaseh v'nishma*, "We will faithfully do" (Exodus 24:7). The ancient covenant is renewed through memory. By observing the mitzvot of Shavuot, our individual memory becomes part of the collective memory of the Jewish people.

For Jews, the inspiring figures in both the remote and recent past remain as constant companions and role models. They teach by precept and example. Their story is our story. Their courage, wisdom, and goodness are a permanent challenge.

Memory roots us firmly in the past. The fertile soil of more than four thousand years of history nurtures us, providing us with a clear sense of who we are. Our lives add new branches to the tree of the Jewish people. A living past provides for a meaningful present and hope for the future.

As we recite the *Yizkor* prayer, we mention in our hearts the names of all who were close to us—grandparents, parents, friends, and relatives. By preserving the memory of those who were our teachers, we are encouraged to continue the tasks they bequeathed to us. The memorial service is an act of faith that proclaims that goodness does not die with a person but exists in the memory of those who remain alive.

Our thoughts also turn to those of our people who sought, through their lives and through their deaths, to testify to the undying spirit of the Jewish people and its mission as a holy nation. In the past, custom dictated that only those whose parents were deceased attended the Memorial Service. But recognizing that so many who died in the Shoah have no one to recite *Kaddish* for them, and realizing that memory helps to forge a chain of solidarity and continuity between our generation and the past, all are encouraged to participate.

The words of the memorial prayer *El Malei Rachamim* ("Fully compassionate God") is a petition for the repose of the deceased and an expression of our faith in the ultimate sacredness of humankind.

Death removes our loved ones from their earthly abode, yet Jewish tradition affirms the faith that the divine spark in every human soul has a permanent dwelling place with the Eternal. The mystery of what lies beyond the grave is shrouded by an impenetrable veil, yet within our hearts is planted the hope for eternity. Memory is the sacred link between past and future and between time and eternity.

Immortality is a word that we can associate only with God, but the blessing of memory and the blessedness of the memory of the righteous can be guaranteed by our devoted recall. The mitzvah of *Yizkor* is a door that opens on eternity, making the present more significant by allowing us to combine memory and hope.

Fasting on Yom Kippur

Yom kippur is a day set apart by the Torah for us to "practice self-denial" (Leviticus 23:27). The "self-denial" that seems to be most expressive of Yom Kippur is fasting, abstaining from food and drink for the entire day.

Fasting is an opportunity for each of us to observe Yom Kippur in a most personal way. It is a day of intense self-searching and earnest communication with the Almighty. This search requires an internal calm that derives from slowing down our biological rhythm. Fasting on Yom Kippur provides the key to our inner awakening.

On Yom Kippur we seek reconciliation with God and humanity. Repentance (*t'shuvah*) involves a critical self-assessment of the past year and the resolve to avoid lapses in sensitivity in the future. *T'shuvah* requires discipline. Our fasting on Yom Kippur demonstrates our willingness to submit to discipline. How can we atone for our excesses toward others unless we can curb appetites that depend on no one but ourselves? To set boundaries for our own conduct in this very private matter is to begin the path toward controlling our public behavior.

The fast of Yom Kippur reaches beyond our inner spiritual awakening and discipline into our ethical behavior. In the Yom Kippur morning haftarah, we read of the prophet Isaiah providing us with the ultimate goal of our fast—to unlock the shackles of injustice, to undo the fetters of bondage, to let the oppressed go free, to share bread with the hungry (Isaiah 58:1–14).

Finally, to fast on the Day of Atonement is an act of solidarity with the suffering of the Jewish people. Through fasting we are drawn closer to all who live lives of deprivation. Our faith demands more of us than twenty-four hours of abstinence from food. It demands that upon the completion of our fast we will turn back to the world prepared to act with love and compassion. In this way fasting touches the biological as well as the spiritual aspects of our being.

Shabbat as Protest

RABBI W. GUNTHER PLAUT, ז״ל

Adapted from W. Gunther Plaut, "The Sabbath as Protest—Thoughts on Work and Leisure in the Automated Society," in Tradition and Change in the Jewish Experience, ed. A. Leland Jamison (Syracuse: Syracuse University Press, 1978), pages 169–183.

IF SHABBAT is to have significance, it must confront one of modern civilization's greatest curses, its internal and external unrest. This unrest arises from the twin facts that the life we lead is frequently without goals and that we are involved in competition without end.

I view Shabbat as potentially an enormous relief from and protest against the basic causes of unrest. Once a week it provides us with an opportunity to address ourselves to the meaning of human existence rather than the struggle for survival, to persons rather than things, to Creation and our part in it, to society and its needs, to ourselves as individuals and yet as social beings. This has been called "the inner source of leisure," the setting of goals that are both realistic and within one's reach, yet also beyond one's self.

There are few better places for such redirection than a religious service, whose major function ought to be not just the repetition of well-worn formulae but the celebration of human goals. If nothing happens to us during this or any Shabbat experience except an enlarging of our vision, we will have gained a new perspective of life's meaning and will have diminished our sense of unrest. That will be Shabbat rest in the sense required by our time.

Endless competition is a specific form of restlessness. Shabbat can be a surcease from and a protest against all forms of competition, even when they come in attractive packages marked "self-advancement" or "self-improvement." Shabbat in this sense may be viewed as a "useless" day. Our ancestors had a keen understanding of the fact that sleep on Shabbat was a form of coming closer to God. We must once again understand that doing nothing, being silent and open to the world, letting things happen inside, can be as important as, and sometimes more important than, what we commonly call useful.

Formerly a person who did not work was considered useless; what we need now is a purposeful uselessness, an activity (or non-activity!) which is important in that it becomes an essential protest against that basic unrest that comes from competition without end. In the Jewish context it may therefore be suggested that on Shabbat one abstains from everything that on one level or another may be considered usefully competitive. Shabbat gives us a quantity of free time and thereby a quality potential of freedom-time, when a person can search for the self and in some area do for self and others what in the work-a-day one cannot.

It has been said that there are four states of human consciousness: imaginative, active, reflexive, and contemplative. The two middle states (activity and reflexive response) characterize our automated society; the other two (imagination and contemplation) are the redeeming features that make life livable. These are the qualities to which Shabbat addresses itself, for imagination is a form of freedom and contemplation is rest from unrest.

M'nuchah and M'lachah
On Observing the Sabbath in Reform Judaism
RABBI MARK WASHOFSKY, PH.D.

IF SOMEONE were to ask us for a concise, standing-on-one-foot definition of the Jewish Sabbath, we would probably reply that it is a day of "rest" (*m'nuchah*) on which one is to abstain from "work" (*m'lachah*).[1] We would say much the same about the major festivals (*chagim* or *yamim tovim*) as well.[2] But if someone asked what those concepts mean to us, as *Reform* Jews, the answer would be much less obvious. Jewish tradition defines the words "rest" and "work" in a very specific way. The Rabbis of old developed that definition into a complex, highly detailed system of rules, principles, and exceptions[3] that fill two Talmudic tractates, nearly two hundred chapters of the great halachic code the *Shulchan Aruch*, and constitute the bulk of what Orthodox Jews mean when they speak of *sh'mirat Shabbat*, the *observance* of the Sabbath.

Our Reform Movement has largely abandoned that system, and we have never replaced it with a single, "official" alternative definition of "work" and "rest." In some ways, of course, this is a positive thing. The absence of an authoritative Reform standard for Shabbat observance allows individuals and congregations to arrive at definitions of *m'nuchah* and *m'lachah* that are meaningful to them. On the other hand, this plethora of personal and local standards might create the impression that we, as an organized movement, are unable to speak with a unified voice about this essential element of Jewish religious life.

That impression is incorrect. I would argue that the Reform Movement, particularly in recent decades, has framed a coherent teaching about Shabbat and Festival observance. This teaching, to be sure, has not been laid down as a code, a set of detailed rules. Rather, in good Reform fashion, it takes the form of guidelines that offer direction to individuals and communities seeking to make their own decisions. It consists of three major elements.

The first element is the publication of books by the Central Conference of American Rabbis, beginning with *A Shabbat Manual* (1972),[4] devoted in part to "the recovery of Shabbat observance" in the Reform Movement,[5] which was later replaced by *Gates of Shabbat* (1991), and the inauguration in 2007 of the Union for Reform Judaism's "Shabbat Initiative."[6] These publications and programs, which demonstrate that *sh'mirat Shabbat* is a major item on our movement's religious agenda, have afforded leading Reform Jewish thinkers the opportunity to express their notions of Shabbat observance, and to consider what *m'nuchah* and *m'lachah* ought to mean in our time. Rabbi W. Gunther Plaut, for example, first defined Shabbat in the earlier edition of this volume as a form of "protest" against the endless struggle and competition that characterize workday human existence. The prohibition of work—which he defined as the abstention from every activity that could be considered "usefully competitive"—affords the individual the opportunity for self-fulfillment: "doing nothing, being silent and open to the world . . . [is] sometimes more important than what we commonly call useful" (pages 124–125).

Rabbi Arnold Jacob Wolf wrote in a similar vein: "The 'work' that is forbidden by Jewish law on the Sabbath is not measured in the expenditure of energy. It takes real effort to pray, to study, to walk to synagogue. They are 'rest' but not restful. Forbidden 'work' is acquisition, aggrandizement, altering the world. On Shabbat we are obliged to be, to reflect, to love and make love, to eat, to enjoy."[7] And Rabbi Eric Yoffie emphasized the value of Shabbat observance for "our stressed-out, sleep-deprived families": "Our tradition does not instruct us to stop working altogether on Shabbat; after all, it takes a certain amount of effort to study, pray and go to synagogue. But we are asked to abstain from the work that we do to earn a living, and instead to reflect, to enjoy, and to take a stroll through the neighborhood. We are asked to put aside those BlackBerries and stop gathering information, just as the ancient Israelites stopped

gathering wood. We are asked to stop running around long enough to see what God is doing."[8] These writers, among others, point to the continuing relevance of the
Torah's instruction concerning *m'nuchah* and *m'lachah*. Our Sabbath, they remind us, cannot truly be "Shabbat" unless we take seriously the demand that we rest and abstain from work on that day.

The second element comprises writings that take these insights to the next logical level. If *m'nuchah* and *m'lachah* are still relevant to us, how might we Reform Jews, who no longer hold strictly to the traditional definition of those concepts, realize them in our personal practice? One such essay, in Rabbi Mark Dov Shapiro's *Gates of Shabbat*, suggests three alternative models of Reform Shabbat observance.[9] "The walker" follows Rabbinic tradition and abstains from driving and the use of money on Shabbat as a means of devoting the day to prayer, study, family, and conversation; "the museum-goer" engages in activities that, while they may run afoul of traditional prohibitions, bring "honor" to the Sabbath and refresh the soul; and "the painter" regards Shabbat as a day to pursue creative activities that affirm our sense of human freedom. These models differ in their details, just as individuals and their needs differ one from the other. What unites them is their conviction that Shabbat observance is central to Reform Jewish life and their invitation to each Reform Jew to construct his or her Shabbat in accordance with that conviction.

The third element includes a series of Reform responsa, advisory rabbinical opinions on issues of Jewish practice, written over the last thirty years to address questions concerning activities that Reform synagogues ought or ought not to schedule on Shabbat. Basing themselves upon two broad conceptual foundations—the Reform Movement's renewed commitment to the importance of Shabbat observance and the value of Jewish tradition as the indispensable starting point of our thinking[10]—the responsa urge that congregations refrain from engaging in activities on Shabbat that, however laudable, tend to violate traditional understandings of the sanctity of the day. These decisions speak specifically to congregational fund-raising efforts that involve commercial activity and to social action projects that entail physical labor. These acts are indeed mitzvot, but then, so is Shabbat. To the extent that we take Shabbat seriously, we should view it not simply as a convenient day on which to do good things but as a mitzvah in its own right, which makes its own legitimate demands upon our attention and which does not give way before other mitzvot unless those causes are emergencies that cannot be addressed on another day of the week.[11]

As I have noted, these Reform Jewish teachings concerning Shabbat observance come not in the form of fixed rules but of general guidelines. Another way to describe them is that they represent an ongoing conversation in our movement over the nature of *sh'mirat Shabbat*. As is the case with all such conversations, we may never reach an absolutely final conclusion. As a movement that prizes individual freedom, we do not seek to impose solutions; rather, we encourage every Reform Jew to arrive at standards that are meaningful to him or her. But to have a conversation at all requires that we speak a common religious language, that we approach the issues within a framework of shared understandings; otherwise, we are not a community at all but a collection of individuals speaking incomprehensibly to (or past) each other. The statements, suggestions, and decisions summarized here offer that sort of framework. Hopefully, they can be of help to us as we continue to explore just what we Reform Jews mean when we speak of *m'nuchah* and *m'lachah*.

Technology and Sacred Time

RABBI LISA J. GRUSHCOW, D.Phil.

SHABBAT AND THE HOLY DAYS demand that we step outside our daily lives and pay attention to a different calendar. Despite their differences from each other, this is something that they share. Whether it is Shabbat that, in Heschel's famous words, calls upon us to build a sanctuary in time; the Pilgrimage Festivals, during which our ancestors left their homes to go to Jerusalem; the High Holy Days, as a spiritual pilgrimage; or holy days like Chanukah, Purim, Tishah B'Av, and Yom HaAtzma-ut, which call upon us to share the story of Jews in other places and times— when we come to these days, time is meant to move differently.

In the language of the Torah (Leviticus 23:2, 4), these are *mo-adei Adonai*, "God's set times," and *mikra-ei kodesh*, "sacred occasions" (or, perhaps, "holy happenings"). Here it is worth noting that the root of the word for holiness, *k'dushah*, denotes separateness. Sacred time is separate time. It is time that is set by God, but also set by us; in the Rabbinic understanding of the biblical verses, we are called upon to determine when the holidays fall. This suggests that there is something intrinsically sacred about these times but also that our actions are essential to how those days take shape.

The question then becomes: how do we make these days holy? How do we mark them as different from our daily lives? This has always been a challenge, all the more so to us who aspire to live in both the Jewish and the modern worlds. In our own time, technology—and especially connectivity, the phenomenon of always being connected—accentuates this challenge. Much has been written in recent years about the effects of constantly being connected to the Internet, primarily through mobile devices, and all that entails: the prevalence of social media, and the constant access to e-mail and work. The argument found in many of these books and articles is that our use of the Internet—and in particular, the practices of multitasking and constantly looking for new information—is altering everything from our brain chemistry to our relationships with our children and spouses. In addition to the growing body of scientific literature is anecdotal evidence. For many of us, our experience of being "connected" is that it is very hard to disconnect—not to check our messages, not to leave the house without our phones. In some ways, the connectivity that comes with technology threatens the actual connections we have with other human beings. In other ways, it offers new opportunities to create and deepen connections. It is easy to say we should turn our phones off for services and at the family table, but it is not clear that the Reform Jewish answer to the issue of technology and sacred time is always to leave our devices at the door.

Our approach instead is a nuanced one. Here, it is essential to explore the commandments and values that shape our observance of sacred time. Using Shabbat as a model, we can delve into the question of what it might mean to connect to sacred time in a world that is permeated by connectivity of a different sort.

There are four ways in which the connectivity question is relevant to a discussion of Shabbat and sacred time: the redefinition of work and rest, the effects on our relationships with other human beings and God, our interaction with the world around us, and the issue of freedom and choice. These four topics correspond to the themes of Shabbat observance that have emerged in Reform Jewish conversations for decades: *m'lachah* and *m'nuchah* (work and rest), *b'rit* (covenant), *maaseih B'reishit* (the works of Creation), and *yitziat Mitzrayim* (going out from Egypt). They also correspond to many of the themes of our other sacred times.

First, work and rest: The new technologies have made the boundaries between our professional and personal lives increasingly permeable. As with any change, there are advantages as well as disadvantages. The ability to take one's work home can mean being able to be at home more, to have more flexibility in our personal and professional lives. But the ability to constantly work makes it much more challenging to carve out time in which work is not done. Traditionally, on some holy days halachic categories of work are permitted, and on others they are not. Here, though, the Reform approach to the question of work may be more expansive. Our concern is not with the technical definitions, but with whether we are removed enough from our everyday occupations to focus on sacred time.

Second, covenant: Insofar as the relationships between human beings, and between human beings and God are central to Shabbat, connectivity poses a challenge here as well. There are clearly positive uses of this technology in terms of connecting to other human beings, whether it be the use of Skype to connect grandparent and grandchild in different places, the ability to use GPS to plan a Shabbat afternoon excursion with one's children, or the opportunity to look up a *d'var Torah*. But whether it is people texting during Shabbat services or at home at the Shabbat table, our use of this technology also is intruding in places that did not have such frequent interruptions before. Studies of parents and children show that children feel most hurt when their parents use their mobile devices at meals, during pickup, and during sports events. These, it could be argued, are covenantal moments between parent and child, just as Shabbat and the holy days are covenantal moments in the Jewish community, and it is precisely at these moments that we are called upon to pay attention to where we are and who we are actually with.

Third, Creation: In terms of the interaction with the world around us, there seem to be two relevant and interrelated elements of Shabbat. One is the challenge to rest and stop creating, and the other is to appreciate nature and the created world. The new technology certainly offers ways to be creative, entirely independent from work. Moreover, there are uses of this technology—for example, an astronomy app that lets a device be held to the sky and map out constellations—that can add to our awe in the face of Creation. This is an area in which the Reform Movement can be most liberal and creative in its halachic approach. Here, the challenge may not be the technology itself as much as the devices, such as smartphones, which are multifunctional and switch easily between functions. One might start off using an astronomy app to appreciate the created world and a moment later be diverted by an e-mail from work, calling on us to create something much more mundane.

This leads to the fourth issue: choice and the question of freedom. For many but not all, the use of these devices can be addictive. Some studies suggest that a dopamine squirt is emitted in the brain when a message is received, and this results in the user checking even more frequently to get the same sense of urgency and excitement. This issue poses a double concern: first, the ways in which the focus on the technology can detract from the creativity and freedom and leisure of sacred time, and second, the ways in which the very addictive nature of the technology can on some level remove our freedom of choice. This is problematic on many levels, among them the incompatibility of a day that remembers the redemption from Egypt being a day on which we are chained to our devices.

In all of these areas, the issue is not the technology itself but how we interact with it. Communities can set their standards for what goes on in the sacred space of the synagogue. Beyond that, each individual must determine how best to celebrate Shabbat and the holy days, whether it be by using technology to see a distant grandparent, using a smartphone to look up a *d'var Torah* at the dinner table, or setting one's phone not to check e-mail from candle lighting on Friday until *Havdalah* Saturday night. This approach is clearly a departure from traditional halachah, but it is in keeping with Reform practice.

Connectivity may pose a unique challenge to our observance of Shabbat and holy days, but the questions we need to ask ourselves are the same questions that Judaism has always asked, based on our interpretation of the biblical and Rabbinic sources. Drawing from the discussion of Shabbat, we are to ask ourselves whether our decisions around the use of technology distance us from *m'lachah*, work, and draw us closer to *m'nuchah*, rest; whether they enhance our sacred times with *k'dushah*, holiness, and *oneg*, joy; whether they remind us of our covenant with God and with each other; whether they increase our appreciation of *maaseih B'reishit*, the created world; and whether they help us to embody *yitziat Mitzrayim*, the fundamental value of freedom. When it comes to the other holy days, there too we can identify the core themes and examine whether and in what ways our connectivity is compatible with our values.

Above all, the sacred time of Shabbat and the holy days offers us a gift. The notion that time can be holy gives us the opportunity—and the obligation—to try to live holy lives. Time is not something that merely passes; it is something that we sanctify by setting it aside. We are called upon to connect in the deepest sense: to ourselves and those we love, to the stories of our history and the rhythms of the year, to our communities, and to our God.

Holiness, Mitzvot, and Justice in Jewish Time

RABBI JONAH PESNER

Holidays are for celebration. The Hebrew word for a Jewish festival is *chag*; the verb *lachgog* means "to celebrate." But what about *holy days*? Perhaps this is a better English term to express what the Torah calls *mikra-ei kodesh* than the standard "holidays." Indeed, the biblical text refers to the most ancient Jewish festivals with these words, which are difficult to translate. *Kodesh* may be more familiar—holy, meaning that which is distinct from the everyday, that which approaches the divine. We declare our festivals sacred, or holy, over a cup of wine by reciting *Kiddush*. The word *mikra-im* (which becomes *mikra-ei* when connected to another modifying word like *kodesh*) relates to the verb "to call" and "to read." It is taken from the ancient tradition of calling the community together for public gatherings to read aloud the law and conduct rituals. Taken together, *mikra-ei kodesh* are literally a call to gather in holiness.

So Jewish holy days aren't just for celebration; they are making holiness. But how? What does it mean to bring holiness into the world by observing our festivals? One way is to understand them as a call to action, animating the Jewish vision of justice in the world. The deeper meanings of Jewish holy day observance can be discovered by paying special attention to the themes of social justice that run through them.

One of the most meaningful memories I have of Sukkot was the year we shared it with Reina Geuvara. Reina is a Latina, Catholic woman who lives and works in Boston as a janitor. She and her coworkers were leading a campaign to demand living wages. At the time, economists explained that it would be hard to live in the Greater Boston area on less than fifteen dollars an hour; these often invisible workers who cleaned at night were paid less than eight dollars an hour, with no health insurance. Their plight truly tested the ancient biblical call "Do not oppress your workers nor wrong them" (Leviticus 19:13).

As part of their campaign, the janitors met with clergy and leaders of diverse congregations to tell their stories and ask us to help call attention to their conditions. They invited us to join them at meetings with building owners and cleaning contractors, to make the moral case with them. These visits were inspiring, as we joined across lines of race, class, and faith to collectively call for the just treatment of those who toil on our behalf.

As they invited us, we invited them. We explained that during the festival of Sukkot, Jews gather in temporary huts decorated with fruits of the harvest. We articulated the Jewish value of blessing God for the bounty and told the story of wandering in the wilderness after our exodus from bondage. Finally, we taught them the tradition of *ushpizin*, the practice of welcoming guests into the sukkah. We could think of no better way to fulfill the mitzvah of *ushpizin* than connecting their redemption to our own.

I will never forget how they cried on the bimah as they stood under the protection of the sanctuary and told their stories to our packed congregation. They were moved by our story of the wilderness, themselves feeling like modern Israelites. Desperately poor, they still joined us in thanking God for all that we have. We cried with them as the translator told the stories of their struggles.

Our tradition offers various paths to holiness, all of which are connected to the mitzvot (commandments). Every time we bless God for giving us the commandments, we acknowledge that "God makes us holy" through them. The mitzvot fall into two categories: ethical and ritual. Most often we think of the ritual mitzvot of holy day observance: lighting candles, blessings over wine and bread, shaking a *lulav*, and many more. How often do we think of the ethical mitzvot related to our festival celebrations? Giving *tzedekah* is one act of righteousness that fulfills a critical commandment on a holy day. But it is only a place to begin.

The stories, themes, prayers, and rituals of each holy day call us to traditional and creative ethical mitzvot that provide diverse and meaningful opportunities to celebrate through acts of justice. Achieving holiness—approaching a place that is a reflection of the Divine—demands no less. God must be as concerned with our ethical actions as with our ritual observances.

In fact, the origins of our festivals generally reflect stories of a repair of an injustice or a recognition of goodness. The obvious examples include Pesach, the master-story of redemption, or Purim and Chanukah, tales of victory in the face of likely destruction. Every holy day has deeper, subtler themes as well. Shavuot is the story of a community standing together, committing to live in covenant. It challenges the modern Jew to question how well we are living in covenant with those around us, locally and globally, many of whom suffer in poverty or with other afflictions. The sweet but profound story of Ruth and Naomi, poor and "other," set during a period of harvest, is a powerful reminder of the fragility of the most vulnerable among us, Jew and non-Jew alike.

Perhaps the best, most important example is Shabbat. In his groundbreaking and inspiring masterwork, *The Sabbath*, Abraham Joshua Heschel describes Shabbat as a cathedral in time. He understands Judaism as a religion in which we discover holiness by marking time, rather than physical space. We say blessings before our actions to elevate them; we live according to the rhythm of daily, weekly, and yearly occasions marking various moments of holiness. During the week, he writes, we work on the creation of the world; on Shabbat we celebrate the work of Creation.

Heschel is well-known for his statement that marching with Dr. Martin Luther King, Jr. was "praying with his legs." As much as Heschel understood Jewish ritual as a way to mark holiness in time, he also understood the underlying call to justice. Shabbat is not merely a ritual category in which we elevate time through prayers; it is an ethical category that seeks to elevate humanity itself. Initially, it is a reminder that to be a free human person with agency and dignity is to be able to refrain from work. We were slaves in Egypt, and we had no Sabbath; Shabbat is a reminder of the true meaning of freedom. This truth applies not only to all human beings, but also to the animal kingdom and the earth itself, all of whom enjoy Shabbat.

On a deeper level, Shabbat is a taste of a world redeemed—the world as it *should* be. It is a glimpse of the world for which we pray throughout our liturgy. It is also a call to action, for though we taste perfection in the sweetness of Shabbat, we know that it is but a taste. When the candle of *Havdalah* is extinguished in the wine, the hiss is a sad sound, as we know we live in the world as it *is*. To honor Shabbat, to fulfill the mitzvot, to heed God's call, is to tirelessly pursue justice in order to help create the repaired world we know it *should* be.

There are times when we celebrate Shabbat through prayer and ritual. And there are times when our sacred obligation to seek justice demands that we celebrate, as Heschel taught, by praying with our feet. Every year, the "pride" rally in our community would fall on Saturday, and lesbian, gay, bisexual, and transgender Jews and their allies would have to choose whether or not to participate. One year, on the eve of a significant legislative fight for marriage equality, my congregation made an important decision: we would honor Shabbat through study, ritual, celebration, and then pray with our feet by marching for justice. Leaders planned a Shabbat worship service, Torah study, and lunch, followed by a march to the pride rally. Longtime Jewish activists came for Shabbat, some for the first time in years, if ever. They wept with pride, not only in their sexuality, but that their Jewish community was fighting with them. We created holiness in time, through meaningful ritual and action for justice.

There are too many examples of the applied, living intersection of celebration of Jewish time through justice to list. Every Jew and community will discover creative ways to fulfill the ethical mitzvot of the festivals. Here are some key questions to help envision action for justice to honor our holy days:

+ What are the moral and ethical implications of the *story* the holy day recounts?
+ What are the *historical contexts* of the festival and corresponding themes of injustice?
+ What symbols and images embodied in the *rituals* reflect our commitments to righteousness?
+ What calls to action are implicit within the language of the particular *prayers*?
+ What are the traditional ethical *customs* associated with each festival? What are modern approaches to practice them?
+ What are the implications for justice found in the traditional *texts* read and studied on the festival? What are other ancient and modern texts are appropriate to lift up the themes of justice relevant to the holy day?

In addition, it is important to ask the following:
+ What are the compelling local and global challenges that deserve attention at this particular sacred moment?
+ What role does Israel play in the festival, and how can our observance both be supportive of, and strengthen our relationship, to the Jewish state?
+ What is the role of world Jewry and the broader global community in the holy day?
+ What opportunities exist for *tzedakah*, direct service, or political advocacy related to those issues and appropriate for the sacred occasion?
+ How can our observance foster stronger relationships, not only among Jews but with our sisters and brothers of all backgrounds?
+ What can we do as individuals, children, families, and wider communities?

This call to seek justice is nothing new for Jews. Many individuals, families, and synagogues have found creative ways to live out the underlying values of our holy days through social action. Indeed, the historical origins of our holy days were acts of repair, as ancient generations sought to draw closer to God as a more righteous community through ritual.

What is new is the question of what *we* will do. The challenge to us and to the next generation is: Will we make our holidays true holy days? Will we bring holiness into the world by elevating our fulfillment of ethical mitzvot alongside our rituals? If we do, not only will we keep our Jewish observance relevant in our lives and impactful on our world, we will also bring about a more just world. That must be what God wants of us, as it is written, "You know what is demanded of you: only to do justice, love mercy, and walk humbly with your God" (Micah 6:8).

The People of the Food

TINA WASSERMAN

THE CHICKEN cooking in the pot with the usual onion, carrot, and celery, and the addition of the turnip and mandatory fresh dill, created an aroma that at once recalled my mother, Pesach, Shabbat, and home. But this soup wasn't to be eaten. Instead, frozen into two gallon-sized freezer bags, it was schlepped through Canadian customs to the URJ Biennial in Toronto—where it also wasn't consumed. It wasn't intended for consumption but rather for evoking memory. Brought to a simmer in a slow cooker and placed right by the door to the assembly room, over two hundred people walked past the soup and subliminally were primed for my talk about historical Jewish cuisine.

Instead of being called "the people of the book," I often feel we should be called "the people of the food," for food has played a pivotal role in our identity. Food sets us apart from others, thus serving historically as a survival technique, and also brings us together as a community. This sense of community has sustained us throughout time and our dispersion. It has allowed us to sometimes thrive but always survive in the face of insurmountable odds.

What makes food Jewish? First and foremost two laws: the laws of kashrut and the laws of Shabbat. The laws of kashrut were designed to separate us from the non-Jew. The command "You shall not boil a kid in its mother's milk" (Deuteronomy 14:21) refers to the culinary practice, in ancient times, of boiling meat in milk to tenderize it. Prohibiting a cooking technique that was commonly followed served to separate the ancients into those who followed the laws of the Torah and those who didn't. Later, the sharing of common food practices served as a way to keep the Jewish community united, separate from the people among whom they lived. Jewish travelers could thus find a welcoming community to whom they were connected through a shared food culture.

A side benefit of observing Shabbat was the establishment of many Jewish communities in remote places. The ninth-century Jewish traders known as Radanites, who found themselves on the road to and from the Far East when Shabbat was nearing, often looked for a home that followed kashrut observance or for an inn that had a separate pot put aside for the Jew. If their skill or trade was lacking in that community, the Jewish traveler often put down roots, and the beginnings of a Jewish community were formed.

One of the most iconic Ashkenazic Shabbat dishes is gefilte fish. Fish was traditionally served for Shabbat and actually was a necessity, since the resourceful, albeit often poor, Jewish cook had already stretched one chicken to provide as many dishes as possible. The classic Shabbat meal readily shows this resourcefulness; one chicken provided the meat, the soup, the fat to spread on the challah, the neck skin to be stuffed, and the liver for the pate. The Rabbis, however, deemed that taking bones out of fish was work, and therefore fish could not be eaten on Shabbat. Our ancestral cooks got around that decree by taking the fish meat out of its carcass, deboning it, and then placing the seasoned chopped fish back into the carcass to be poached in a large pot of water with a few meager vegetables. *Gefilte* literally means "stuffed"! Over time recipes were modernized to accommodate the time allotted to cooking and the newer equipment available. The whole stuffed fish morphed into balls of ground, seasoned fish steamed on top of the fish carcass with a few vegetables poached in water, broth, or white wine or baked in a loaf.

The tales and myths of our heritage lent many opportunities for creative interpretation in the foods we prepared for specific holidays. The kreplach that swim in our bowl of golden chicken soup during the High Holy Days, and most specifically for Erev Yom Kippur, can be traced to the medieval custom of writing one's wish for the new year on a piece of paper, tucking it into the center of a piece of dough, and wearing it around one's neck as an amulet. Although there is no proof, I suggest that a frugal housewife decided not to waste good milled flour on an amulet, and the symbol of being "sealed" in the Book of Life for the coming year wound up in our soup!

Chanukah, for most of the Jewish world, is associated with fried foods and the tale of the vial of oil lasting for eight days instead of one. The question is, which came first, the story that needed a recipe to commemorate itself or the daily affairs of the Jews that easily lent themselves to the creation of a tale? The establishment of the Chanukah celebration in late fall coincided with the "harvest" of the geese that had been methodically fattened for the previous three months. The down and feathers were used for warmth, the meat was preserved as a confit to be eaten throughout the winter months ahead, and the fat was rendered to provide cooking oil for the next year. With the newly rendered fat readily available, the Jewish cook could always find some potatoes and onion, and a simple preparation was transformed into a culinary legend.

Centuries ago a large portion of the Jewish world occupied the Middle East and Orient, where they created a culinary legend around the story of Judith that is associated with Chanukah. As the story goes, Judith avoided annihilation of her community at the hands of General Holofernes and his army by daring to go into his tent and seducing him with cheese and wine. After Judith plied him with salty cheese and copious amounts of wine, the general got drunk and fell asleep. Judith, according to legend, cut off his head, placed it on a staff, came out of the tent, and scared off the general's troops and saved the Jews of her village. Because of this legend, it became a custom to eat dairy foods on Chanukah. The story of one person craftily saving an entire village was very popular in the Sephardic Jewish community in Holland as well, so much so that in the sixteenth century the Jewish community celebrated the defeat of the invading Spanish army at the hands of a small band of soldiers by adopting and adapting the recipe for a stew that was left simmering in the deserted camp when they fled.

Haman's physiognomy was the culinary basis for enacting his

defeat. Italians would pinch thin strips of dough together and fry them to resemble Haman's misshapen ears. French Jews served palmiers to commemorate Haman's aural appendage. German Jews would often bite off the head of the ubiquitous gingerbread man in order to display their disgust for the villain. But, the most iconic food for Purim are the hamantaschen, "Haman's pockets." This pastry was originally adapted from the non-Jewish food customs of Bavaria. Filled with poppy seed, the *mohntaschen* (poppy seed pockets) sounded like *hamantaschen*, and the seeds paralleled the promise of God in Genesis 22:17 to make the seed of the offspring of Abraham as extensive as the sands on the seashore. In the eighteenth century, a Bavarian prune merchant named David Brandeis was accused of poisoning a magistrate and was scheduled to be hanged (an odd parallel to Purim). At the last minute the *povidl*, or prune, merchant was acquitted, and the townspeople celebrated by making their hamantaschen with prune filling that year, starting a new tradition that has endured to this day.

Matzah is one of the few foods actually prescribed in the Torah as a commandment. Any other food associated with a holiday is based on custom. *Charoset* is made to resemble the mortar that held the bricks together on the pyramids built by Jewish slaves. Preferably dark and brownish in color, the mixture itself often gave clues to its origin. Contains apples? Must be an Ashkenazic recipe from lands where apples were a mainstay. Bananas and oranges? From the Maghreb region, where Romans planted orange trees all along the shores of the Mediterranean before the empire fell. The trees' cultivation was renewed when the Moors conquered Spain. Dates? From the Middle East. Walnuts? From Georgia and Eastern Europe. Pecans? Why, the southern United States, of course!

As you make your way through the culinary traditions of our heritage, may you hear and taste the stories of the survival and perseverance of our people. The recipes are stories, and the stories are recipes.

Eat in good health! B'tei-avon!

Eating Our Values

RABBI MARY L. ZAMORE

At the holidays, we break out of our normal patterns to appreciate the time and season. Often we celebrate by bringing out our best: a new dress, fresh flowers, grandma's china, home cooking. In many ways, we strive to live during holidays in the manner we aspire to live every day. However, as we clean our homes, gather family around us, and invite guests over, we should be polishing not only our silver but also our values. Since our Jewish holidays are frequently centered on food, these moments are wonderful times to live out the food values that we wish to incorporate every day. Integrating Jewish ethical and spiritual food values into our holiday celebrations will only deepen the significance of these special times for our families and communities. Eight values central to Jewish eating are outlined in alphabetical order below. With limitless applications, each of these values represents a rich opportunity to infuse holiday celebrations with meaning. Holiday eating can be a beginning to living these values every day.

Bal Tashchit—Environmentalism

While the Rabbinic term *bal tashchit* literally means "do not destroy," it is rooted in the biblical commandment *lo tashchit* (Deuteronomy 20:19–20), meaning the same. *Bal tashchit* is often used synonymously with *shomrei adamah*, "guardians of the earth," a term that describes humanity's relationship to the earth. Both terms become the heading under which environmental issues are addressed. The application of the value of environmentalism to Jewish eating is boundless. It can be invoked as an argument in favor of reducing meat consumption through Jewish vegetarianism or meat minimalism; it can support the call for reduced packaging of kosher food and minimal use of disposable items at Jewish communal meals.

Rather than being on vacation from our values, we must uphold our commitment to the environment, especially at holidays. Since festive meals are usually planned well in advance, we have the opportunity to think ahead about how to reduce our dependency on disposable serving pieces (e.g., cups, plates, tablecloths, forks). We can borrow items from family and guests to reduce the use of disposables, which merely become landfill after one meal; we can organize volunteers to wash dishes in order to share the burden of reusable dishes.

The choice of our food can also have an impact on the environment. Many Jews are reducing the role of meat, especially red meat, in their diets. Reconsider the amount of meat served at holiday meals. While some Jews cling to the Talmudic statement "There could be no joy without meat,"[1] many are learning that meat does not need to be the center of every holiday meal. The meat course can be one choice among many other dishes, or a festive, completely vegetarian menu can be created. Eating seasonal and local food is also good for the environment, as this reduces the impact of transport, also known as the carbon footprint, of our food. Choosing a fruit or vegetable that is in season and grown locally is a better choice than picking one that has been transported across the world. A bonus is that seasonal and local produce usually tastes better.

B'rachot—Blessing

While it is a mitzvah to recite *b'rachot*, blessings, every time we eat, this may not be part of our individual daily practice. However, holidays are a wonderful time to sanctify our food and table by reciting *Kiddush*, the blessing over wine, *HaMotzi*, the blessing over bread, and *Birkat HaMazon*, the blessing after we eat. These blessings allow us to pause before we eat and to reflect gratefully on the gifts of food and company. We connect to God through this contemplative practice. We set the mood at our holiday table, reminding ourselves why this meal is different from all other meals.

These blessings can be recited according to our ability. For example, while there are long versions of the evening *Kiddush* specifically for the Festivals, if no one knows the full blessing, it is fine to sing the part you do know in Hebrew and then read the rest in English or sing along with a recording, online video, or app. The same can be applied to *Birkat HaMazon*, the blessing after we eat. It should be noted that one does not require a challah in order to say *HaMotzi*, the blessing over any type of bread. Before you recite these prayers, you can add some personal, spontaneous prayers that are tailored to the specific holiday and people around the table.

Kashrut—Kosher Food and Wine

If kashrut is an unfamiliar practice, it need not seem foreign or intimidating, for ultimately kashrut is our Jewish relationship with food. Any time we allow Jewish law and values to inform our food choices, we are keeping Jewish dietary laws. Therefore, when we eat matzah on Passover, fruits and vegetables on Tu BiSh'vat, or we fast on Yom Kippur, we allow our rich tradition to shape our food choices. When Jewish dietary laws influence our eating habits, we affirm our Jewish identities and connect to our greater Jewish community, our sacred tradition, and God.

Traditional Jewish holiday recipes reflect kashrut, the Jewish dietary laws, by excluding nonkosher foods like pork, shellfish, and nonkosher meats and by separating milk from meat foods and their related products. While you may or may not keep kosher during the rest of the year, you can sanctify your holiday table by following some or all of the Jewish dietary laws. Making a kosher-style meal is a good place to start for Jews who do not regularly keep kosher. For example, you can avoid mixing milk and meat by using oil and oil-based margarine in recipes, by not serving glasses of milk, and by skipping cream or cheese sauces at a meat meal. Keeping some or all of the laws of kashrut will distinguish your Jewish holiday table from the other daily and festive meals you serve throughout the year, it will connect your home to Jews throughout the world, and it will model living Judaism for your family.

Another way to bring kashrut to your table is to use kosher wine.

While it is acceptable from a Reform Jewish outlook to say *kiddush* over any wine, Jewish holidays are wonderful times to try kosher wine. While some Jews look forward to the unique taste of kosher wine labeled "heavy Concord grape," others will appreciate the wonderful variety of fine kosher wines now available. In particular, Israel produces an amazing variety of kosher wines in many different price ranges. You can take the opportunity to connect to and support Israel by making a point to buy Israeli kosher wine.

Kesher—Connection through Food

Eating together creates connection among people. The value of *hachnasat or'chim*, welcoming guests, teaches us to gather friends and family around our tables. We should especially try to remember those who may be alone or do not have the means to make a holiday meal. While entertaining can add extra work to already full lives, it is a great joy to nurture family and friends, especially on a holiday, and to draw them closer to us and each other over good food. As hosts, we bond with our families and friends, but we also connect to our food through our meal preparation. During the regular week, we often cook on autopilot, depending on a rotation of familiar and fast recipes or, even more often, prepared foods. Holidays bring a fresh inspiration to our menus and give us an opportunity to prepare food from scratch.

In planning and preparing our holiday meals, we can connect to our food and through food to the Source of our food. The Torah teaches us, "God Eternal took the man, placing him in the Garden of Eden to work it and keep it" (Genesis 2:15). Recalling our ancient connection to the soil, we can also encounter God in the garden. However, gardener or not, we all have the blessing of rejoicing in the beauty, variety, and miracle of food. As we prepare and cook our holiday meal, we can pause to reflect on the food before us, appreciating the beautiful partnership that is intrinsic to cooking. Food preparation offers an awesome intersection among Creator—God, the Source of our nourishment; food workers—those who toil to bring food to our markets; and cooks—we who draw upon communal human history and knowledge to prepare the food. As we shape our menus, we also connect to our personal histories when we select recipes handed down through our families or cultural traditions. When we cook, we can acknowledge the spirituality that infuses food preparation. We can know that we are not simply alone with our pots and pans.

Oshek—Worker's Rights

Oshek, the oppression of a worker, is expressly forbidden in the Torah. The Torah instructs, "You shall not defraud your fellow. You shall not commit robbery. The wages of a laborer shall not remain with you until morning" (Leviticus 19:13–14). In addition, "You shall not abuse a needy and destitute laborer, whether a fellow Israelite or a stranger. . . . You must pay out the wages due on the same day" (Deuteronomy 24:14–15). In a modern context, the concept *oshek* is readily applied to the workers who produce and help serve our food. We must treat and pay our help fairly, whether they work in our Jewish institutions or homes. Being clear about work duties, hours, and pay is important. Making sure those who work for us have a safe way of getting home, especially at night, is also vital. Thanking our employees privately and publicly is also respectful of their role in creating a beautiful holiday.

When we buy our food, whether prepared or unprepared, we can look for certifications that assure that agricultural and food workers involved in its production have been fairly paid. There are a growing number of secular and specifically Jewish certifications that attest to food workers' conditions. These include Fair Trade, a secular agency that certifies the payment of living wages to workers, especially in the notorious coffee, tea, chocolate, and nut industries;[2] Magen Tzedek (originally named Hechsher Tzedek), which was created by Rabbi Morris Allen through the Conservative Movement to certify that kosher products adhere to additional ethical guidelines, including *oshek*;[3] the Israeli Orthodox social justice organization Bema'aglei Tzedek's *Tav Chevrati*, a seal of approval granted free of charge to restaurants and other businesses that respect the legally mandated rights of their employees;"[4] and the American Orthodox social justice organization Uri L'Tzedek's *Tav haYosher*, which seeks to certify kosher restaurants that uphold "the right to fair pay, the right to fair time, and the right to a safe work environment."[5] While it is extremely difficult to find a large range of food products with these certifications, we can support this value by seeking out such products, especially when we buy coffee, tea, and chocolate.

Sh'mirat HaGuf—Preserving Our Health

Sh'mirat haguf, the value of caring for our bodies, is rooted in the concept that we were created *b'tzelem Elohim*, "in the image of God" (Genesis 1:27). To honor God is to care for God's handiwork. *Sh'mirat haguf* commands us to tend to our own bodies, but also to feel responsible for our fellow beings. Therefore, if the food we eat is produced with chemicals that can harm the agricultural workers, we should have two concerns—the effect of the chemicals on our health and on the workers' health. Emphasizing organically produced foods will benefit our health, the workers' health, and the environment.

Holidays can be a time of great indulgence. While some treats are certainly called for, it is possible to lighten the health impact of our festive meals by choosing lighter versions of our favorite recipes, emphasizing fruits and vegetables in our menus, and avoiding the subtle (and sometimes not so subtle) message that everyone has to become members of the clean plate club. Urging family and friends to eat too much or to eat foods that may harm their health is not considerate or loving. A kind host will inquire about guests' allergies, dietary needs, and do the best to accommodate them. If particular guests' diets are too complicated, it is perfectly fine to politely explain the situation and invite them to bring their own food.

Tzaar Baalei Chayim—Animal Rights

Tzaar baalei chayim, "the prevention of suffering to animals," is considered to be a biblical commandment, based on the verse "When you see the ass of your enemy lying under its burden and would refrain from raising it, you must nevertheless help raise it" (Exodus 23:5).[6] While a good part of the laws under this heading have to do with the treatment of work animals, the treatment of food source animals is reflected in the traditional dietary laws, kashrut. For example, in ritual kashrut, the separation of milk and meat are based on the thrice repeated command "You shall not boil a kid [young goat] in its mother's milk" (Exodus 23:19, 34:26; Deuteronomy 14:21). While this verse is widely used to support the ritual practice of separating milk and meat, its ethical dimension is frequently recognized for teaching the humane treatment of animals. In our daily and holiday eating, we can live this value by reducing the role of meat in our diets or by choosing sources for our meat, dairy, and eggs that are dedicated to the humane treatment of animals. We can also shun foods, like veal and foie gras, that are technically kosher yet violate the value of tzaar baalei chayim.

Tzedakah and Tzedek—Charity and Social Justice

The work of tzedek (social justice), including the concern for the oppressed and hungry, can be expressed through many of the values discussed, as it is intrinsic to Judaism's daily observance. Nutritious food is not a privilege, but a right. Judaism also considers the joy of celebrating holidays as a right deserved by all Jews. Some people do not have the financial means to make a proper holiday; others do not have family and friends. We can open our homes to community members who may find themselves alone at the holidays. Your rabbi can help make a match if you are not sure who may need support. If you are not in a position to invite acquaintances or strangers to your home, you can buy gift cards at local grocery stores and let your rabbi distribute them without you or the recipient knowing each other (a modern twist on Maimonides's ladder of *tzedekah*). Better yet, lead your synagogue in organizing a collection of gift cards or holiday foods to be anonymously distributed. Many grocery stores give away turkeys (and other foods) at certain holiday seasons. If you are not using yours, claim it anyway and donate it. Include a foil pan and nonperishable side dishes to ensure the recipient has the means to cook the meal. Again, this can be a community-wide collection.

When we celebrate holidays, we can remember the poor of our communities by volunteering at local soup kitchens, food pantries, or meals-on-wheels programs. Clearly, these acts of kindness do not have to be done on the actual holiday, although they often can be. Giving a donation to your favorite feeding program is also an appropriate way to sanctify your holiday. Finally, when you are planning your festive meal, think about the leftovers. Distributing the leftovers in a meaningful way should always be on your checklist of hosting responsibilities. Many local feeding programs will take fresh leftovers. Just make sure that you are giving away something that you are willing to eat yourself.

Where to Start

Each of these values is worthy in its own right; many intersect in their practical application. Do not get overwhelmed by trying to incorporate every value to its fullest extent into your holiday meals. Start with the ones that speak to you and are easy to achieve. Make sure you have a good mix of the spiritual and ethical, as these reinforce one another. Then, build from there, adding as you can. Most of all, enjoy your holiday table, fill it with good food, and surround yourself with family and friends.

For more information about Jewish food ethics, see The Sacred Table: Creating a Jewish Food Ethic, *edited by Mary L. Zamore (New York: CCAR Press, 2011).*

Passover Kashrut
A Reform Approach
RABBI MARY L. ZAMORE

Set Yourself Up for Success
Many liberal Jews mark Passover by adjusting their regular eating habits, yet they claim no connection to regular kashrut. But Reform kashrut is not an all-or-nothing matter. Jews who sanctify Passover through the eating of matzah and refrain from eating *chameitz* should proudly embrace these rituals, even if they eschew regular kashrut. (The same attitude should be held by those who keep kosher in their homes but do not restrict their diets outside.)

At the same time, Jewish leaders must make Passover kashrut accessible by educating their communities and helping them plan in advance for the holiday. Clarifying the laws and providing easy solutions to logistical barriers help families to keep and enjoy Passover kashrut. Many Jews become overwhelmed and, despite good intentions, give up in the middle of the holiday. Often they have not prepared their kitchens in a way that makes Passover easier to keep; they have not taken the time to excite their children about the holiday. Therefore, they start the holiday at a handicap. There are ways to help individuals, families, or communities clarify their expectations for Passover eating, some of which are discussed in *The Sacred Table: Creating a Jewish Food Ethic* (CCAR Press, 2011).

For all dietary practice, but especially for Passover, it is important to know that one mistake does not signal the end of the ritual. Rather, mistakes are an invitation to evaluate what went wrong and to correct expectations or logistics for the future.

The Laws
A gastronomic reminder of the Exodus from Egypt, the foundation of Passover kashrut, is found in the following verses:

*This day shall be to you one of remembrance: you shall cel-
ebrate it as a festival to the Eternal throughout the ages; you
shall celebrate it as an institution for all time. Seven days you
shall eat unleavened bread; on the very first day you shall
remove leaven from your houses, for whoever eats leavened
bread from the first day to the seventh day, that person shall
be cut off from Israel. You shall celebrate a sacred occasion
on the first day, and a sacred occasion on the seventh day; no
work at all shall be done on them; only what every person is to
eat, that alone may be prepared for you. You shall observe the
[Feast of] Unleavened Bread, for on this very day I brought
your ranks out of the land of Egypt; you shall observe this day
throughout the ages as an institution for all time. In the first
month, from the fourteenth day of the month at evening, you
shall eat unleavened bread until the twenty-first day of the
month at evening. No leaven shall be found in your houses for
seven days. For whoever eats what is leavened, that person—
whether a stranger or a citizen of the country—shall be cut off
from the community of Israel. You shall eat nothing leavened;
in all your settlements you shall eat unleavened bread.*
(Exodus 12:14–20)

These verses establish the holiday of Passover and command that
we should eat matzah and refrain from eating *chameitz*, leavened
bread, during the seven days. The Rabbis define *chameitz* as five
grains—wheat, barley, spelt, rye, and oats (BT *P'sachim* 35a)—that
are exposed to water for more than eighteen minutes. This time
frame is counted from the minute the water touches the flour to the
time it is fully baked. Although the time frame was debated through
the development of this law, eighteen minutes is considered the
boundary between matzah and *chameitz* (BT *P'sachim* 46a; *Shulchan Aruch, Orach Chayim* 459). Therefore, matzah is produced
from start to finish in under eighteen minutes. Kosher-for-Passover
foods that contain these grains (e.g., cookies, cakes, crackers, pasta)
are usually made from matzah meal (finely ground matzah) rather
than flour to ensure that there is no *chameitz* in the product.

In the strictest observance of Passover, the entire household is thoroughly cleaned. All dishes, pots, and utensils are switched to sets reserved for Passover use. All food products containing any morsel of *chameitz* are used up before the holiday or are removed from use and stored away. Then, these forbidden foods are symbolically sold (see CCAR Responsum 5756.9). All food brought into the cleaned home must be certified kosher for Passover. This level of observance may be overwhelming to Jews who did not grow up with these practices; it may seem unnecessary to others.

Therefore, the following approach is for those who are just beginning to keep Passover and those seeking a simpler way to keep Passover. It can also be used as a paradigm as to how to teach Passover kashrut within the liberal community. Clearly, this can be adjusted to incorporate more or fewer observances; it can be adjusted according to the age and knowledge levels of the students.

A Simple Model for Keeping Passover Kashrut

Clean your kitchen and eating areas to remove crumbs, etc. (If you eat in your car, you may want to vacuum it.)

1. Go through your pantries, refrigerator, and freezer, removing all obvious *chameitz*. (*Kitniyot* are discussed CCAR responsum 5756.9.) Children love to sort things; engage their help. It will help them learn the laws of Passover and excite them about the holiday.

2. Store away nonperishable foods in closed bags, boxes, or cabinets, so they are not a temptation. Many people mistakenly believe that Jews must throw out all of their unused food before Passover. This is not true and would be wasteful. However, if you can afford it, Passover cleaning provides a wonderful opportunity to donate unused food to a local food pantry. It is also a good time to support your local kosher food pantry so that other Jews can celebrate Passover.

3. If you have an extra refrigerator and/or freezer, put perishable foods in it and tape it shut. If you have only one refrigerator/

freezer, designate a particular drawer or shelf for *chameitz*. Place *chameitz* in black plastic bags and then place in the refrigerator/freezer. It is easier to keep the holiday if you are not looking at *chameitz*.

4. Go shopping, buying lots of delicious foods. If you are short on time, consider what is easy to prepare. You do not need to limit yourself to the Passover aisle. There are plenty of foods found throughout the store that are good for the holiday. You can either buy foods that are certified for Passover or read labels to stay away from the five grains. Consider allowing a few treats like sugary Passover cereal if that helps motivate your family. Also, remember that fresh fruits and vegetables are all kosher for Passover, making Passover a great time to return to a back-to-basics diet, avoiding commercially processed foods.

As you feel comfortable with your level of observance, you can evaluate and adjust your practices, adding more rituals as you see fit.

The Journey to Judaism
Choosing Judaism, Choosing Mitzvot

RABBI JUDITH SCHINDLER

Becoming jewish is a journey. It is a process of becoming at
home with Jewish learning, with mitzvot, with Jewish holidays,
with the Jewish people, and with one's own Jewish soul. Unlike
many other faiths, where conversion can be an instantaneous process of revelation, becoming Jewish does not occur overnight. It
requires an extended process of learning and living the Jewish faith
and culture, of exploring the vast array of mitzvot, the Jewish acts
that can enrich and elevate one's life, and incorporating them into
one's routine and into the fabric of one's being.

An essential step on the journey to Judaism is entering the synagogue. In biblical times, Abraham and Sarah kept their tent open on
all four sides so that any passerby could be drawn into their midst
and learn about Jewish ways of believing and acting. In Talmudic times, the great Rabbi Hillel was renowned for his welcoming
stance. Similarly today, the liberal synagogue warmly embraces
those who yearn to deepen their relationship with Judaism. While
ancient anti-Semitism and the persecution of those who converted
and those who facilitated conversion in medieval times led Jewish
communities to become more closed, that reality began to change
in the modern era. The new approach was aptly articulated by
Rabbi Alexander Schindler, of blessed memory, president of the
Union of American Hebrew Congregations (the former name of the
Union for Reform Judaism). He called upon the Reform Movement
to cast open its closed doors to the non-Jew who married a Jew
and to all: "My dream is to see our Judaism unleashed as a resource
for a world in need: not as the exclusive inheritance of the few, but
as a renewable resource for the many; not as a religious stream too
small to be seen on the map of the world, but as a deep flowing

river, hidden by the overgrown confusion of modern times, that could nourish humanity's highest aspirations."[1]

Once inside the tent of Judaism, one will learn that the path to living a Jewish life is paved by mitzvot. They surround every aspect of one's day, year, and life. There are mitzvot that sanctify time, food, milestone moments, and one's encounters with every human being.

The mitzvot surrounding Shabbat teach us to stop and celebrate the lives that we have. By celebrating the Sabbath each week, we can escape the potentially oppressive nature of work and our week-day demands so that we can absorb the holiness of our labor and get in touch with what matters most—ourselves, our souls, our families, our community, and God.

The mitzvot surrounding the sacred cycle of holidays not only enable one to connect with God through the words of liturgy and with family through home celebrations, they enable one to connect with the cycle of the seasons, with the awe of nature, and with the significant historic moments of the Jewish people. Through the diverse mitzvot surrounding Sukkot, Pesach, Shavuot, Chanukah, and Tu BiSh'vat, we connect with Israel's agricultural times and seasons. As we reap our harvest in the fall, as we pray for rain and dew (each in its time), as we seek to bring light to the dark days of winter, and as we celebrate the earth's turning to spring, we affirm our connectedness to the earth, to God, and to the land and people of Israel.

Mitzvot surrounding food elevate our eating. One who chooses to embrace the mitzvot of traditional kashrut can find God by iden-tifying with Jews of generations before and with the wider Jew-ish world. By choosing to observe ethical kashrut (or eco-kashrut, as many call it), one ensures that one's food choices do not harm our environment or the ethical treatment of those who produce what we eat. Additionally, one can connect with God by taking on mitzvot that treat our bodies with care, for just as the synagogue's ark houses the sacred scroll of the Torah, so does the human body house the soul.

There are also ethical mitzvot. Judaism teaches that every human being is created *b'tzelem Elohim*, "in the image of God." God is found in relationships and in the commandments that guide the connections between parent and child, as children honor parents and as parents bless and teach children. God is found in the fulfillment of commandments that guide one's relationships with neighbors, with coworkers or employees, with the homeless, the needy, and the stranger on the city street. The Holiness Code at the heart of Leviticus teaches that God is found most powerfully not only in sanctuaries but also in the simple moments of everyday living. There are mitzvot surrounding sexuality that call the Jew to achieve holiness in our most private moments of intimacy, and there are mitzvot surrounding social justice calling the Jew to continually work to repair that which is broken in the world.

The majority of mitzvot are given in the Torah without reason or reward. Whether performing mitzvot brings the God-given rewards to one's present life or afterlife, we cannot know. Truly, Jewish tradition asks us not to consider any otherworldly reward in the doing of mitzvot. Yet we can know the human rewards of blessing, healing, and connection that the fulfillment of mitzvot bring.

The passage to becoming part of the Jewish religion requires studying each mitzvah of modern life and incorporating those that will ground and fill your daily routine, your holiday cycle, and the milestone moments of your life with meaning and with purpose. By weaving mitzvot into your days, Jewish memory will be created within you, and you will find your Jewish soul connected with Jews who surround you in the synagogue and with the generations of Jews who came before you. When the building blocks of mitzvot become a natural part of your life, it is then that your clergy will likely affirm that you are ready to finalize your conversion and formally count your soul among those who once stood at Sinai.

In the Mishnah, Joshua ben Perachyah said, "Find yourself a teacher; get yourself a friend to study with you."[2] Judaism is learned not only from rabbis, but also with peers and mentors. Find a community from whom you can learn the meaning behind the many mitzvot presented in this book. They will be better understood as you see them lived by community.

Rabbi Arnold Jacob Wolf, of blessed memory, compares the mitzvot to jewels:

> I try to walk the road of Judaism. Embedded in that road there are many jewels. One is marked "Sabbath" and one "Civil Rights" and one "Kashrut" and one "Honor Your Parents" and one "You Shall Be Holy." There are at least 613 of them and they are different shapes and sizes and weights. Some are light and easy to pick up, and I pick them up. Some are too deeply embedded for me, so far at least, though I get a little stronger by trying to extricate the jewels as I walk the street. Some, perhaps, I shall never be able to pick up. I believe that God expects me to keep on walking Judaism Street and to carry away whatever I can of its commandments. I do not believe that God expects me to lift what I cannot, nor may I condemn my fellow Jew who may not be able to pick up even as much as I can."[3]

There are many who are born Jewish who have failed to receive the richness of their inheritance. One-third of the Jewish population is secular and has not embraced Judaism as a way of life. Yet the truth remains that all Jews, whether they convert (Jews-by-choice) or whether they are born Jewish, need to *choose* Judaism and choose mitzvot to live their faith.

The Book of Exodus notes that when Moses first presented the Israelites with the Torah and the mitzvot within it, they responded, "*Naaseh v'nishma*—We will do and we will understand" (Exodus 24:7). Inquisitiveness, patience, perseverance, humility, and a sense of awe are all required on one's journey to living a Jewish life for one to uncover the valued treasure of mitzvot. Oftentimes trying mitzvot will precede understanding them.

Relationships command us. The actions that fill our days are determined by the relationships that we have or have had—with our parents, our teachers, our colleagues, our community, and even with the stranger who dwells within our highly connected modern world. Choosing Judaism means choosing to be in partnership with God and with the Jewish people and taking on the responsibilities, the mitzvot, upon which those relationships rest.

According to the midrash, Abraham faced ten trials on his path to becoming the first Jew. Similarly, those who join Judaism face trials. Among them may be recognizing that one is religiously not at home where one currently is; entering a synagogue for the first time; meeting the rabbi; telling family members, friends, and colleagues that one is on the path to conversion; learning; living the mitzvot; becoming part of the Jewish community; and standing before the clergy as one becomes a Jew.

At a pivotal point on Abraham's journey to Judaism, his name was changed from Abram, acknowledging God's place in his name and his life (Genesis 17:5). In the process of that name change, Abraham's fate and future were transformed, and his life became filled with holiness. Similarly, every person can choose Judaism and choose mitzvot as a means of creating a happy, whole, and holy life. They need only to take the first steps toward leaving the wilderness, finding the open tent of a welcoming synagogue, and seeking the wisdom and warmth that lie within.

Tzedakah

GIVING TZEDAKAH is an important mitzvah. We are commanded to use our resources to provide decent lives for ourselves and our families and to help make the world a more just and compassionate place. Judaism teaches that everyone, even the poorest member of society, has the responsibility to give *tzedakah*.[1] While *tzedakah* is often translated as "charity," it is derived from the Hebrew root *tzadi-dalet-kuf*, which means "justice" or "righteousness." It is such a central Jewish value that we are supposed to seek out opportunities to perform this mitzvah and not wait passively for them to appear.

One classic description of this concept is Maimonides's Eight Levels of *Tzedakah*.[2] This "ladder" ranks the different levels of *tzedakah*, with the highest level being the first in this list and going in descending order:

+ Giving an interest-free loan to a person in need, forming a partnership with a person in need, giving a grant to a person in need, or finding a job for a person in need, so long as that loan, grant, partnership, or job results in the person no longer living by relying upon others.
+ Giving *tzedakah* anonymously to an unknown recipient via a person (or public fund) who is trustworthy, wise, and can perform acts of *tzedakah* with your money in a most impeccable fashion.
+ Giving *tzedakah* anonymously to a known recipient.
+ Giving *tzedakah* publicly to an unknown recipient.
+ Giving *tzedakah* before being asked.
+ Giving adequately after being asked.
+ Giving willingly, but inadequately.
+ Giving "in sadness" or giving out of pity. (It is thought that Maimonides was referring to giving because of the sad feelings one might have in seeing people in need, as opposed to

giving because it is a religious obligation. Other translations say, "Giving unwillingly.")

Helping someone to achieve independence and therefore no longer needing to be a recipient of *tzedakah* is the highest level. Giving sadly or unwillingly is the lowest level but is still a valid form of *tzedakah*. This ladder in many ways acts as a summary of Jewish teachings on *tzedakah*. While some levels are higher than others, all fulfill the obligation inherent in the mitzvah of *tzedakah*.

The verse *Tzedek, tzedek tirdof*, "Justice, justice shall you pursue" from the Torah (Deuteronomy 16:20), is interpreted by the midrash to mean that we are supposed to perform the mitzvah of *tzedakah* where we are, but we are obligated to also pursue opportunities beyond our immediate environs. Because of the additional emphasis on helping beyond one's own circle, it has come to mean not only giving direct aid to the poor but also supporting an array of causes and organizations involved in *tikkun olam* (repairing the world), which could include both direct service and advocacy. Therefore, *tzedakah* can also mean supporting those organizations and causes that perpetuate Jewish life and create a more just, peaceful, and compassionate society.

For many, the observance of the sacred days of the Jewish calendar prohibited acts of *tzedakah* on those days, as giving gifts of money or supporting causes were considered to be work and therefore not appropriate activities. However, an expanded concept of *m'lachah* (work) and *m'nuchah* (rest), *oneg* (delight), and *k'dushah* (holiness) suggests that for some people, observance of the sacred times is enhanced by acts of *tzedakah*, especially when doing so is understood as a subcategory of *tikkun olam* and *g'milut chasadim* (acts of loving-kindness). This is derived from the Mishnah: *Al sh'loshah d'varim haolam omeid: al haTorah, v'al haavodah, v'al g'milut chasadim*, "The world stands on three things: on Torah, worship, and deeds of loving-kindness."[3] Since study and worship are essential to our observance, it would seem natural that an act of *g'milut chasadim* would also complete and enhance our observance.

Therefore, Shabbat, the Festivals, and other sacred days, outside of communal worship hours, are very appropriate times for special acts of *tzedakah*. Ideally they ought to be tailored to the specific values most connected to the sacred day. A time-honored custom is for each household to have a *tzedakah* box, or perhaps even multiple *tzedakah* boxes, and to deposit money before candle lighting or beginning the observance of the sacred occasion. The members of the household can then determine where to give the money.

Specific occasions can engender conversation about where money might be donated to mark the ideas and values that are commemorated by the day. For example, for Yom HaAtzma-ut (Israel Independence Day), money could be donated to an Israel-related cause. On Yom Kippur one might donate food or the money that was not used that day (because of the fast) to feed the hungry. But beyond the giving of money, since Sukkot is a time of thanksgiving for the bountiful harvest, a time of hospitality, and a reminder of the fragility of providence, one might collect food for distribution to the poor, or volunteer to prepare or deliver meals to hungry. Participating in a rally on Sukkot afternoon to preserve the quality of the air and water that make bountiful harvests possible would be considered by some an appropriate observance of the festival. The possibilities are endless. The key to understanding the concept of *tzedakah*, and incorporating it into our observance on the sacred days themselves, is to consciously perform these acts *lichvod Shabbat*, "in honor of Shabbat," and *lichvod Yom Tov*, "in honor of the festival." Part of observance is to recognize the unique character of each sacred day.

Notes

The Cycle of the Jewish Year

1 In the Hebrew calendar, the days of the week do not have names, but are numbered according to their relationship to Shabbat—Sunday is *Yom Rishon l'Shabbat*, "the first day toward Shabbat"; Monday is *Yom Sheini l'Shabbat*, "the second day toward Shabbat"; etc. Shabbat is unique among the holy days, because it is independent of the cyclical changes of nature:

> Since the rhythm of the Sabbath is the only exception to the prevailing natural rhythm and since the exception in no way derives from time as such nor is traceable to any aspect of time experienced in the ancient Near East, it is likely that the opposition between the Sabbath on the one hand and nature on the other hand was not unintentional. The intention was, I suggest, to fill time with a contact that is uncontaminated by, and distinct from anything related to natural time, i.e., time as agricultural season or astronomical phase . . . that content, displacing the various ideas and phenomena associated with natural time is the idea of the absolute sovereignty of God, a sovereignty unqualified even by an indirect cognizance of the rule of other powers. As man takes heed of the Sabbath day and keeps it holy, he not only relinquishes the opportunity of using part of his time as he pleases but also forgoes the option of tying it to the secure and beneficial order of nature. (Matitiahu Tsevat, "The Meaning of the Sabbath," in *The Meaning of the Book of Job and Other Biblical Studies* [New York: KTAV, 1980], pages 50–52).

2 *Pirkei Avot* 4:2.

The Jewish Calendar

3 BT *Sanhedrin* 11a–b.

4 Ibid., 12a.

5 Genesis 1:5, "And there was evening and there was morning, [the] first day."

6 To determine if a given year is a leap year, one divides the date by 19, and if the remainder is 0, 3, 6, 8, 11, 14, or 17, it is a leap year.

7 It should be noted that the names Kislev, Tevet, Adar, Nisan, Sivan, and Elul are found only in the Books of Zechariah, Nehemiah, and Esther, all of which were written after the Babylonian exile.

8 BT *Sanhedrin* 97b; BT *Avodah Zarah* 9b.

9 *Mishnah Rosh HaShanah* 2:2.

10 JT *Rosh HaShanah* 2:1, 58a.

11 *Mishnah Rosh HaShanah* 2:7.

12 Solomon Zeitlin, "The Second Day of the Holidays in the Diaspora and the Second Day of Rosh Ha-Shanah in Israel," *CCAR Journal*, 16, (April 1969): 48–57.

13 JT *P'sachim* 4:1, 30d.

14 W. Gunther Plaut, *The Rise of Reform Judaism* (New York: World Union for Progressive Judaism, 1963), pages 195–198.

Every Day

1 *Gates of Mitzvah,* page 38, E-3, and page 83, notes 68–69. Daily services may be found in *Mishkan T'filah*, pages 1–117. Also, evening and morning prayers and private weekday prayers may be found in *On the Doorposts of Your House* (revised edition, 2010), pages 3–20. Private prayer is an important part of daily living. However, in some congregations there is a daily service that provides the opportunity to fulfill the mitzvah with other members of the community.

2 *Gates of Mitzvah*, pages 40–41, E-7. The text of table blessings may be found in *Mishkan T'filah*, pages 606–609, and *On the Doorposts of Your House* (revised edition), pages 23–40.

3 *Gates of Mitzvah*, page 19, E-1, and page 22, F-1.

4 The mitzvah of honoring one's parents is found in both versions of the Ten Commandments (Exodus 20:12 and Deuteronomy 5:16).

5 Leviticus 19, which is part of a section of the Torah known as the Holiness Code, is a rich source of mitzvot that regulate relationships among human beings. For example, "You shall not falsify measures of length, weight, or capacity. You shall have an honest balance, honest weights, an honest *eifah*, and an honest *hin*" (Leviticus 19:35–36).

6 Leviticus 19:18, "Love your fellow as yourself."

7 Leviticus 19:15, "You shall not render an unfair decision: do not favor the poor or show deference to the rich; judge your kin fairly."

8 For example, Amos 5:21–24: "I loathe, I spurn your festivals, I am not appeased by your solemn assemblies. If you offer Me burnt offerings—or your meal offerings—I will not accept them. I will pay no heed to your gifts of fatlings. Spare Me the sound of your hymns, and let Me not hear the music of your lutes. But let justice well up like water, righteousness like an unfailing stream."

9 *Avot D'Rabbi Natan*, chapter 15.

Shabbat

1 As quoted in *Mishkan T'filah: A Reform Siddur*, pages 149 and 251, deriving from Achad Ha-am's "Shabbat Vetziyonut," *HaShiloach* 3, no. 6 (1898), reprinted in *Al Parashat Derachim* (Tel Aviv, 1955), page 496.

2 "For in six days the Eternal made heaven and earth and sea—and all that is

in them—and then rested on the seventh day; therefore the Eternal blessed the Sabbath day and hallowed it" (Exodus 20:11).

3   "Remember that you were a slave in the land of Egypt and the Eternal your God freed you from there with a mighty hand and an outstretched arm; therefore the Eternal your God has commanded you to observe the Sabbath day" (Deuteronomy 5:15).

4   *Mishkan T'filah*, page 123: "In love and favor, You made the holy Shabbat our heritage as a reminder of the work of Creation."

5   Ibid.: "As first among our sacred days, it recalls the Exodus from Egypt."

6   According to Rabbinic legend, an additional soul (*n'shamah y'teirah*) dwells in the Jew during Shabbat (BT *Beitzah* 16a; *Taanit* 27b).

7   *Mishnah Tamid* 7:4; BT *Rosh HaShanah* 31a.

8   Exodus 20:8; Deuteronomy 5:12.

9   The Talmud (BT *K'tubot* 62b) designates Friday night as the appropriate time for scholars and their wives to have sexual intercourse. Rashi, in his commentary, explains that the reason for the injunction is that Shabbat is a time of "pleasure, rest, and physical enjoyment." Furthermore, a thirteenth-century kabbalistic text, *Igeret HaKodesh*, views sexual intercourse as being in keeping with the spiritual nature of Shabbat (*The Holy Letter* [New York: KTAV, 1976], pages 66–79). The *Shulchan Aruch* (*Orach Chayim* 280:1) adds, "Sexual relations are one of Shabbat's joys."

10   "On the seventh day, God had completed the work that had been done, ceasing then on the seventh day from all the work that [God] had done. Then God blessed the seventh day and made it holy, and ceased from all the creative work that God [had chosen] to do" (Genesis 2:2–3). We should be aware that the original meaning of the Hebrew word *kadosh* (holy) is "to be set aside or apart as special." It is only when Shabbat is in fact different from the other days of the week that we can say it is *kadosh* (holy) for us.

11   According to Rabbinic lore, the world was still incomplete on the sixth day. "What did the world lack? It lacked *m'nuchah* [rest]. Shabbat came and rest came and the world was now complete" (Rashi's commentary to Genesis 2:2; BT *M'gilah* 6a). The midrash (*B'reishit Rabbah* 10:9) adds that tranquility, ease, peace, and quiet were created on the first Shabbat. *M'nuchah* is a positive concept that required a special act of creation. Each Shabbat, the individual has the opportunity to experience *m'nuchah* which refreshes both body and spirit.

12   BT *Shabbat* 113b: "Your conversation on Shabbat shall not be like your conversation on weekdays." Rashi comments that one should not discuss business on Shabbat. In order to experience the tranquility that Shabbat can bring, one should refrain from discussing those things that will deflect one's attention from the special character of Shabbat.

13   BT *Shabbat* 113a: "Your walking on Shabbat shall not be like your walk-

ing on a weekday." On Shabbat there is no need to hurry. By walking more slowly, one adds to the restfulness of the day. Everything is slower on Shabbat because there is plenty of time. It is a day of being rather than a day of doing.

14 The midrash (*B'reishit Rabbah* 17:5, 44:17) and the Talmud (BT *B'rachot* 57b) describe Shabbat as a reflection of the world-to-come. Shabbat's ability to transform the world from the real to the ideal, even for just a little while, fills the Jew with new hope and new resolve.

15 The Mishnah (*Shabbat* 7:2) lists thirty-nine classes of activities that are to be categorized as work and prohibited on Shabbat. The Talmud, codes, and responsa literature have elaborated and refined this list. While there are some Jews who choose to define work in accord with these definitions, many no longer consider certain prohibited activities as work. A renewal of Shabbat observance requires a new definition of work and rest. An attempt at such a definition is to be found in "Shabbat as Protest" by W. Gunther Plaut, pages 124–125. This book affirms the principle that a Jew should not work on Shabbat. A person's gainful occupation is classified as work and should not be engaged in on Shabbat. All other activities must be judged in light of the way they contribute to or detract from Shabbat as a day of *oneg* (delight), *m'nuchah* (rest), and *k'dushah* (holiness). This means that there may be a wide variation in the specific activities that individual Jews will do and refrain from doing on Shabbat. Such a rethinking of the definitions of work and rest will make it possible for many to reconsider their own observance and return to Shabbat.

16 The Talmud (BT *Beitzah* 9a–b) discusses actions that are not actual violations of Shabbat or the Festivals but that give the appearance of a violation. This is called *marit ayin* (appearance of the eye). This concept should sensitize Jews to the need to make sure that their public posture is one of respect for Shabbat observance.

17 In the *M'chilta* (*BaChodesh* 7, ed. Lauterbach, pages 252–253): "Eleazar b. Chananiah b. Chezekiah b. Garon says, 'Remember the Sabbath day to keep it holy.' Keep it in mind from the first day of the week on, so if something good happens to come your way, prepare it for Shabbat."

18 The Talmud (BT *Beitzah* 16a) records the practice of Shammai the Elder, who always sought the choicest food for the Shabbat table. If earlier in the week he found a particularly fine animal, he set it aside for Shabbat, and if later in the week he found a better animal, he would eat the first and set aside the second. In this manner he prepared for Shabbat. Today one may follow his example by planning the Shabbat meal to include something special—for example, the first fruit of the new season, or even a fruit out of season, a particularly choice cut of meat, or any dish that those gathered at the table would find especially enjoyable.

19 The Talmud (BT *Shabbat* 113a) states, "Your Shabbat garments should not be like your weekday garments." Dressing up for Shabbat adds to its festive character and distinguishes it from the other days of the week. If during the week one purchases a new garment that is appropriate for Shabbat, then waiting to wear it for the first time on Shabbat can contribute to one's enjoyment of Shabbat.

20 The Talmud (BT *Shabbat* 119a) compares Shabbat to a bride or queen. Almost all of the specifics of Shabbat preparation can be derived from the concept of Shabbat as an important guest.

21 The Talmud (BT *Shabbat* 119a) describes the individual preparations of the Sages. Their personal involvement included chopping wood and cooking the meal. The *Shulchan Aruch* (*Orach Chayim* 250:1) emphasizes the need for each individual to participate by stating that even those who have servants should assume some of the tasks of preparation.

22 The Talmud (BT *Shabbat* 127a), elaborating on the Mishnah (*Pei-ah* 1:1), lists *hachnasat or'chim* among those mitzvot for which "a person is rewarded in this world and in the world-to-come." One does not have to believe in literal reward and punishment to accept the idea that the performance of *hachnasat or'chim* (and the other humanitarian mitzvot on this list; see also *Mishkan T'filah*, page 206) is eternally rewarding.

In the same Talmudic passage, Rabbi Judah went even further in praise of *hachnasat or'chim,* teaching that "welcoming guests is of greater merit even than welcoming the presence of God." Today, considering the great number of fragmented families and single adults in our society (see *Gates of Mitzvah*, "The Single Person, the Single-Parent Family, and *Mitzvot*," page 119) and the particular difficulty that such people have in observing home-centered mitzvot, it is of the greatest importance to invite them into the family circle and to include them in *chavurot* (congregational subgroups that meet to study Judaism and/or celebrate Shabbat and the Festivals).

23 The mitzvah of *tzedakah* has its roots in the biblical injunction "Open your hand to the poor and needy kin" (Deuteronomy 15:11). Maimonides (*Sefer HaMitzvot, Mitzvot Aseh* 195) states that this means "we are to help our poor and support them according to their needs." In Jewish tradition, holy days and life-cycle events provide additional opportunities to perform this mitzvah.

24 For example, every Friday afternoon Rabbi Chaninah would send four *zuzim* to the poor (BT *K'tubot* 64a).

25 The Talmud (BT *Shabbat* 25b) states explicitly that the kindling of Shabbat lights is a mitzvah, and it is clear that by Mishnaic times it was already a well-established practice (*Mishnah Shabbat* 2:6–7). The midrash (*Tanchuma, Noach* 1) connects the lighting of Shabbat lights with the concept

of Shabbat delight (*oneg*): "'And you shall call Shabbat a delight' (Isaiah 58:12): This is kindling the lights on Shabbat."

26 Usually when one performs a mitzvah that requires the recitation of a blessing, one recites the blessing and then performs the mitzvah; e.g., in *Kiddush*, the blessing is recited first, and then the wine is drunk. However, the lighting of Shabbat candles requires a different procedure. Since the recitation of the blessing marks the formal beginning of Shabbat, and since according to the traditional definition of work, the lighting of a fire on Shabbat is prohibited, one first lights the candles and then covers one's eyes and recites the blessing.

27 While the lighting of candles is more closely associated with women, men are also responsible for performing the mitzvah (Maimonides, *Mishneh Torah, Hilchot Shabbat* 5:2).

28 Jewish calendars specify the traditional time for lighting candles as eighteen minutes before sunset. This is to ensure that they are lit before the beginning of Shabbat.

29 *Shulchan Aruch, Orach Chayim* 263:1.

30 Exodus 20:8; Deuteronomy 5:12.

31 In the *M'chilta* (*BaChodesh* 7, ed. Lauterbach, page 253), the mitzvah of *Kiddush* is derived from Exodus 20:8: "'To keep it holy' means to hallow it with a benediction. On the basis of this passage the Sages said: At the beginning of the Sabbath we hallow it by reciting the *Kiddush* [sanctification] over wine." (Also BT *P'sachim* 106a.)

   The *Kiddush* consists of two blessings: the blessing over the wine and the blessing over the day. If one does not have wine or grape juice for *Kiddush*, then one may substitute bread for wine and recite *HaMotzi* followed by the blessing over the day.

32 *Gates of Mitzvah*, pages 41–42 , E-9, and page 85, note 77.

33 Joseph Hertz, *Authorized Daily Prayer Book*, (New York: Bloch Publishing Company, 1948, 1975), page 977.

34 In Rabbinic writings, the family table is often compared to the altar of the Temple. It is for this reason that the custom arose to sprinkle salt on the bread or challah after *HaMotzi*, as we read in Leviticus 2:13, "With all your offerings you must offer salt."

35 Interpreting Isaiah 58:13, "And you shall call Shabbat a delight," the Talmud (BT *Shabbat* 118b) asks, "In what does one express one's delight?" and proceeds to describe delight as eating food especially prepared for Shabbat. Jewish lore records many examples of the special character of the Shabbat meal throughout Jewish literature—e.g., food tasted better on Shabbat (midrash, *B'reishit Rabbah* 11:4; BT *Shabbat* 119a).

36 BT *Shabbat* 113b.

37 "When you have eaten your fill, give thanks to the Eternal your God . . ."

(Deuteronomy 8:10). See *Gates of Mitzvah*, pages 84–85, note 74.

38 On the mitzvah of daily prayer, see *Gates of Mitzvah*, page 20, E-3, and page 38, E-3. While private prayer is a mitzvah and always desirable, worship with a congregation is a mitzvah of superior importance. The Talmud (BT *B'rachot* 6a) says:

> Rabin ben Rabbi Adda says in the name of Rabbi Isaac: How do we know that the Holy One, blessed be He, is to be found in the Synagogue? For it is said, "God stands in the congregation of God" (Psalm 82:1). And how do we know that if ten people pray together the Divine Presence is with them? For it is said, "God stands in the congregation of God."

39 The "long" *Kiddush* is recited only at night (BT *P'sachim* 106b). The *Kiddush* for the Shabbat noon meal consists of *V'shamru* (Exodus 31:16–17) and the blessing over wine (*Shulchan Aruch, Orach Chayim* 289:1).

40 *Gates of Mitzvah*, page 19, E-l; page 22, F-l , F-3; page 73, note 26.

41 The Talmud (BT *Bava Kama* 82a) offers the following explanation for the origin of the public reading of Torah on Shabbat:

> "They traveled three days in the wilderness and found no water" (Exodus 15:22), upon which those who expound verses metaphorically said: "Water means nothing but Torah, as it says, 'All who are thirsty, come for water' (Isaiah 55:1). It thus means that as they went three days without Torah they immediately became exhausted. The prophets among them thereupon rose and enacted that they should publicly read the law on Shabbat, make a break on Sunday, read again on Monday, make a break again on Tuesday and Wednesday, read again on Thursday, and then make a break on Friday, so that they should not be kept for three days without Torah."

42 For example, W. Gunther Plaut (ed.), *The Torah: A Modern Commentary*, Revised Edition (New York: Union for Reform Judaism, 2005).

43 *Gates of Mitzvah*, page 49, A-3; page 88, notes 87 and 88.

44 The Talmud (BT *Moeid Katan* 9a) prohibits marriage on a Festival because one may not mix two joyous occasions: *"Ein m'ar'vin simchah b'simchah,"* i.e., a wedding is a *simchah* and the festival is a *simchah*. Further, the *Shulchan Aruch* (*Orach Chayim* 339a; *Even HaEizer* 64:3) states that marriages may not be performed on Shabbat and the Festivals. This prohibition is based on the statement in the Talmud (BT *Beitzah* 36b) and the underlying mishnah (5:2). These prohibitions do not relate to biblically prohibited work but were issued by the Rabbis in an effort to protect the sanctity of Shabbat.

The Responsa Committee of the CCAR (*CCAR Yearbook*, vol. 87 [1977], pages 96–99) opposed the performance of marriages on Shabbat and the

Festivals for the following reasons:

(1) Since the avoidance of weddings on Shabbat has the weight of a widely observed *minhag* which supports the spirit of Shabbat, it should not be dismissed or disregarded.

(2) The Reform movement has encouraged Shabbat observance in creative ways for more than a decade. We have published *Gates of Shabbat,* and we encourage our members to make this a "special day" upon which we do not carry out duties and acts performed on other days. Countenancing marriages on Shabbat would detract from this objective and weaken our efforts.

(3) We have a great respect for *K'lal Yisrael* and wish to do everything possible to advance the unity of the Jewish people.

(4) Our tradition has always emphasized that in addition to all else, marriage has companionship, procreation, and family life as its basis, but there are also various economic aspects which form an important element of the traditional *ketubah,* although these aspects are not stressed by Reform Jews. However, economic considerations do play a considerable role at a time when the family is about to be established in terms of property rights, insurance benefits, etc., and an equally large role when such a family is dissolved. These may not be readily apparent to the couple; although they may not be "transactions" in the ordinary sense, Shabbat is not the time to initiate them.

(5) We are opposed to the performance of marriages on Shabbat as we prefer allegiance to a hallowed tradition rather than mere convenience.

45 While Shabbat is counted as part of the shivah (i.e., the first seven days of mourning), all formal mourning is suspended, and the basic mitzvot of Shabbat are observed (BT *Moeid Katan* 19a; *S'machot* 7:1).

46 Funerals are not conducted on Shabbat, nor on the first day or last day of a major Festival, since no work may be performed, and the mood of the funeral is contrary to the spirit of rejoicing (*oneg*) that characterizes Shabbat and the Festivals.

47 *Havdalah* was already a well-established practice in early Mishnaic times (*Mishnah B'rachot* 8:5; *Tosefta B'rachot* 6:7). The principal blessing, the blessing of *Havdalah* (separation), is mentioned in the Talmud (BT *P'sachim* 103b). A detailed explanation of and sources for *Havdalah* can be found in *Gates of Understanding,* pages 253–255.

Maimonides (*Mishneh Torah, Hilchot Shabbat* 29:1) derives the mitzvah of *Havdalah* from Exodus 20:8: "'Remember Shabbat to keep it holy.' . . . It is obligatory to remember Shabbat both when it commences and when it terminates; by reciting *Kiddush* when it commences, and *Havdalah* when it terminates."

Shabbat ends at sunset. It is customary to wait until one can see three stars in the sky. Many prefer to delay *Havdalah* as late as possible, thereby holding onto Shabbat as long as possible.

48 The Talmud (BT *P'sachim* 103a) stipulates that a torch be used for *Havdalah*. In the blessing over the light, the word for "light"—*m'orei*—is plural; this has been interpreted to mean that the *Havdalah* candle must have two or more wicks.

The Days of Awe (*Yamim Noraim*)

ROSH HASHANAH

1 While the first of Tishrei is designated by the Torah as "a day when the horn is sounded" (Numbers 29:1), it is the Mishnah (*Rosh HaShanah* 1:1) that first identifies it as the New Year. Not only is the first of Tishrei the first day of the new year, but it is also the birthday of the world (BT *Rosh HaShanah* 11a). It is the complex interconnection of New Year, Creation, and judgment that provides the conceptual framework for understanding the mitzvot and customs of Rosh HaShanah.

2 According to the Mishnah (*Rosh HaShanah* 1:2), Rosh HaShanah is one of the four times during the year that the world is judged. The *Tosefta* (ibid.) conceives of judgment commencing on Rosh HaShanah, but the final verdict remains open until Yom Kippur. Therefore, the period between Rosh HaShanah and Yom Kippur became an especially appropriate time for self-examination and repentance.

3 The midrash (*Pirkei D'Rabbi Eliezer* 46) identifies the first of Elul as the day on which Moses ascended Mount Sinai to receive the second set of tablets containing the Ten Commandments. Since Moses remained on the mountain for forty days, the Rabbis identified this whole period, from the first of Elul until Yom Kippur, as a period of penitential prayer and repentance.

Traditional Rabbinic exegesis considers the Song of Songs to be an allegorical description of God's love for Israel. The name of the month Elul consists of the four Hebrew letters *alef, lamed, vav, lamed*. These four letters were interpreted as referring to the first letters of the words in Song of Songs 6:3, *Ani l'dodi v'dodi li*, "I am my beloved's, and my beloved is mine." Therefore, Elul is the period of reconciliation between God and Israel.

4 In Jewish tradition many reasons have been offered for the sounding of the shofar. The ram's horn is identified with the ram that became the substitute sacrifice for Isaac (Genesis 22:1–19); the giving of the Torah at Sinai

was accompanied by the sounding of the shofar (Exodus 19:16–20); the proclamation of the Jubilee was heralded by the blast of the shofar (Leviticus 25:9–11); and the commencement of messianic times is to be announced by the sound of the great shofar (Isaiah 27:13). Our liturgy (*Gates of Repentance*, page 139) cites Maimonides's call to awaken from our spiritual slumber:

> Awake, you sleepers, from your sleep! Rouse yourselves, you slumberers, out of your slumber! Examine your deeds, and turn to God in repentance. Remember your Creator, you who are caught up in the daily round, losing sight of eternal truth; you who are wasting your years in vain pursuits that neither profit nor save. Look closely at yourselves; improve your ways and your deeds. Abandon your evil ways, your unworthy schemes, every one of you! (*Mishneh Torah, Hilchot T'shuvah* 3:4).

5   BT *Rosh HaShanah* 16b.

6   The Talmud (BT *Kiddushin* 40a–b) teaches the following:

> Our Rabbis taught: A man should regard himself as though he were half guilty and half meritorious—if he performs one precept, happy is he for weighting himself down in the scale of merit; if he commits one transgression, woe to him for weighting himself down in the scale of guilt, for it is said, "But one sinner destroys much good" (Ecclesiastes 9:18), [i.e.], on account of a single sin that he commits much good is lost to him. Rabbi Eleazar, son of Rabbi Simeon, said: Because the world is judged by its majority, and an individual [too] is judged by his majority [of deeds, good or bad]—if he performs one good deed, happy is he for turning the scale both for himself and for the whole world on the side of merit; if he commits one transgression, woe to him for weighting himself and the whole world in the scale of guilt, for it is said, "But one sinner" [ibid.]; on account of the single sin that this man commits he and the whole world lose much good.

7   Midrash, *B'reishit Rabbah* 44:12. It is found in a slightly different version in the Talmud (BT *Rosh HaShanah* 16b), and in the Rosh HaShanah liturgy (*Gates of Repentance*, page 109).

8   *D'varim Rabbah* 2:12. The midrash (*Sh'mot Rabbah* 19:4) enlarges on the concept of God's openness to repentance in its exegesis of Job 31:32: "'No stranger need lodge in the street.' The Holy One, blessed be God, does not reject a single creature. Rather, all are acceptable to God. The gates are open at all times and all who wish may enter."

9   See note 3 above.

10 The word *s'lichot* is the plural form of the Hebrew word *s'lichah*, which means "forgiveness." Since most Reform congregations do not have daily

services, the *S'lichot* liturgy is often only recited late on the Saturday night before Rosh HaShanah.

11 If Rosh HaShanah falls on a Monday or Tuesday, *S'lichot* services are held on the Saturday night prior, meaning 8 to 9 days preceding Rosh HaShanah (Rama on *Orach Chayim* 581:1).

12 The custom of blowing the shofar from the first of Elul is based on the same midrashic passage from *Pirkei D'Rabbi Eliezer* cited in note 3 above. The shofar is not sounded on the day before Rosh HaShanah, to make a distinction between the end of Elul and Rosh HaShanah.

13 Rama on *Orach Chayim* 581:4.

14 See note 2 above.

15 See page 162, "*Tzedakah,*" and page 169, note 23. The practice of giving *tzedakah* on Erev Rosh HaShanah is mentioned by the Rama in *Orach Chayim* 581:4.

16 Rosh HaShanah is included in Leviticus 23 along with Shabbat, Pesach, Shavuot, Yom Kippur, Sukkot, and Sh'mini Atzeret as a major festival. The *M'chilta* (*BaChodesh* 7, ed. Lauterbach, vol. 2, page 253) links the Shabbat *Kiddush* and the Festival *Kiddush* on the basis of Leviticus 23:4: "These are the set times of the Eternal, the sacred occasions." Maimonides (*Mishneh Torah, Hilchot Shabbat* 29:18) states, "Just as *Kiddush* is said on Friday night and *Havdalah* at the termination of the Sabbath, so also is *Kiddush* recited on the night of a festival and *Havdalah* at the termination of the festival and Yom Kippur, for all these are 'Sabbaths of the Eternal' (Leviticus 23:38)." The lighting of candles is also based on this analogy.

17 Customs vary as to the shape of the challot for Rosh HaShanah. In some places round challot with raisins signifying a full and sweet year are used, and in other places challot in the form of a ladder symbolically reaching toward heaven are used.

18 See page 22, "The Mitzvah of Congregational Worship," and page 171, note 38.

19 It is a common Reform practice to blow the shofar on Rosh HaShanah even when it falls on Shabbat. Conservative and Orthodox congregations, however, following the ruling of the *Shulchan Aruch* (*Orach Chayim* 588:5), do not sound the shofar on the first day of Rosh HaShanah when it falls on Shabbat. In such a case they sound it only on the second day, which can never fall on Shabbat. The reasons for current Reform practice are discussed in the *CCAR Yearbook*, vol. 23, pages 182–183 and vol. 33, pages 60–61, and by Solomon B. Freehof in *Recent Reform Responsa*, pages 36–41. At the end of his discussion, Rabbi Freehof summarizes the matter as follows (pages 40–41): "Since the sounding of the shofar on the Sabbath is not really prohibited in itself, since the sounding of the shofar on the New Year is a Biblical mandate, and since some authorities at least permitted

the shofar to be sounded on the New Year Sabbath even though the people would have heard it on the second day anyway, we, who observe only one day [see page 35, "The Second Day of Rosh HaShanah"], should not, in my judgment, deprive our people of the spiritual benefit of hearing the sound of the shofar when the New Year comes on the Sabbath."

20 See page 173, note 4.

21 Essential to the fulfillment of this mitzvah is the concept *of kavanah*, the directing of one's mind toward the meaning and significance of the sounding of the shofar (*Mishnah Rosh HaShanah* 3:7; BT *Rosh HaShanah* 28b, where the mishnah is discussed).

22 BT *Moeid Katan* 19a; *Mishnah S'machot* 7:1.

23 See page 175, note 16.

ASERET Y'MEI T'SHUVAH (TEN DAYS OF REPENTANCE)

24 The Talmud (BT, *Rosh HaShanah* 18a) designates the period from Rosh HaShanah to Yom Kippur as being a particularly propitious time for repentance: "'Seek the Eternal while God may be found' (Isaiah 55:6). Where can the individual find God? Rabbah ben Abuha replied, 'These are the ten days from Rosh HaShanah to Yom Kippur.'"

25 Complete repentance, according to the Talmud (BT *Yoma* 86b), involves having both the ability and opportunity to repeat a sin for which one has repented and to refrain from repeating it. In addition, one must make restitution and seek the forgiveness of the aggrieved persons (*Mishnah Bava Kama* 9:7).

26 *Mishnah Yoma* 8:9. See also note 29, below.

27 The Talmudic concept of repentance involves the explicit confession of sins (BT *Yoma* 36b, 86b). Such a process requires a careful review of our behavior in order to determine where we have failed to live up to the standards that we set for ourselves and that are based on the mitzvot of Jewish living.

28 *Mishnah Yoma* 8:9.

29 Seeking forgiveness and being forgiving is part of the Talmudic understanding of the process of repentance (*Mishnah Bava Kama* 9:7). Maimonides, in his code (*Mishneh Torah, Hilchot T'shuvah* 2:8–9), basing himself on Leviticus 19:18, "Do not bear a grudge and do not take vengeance," considers the one who is unwilling to forgive as a sinner. The duality of this procedure is a recognition of the potential destructiveness of unresolved conflict as well as the power of repentance to rebuild relationships, renew the individual, and strengthen the community.

30 BT *Taanit* 20a.

31 *Shulchan Aruch, Orach Chayim* 581:4.

32 Only Shabbat (Exodus 31:15, 35:2; Leviticus 23:3) and Yom Kippur (Leviticus 16:31, 23:32) are called *Shabbat Shabbaton*, "Sabbath of Sabbaths."

33 The biblical formula that was recited by King Solomon (I Kings 8:47) is part of the *Vidui*, confessional prayers, of Yom Kippur (*Gates of Repentance*, pages 269, 324, and 512).

34 According to the Mishnah (*Yoma* 8:8), Yom Kippur brings about atonement when accompanied by repentance.

35 This concept of mutual turning is suggested in the statement of the prophet Malachi (3:7), "Return to Me, and I will return to you, says the God of heavenly hosts."

36 See pages 36–37, "The Mitzvah of Reconciliation." During the Ten Days of Repentance, one should have made contact in person, in writing, or by telephone with all of the people one believes one may have offended. The dinner on Erev Yom Kippur should then be seen as a final opportunity to effect reconciliation with the family and friends who are gathered around the table.

37 See page 162, "*Tzedakah*."

38 The concept of *kaparah* (means of expiation) is probably based on the ancient scapegoat ritual for Yom Kippur (Leviticus 16:5–22). In later times the custom of *kaparot* (plural of *kaparah*) developed. One day before Yom Kippur a person would swing a fowl around his/her head three times and recite the following formula: "This is my substitute, my vicarious offering, my atonement; this cock [or hen] shall meet death, but I shall find a long and pleasant life of peace." The fowl was then slaughtered and given to the poor. There has been much rabbinic opposition to this custom, and today it is practiced only among some Orthodox Jews. A variation of this rite was the substitution of money for the fowl. While Reform Jews do not practice the ritual of *kaparot*, the basic connection between charity and repentance is integral to atonement and to the observance of Yom Kippur.

39 The Talmud (BT *Yoma* 81b) enunciates the principle of adding ordinary time to sacred time in order to lengthen the observance of a festival or holy day. Therefore, it is customary to begin the final meal early.

40 *Shulchan Aruch, Orach Chayim* 610:1–3.

41 *V'initem et nafshoteichem*, "you shall practice self-denial" (Leviticus 23:27), is interpreted by the Mishnah (*Yoma* 8:1) to include refraining not only from eating and drinking but also from washing, anointing, sexual intercourse, and wearing leather shoes. The majority of Reform Jews understand "self-denial" as abstaining from eating and drinking only.

42 *Mishnah Yoma* 8:4; BT *Yoma* 82a.

43 The Mishnah (*Yoma* 8:5–6) and the Talmud (*Yoma* 82a ff.) give examples of people who should not fast. The general principle is that when there

is danger to human life, the laws of Shabbat are suspended—not only for actual danger but even for possible danger. Since Yom Kippur is *Shabbat Shabbaton*, the Sabbath of Sabbaths, the principle applies to it as well (BT *Yoma* 84b). Obviously the same principle applies to the other festivals.

44 See page 22, "The Mitzvah of Congregational Worship," and page 171, note 38.

45 *Yizkor* (literally, "May He remember") is the popular name of the special prayer prescribed in the liturgy for recitation on certain holy days, especially Yom Kippur, in memory of the dead. *Yizkor* as recited in the Ashkenazic congregation probably dates only from after the Crusades. *Yizkor* is recited in all Reform congregations on Yom Kippur and on the seventh day of Pesach, and on Shavuot and Sh'mini Atzeret–Simchat Torah as well. (For the text of the service, see *Gates of Repentance,* pages 477–494, and *Mishkan T'filah: A Reform Siddur,* pages 574–583.)

46 See page 175, note 16.

47 The custom of symbolically starting to build the sukkah at the conclusion of Yom Kippur is based on the principle, "If a mitzvah comes your way, perform it immediately" (*M'chilta Pischa* 9, ed. Lauterbach, page 74). The *Shulchan Aruch* (*Orach Chayim* 24:1) applies this principle to the building of the sukkah.

48 Ecclesiastes 9:7. The midrash (*Kohelet Rabbah* 9:7) applies this verse to Yom Kippur.

The Pilgrimage Festivals (*Shalosh R'galim*)

1 The phrase *Shalosh R'galim* is first attested to in Exodus 23:14.

2 While Sh'mini Atzeret is the eighth day of Sukkot, it is considered a separate festival by the Talmud (BT *Sukkot* 47a–b). Simchat Torah is the second day of Sh'mini Atzeret. Since Reform Jews follow the calendar of Israel, Sh'mini Atzeret and Simchat Torah are celebrated on the same day (see "The Jewish Calendar," pages 5–9).

3 Rejoicing (*simchah*) on the Festivals is similar to delight (*oneg*) and rest (*m'nuchah*) on Shabbat (see page 14, "The Mitzvah of Delight [*Oneg*]," and page 15, "The Mitzvah of Rest [*M'nuchah*]"). Special meals, wine, new clothes, and Torah study are part of the joyous celebration of the Festivals (see BT *P'sachim* 109; BT *Beitzah* 15b). However, the key to Festival rejoicing is the turning away from everyday activities to observe the mitzvot of the day.

4 See page 175, note 16.

5 The tradition makes only a minor distinction between the prohibition against work on Shabbat and on the Festivals: "The Festivals differ from Shabbat only in the preparation of necessary food" (*Mishnah M'gilah* 1:5; *Mishnah Beitzah* 5:2). However, the basic principle is that no work should

be done on the Festival that interferes with the joy or sanctity of the Festival (Maimonides, *Mishneh Torah, Hilchot Yom Tov* 1:5; *Shulchan Aruch, Orach Chayim* 195:1, 510:8).

6 See Shabbat, page 171, note 38.

7 The mitzvah of rejoicing on the Festivals (see page 48, "The Mitzvah of Rejoicing (*Simchah*) on the Festivals," and page 178, note 3, above) is incompatible with the mitzvah of mourning. Since the observance of the festival is a communal obligation, it takes precedence over mourning, which is an individual obligation; therefore, formal mourning is suspended for the duration of the festival (BT *Moeid Katan* 14b).

8 See page 171, note 44.

9 BT *Moeid Katan* 8b.

10 See Shabbat, page 172, note 47.

PESACH

11 There are four special Sabbaths that precede Pesach: Shabbat Sh'kalim (see page 188, note 19), Shabbat Zachor (see page 187, note 12), Shabbat Parah, and Shabbat HaChodesh.

Shabbat Parah recalls the purification ritual of the red heifer (*parah adumah*). The additional Torah reading in Numbers 19:1–22 describes the ritual. The haftarah, taken from Ezekiel 36:22–36, is an eschatological description of Israel's future purification. Shabbat Parah served as a reminder that the *pesach* (paschal sacrifice) had to be eaten in a state of ritual purity.

Shabbat HaChodesh is the Shabbat immediately preceding the month of Nisan. In addition to the weekly Torah portion, Exodus 12:1–20 is also read. It describes the arrival of Nisan and the preparations for Pesach. Shabbat HaChodesh announces the arrival of Nisan and serves as part of the preparation for Pesach.

Additionally, the Sabbath immediately preceding Pesach is known as Shabbat HaGadol (the Great Sabbath). According to some authorities, the name is derived from one of the verses in the haftarah (Malachi 3:4–24), "Behold, I will send you Elijah the prophet, before the coming of the great and terrible day of the Eternal" (3:23). This haftarah was selected in accordance with the Talmudic statement: "In Nisan they were delivered; in Nisan they will be delivered in the future" (BT *Rosh HaShanah* 11b). Since the redemption from Egypt occurred in Nisan, so the messianic redemption will occur in Nisan. On Shabbat HaGadol, it was customary for the rabbi to instruct the people on the proper observance of Pesach.

12 The development of the historical Passover is explained in *The Torah: A Modern Commentary*, Revised Edition (New York: URJ Press, 2005), pages 419–421.

13 The principle that governs the narration of the Passover story is that "one

begins with degradation and rises to dignity" (*Mishnah P'sachim* 10:4). Therefore, according to the Talmud (BT *P'sachim* 116b), Samuel began the narration with the passage "We were slaves to Pharaoh in Egypt . . ." (*A Passover Haggadah*, page 34), giving primacy to the notion of physical bondage. However, Samuel's contemporary, Rav, began the narration with the passage "For in the beginning our ancestors were idolators . . ." (*A Passover Haggadah*, page 35), placing the emphasis on spiritual rather than physical slavery. The Mishnah (*P'sachim* 10:4), however, proposes a third possibility, that the narrative should begin with an exposition of Deuteronomy 26:5, "My father was a fugitive Aramean . . ." (*A Passover Haggadah*, page 37), interpreting slavery as social degradation. The present Haggadah contains all three passages, making it clear that slavery has physical, ideological, and social components.

14 *Mishnah P'sachim* 10:5; *A Passover Haggadah*, page 56.

15 Midrash, *Sh'mot Rabbah* 21:10.

16 "The fourteenth day of the month at evening" is understood as the eve of the fifteenth, because the Jewish day begins at sundown.

17 According to the Talmud (BT *P'sachim* 35a), these are the only grains from which matzah can be made and therefore, strictly speaking, the only ones that are subject to the prohibition of leaven. While the tradition developed many complex rules concerning what may be eaten and what may not be eaten during Pesach, the basic principle is that all leaven and all products containing leaven are not to be eaten.

18 There is much debate today about the relevance of *kitniyot* for Reform Jews. A full discussion of the *kitniyot* issue is explored in CCAR Responsum 5756.9.

19 When it became economically unfeasible to dispose of all one's leaven during Pesach, the Rabbis developed a legal fiction whereby one sold the leaven to a non-Jew, with the understanding that it would be returned after Pesach. This method became especially important to Jews whose businesses involved the extensive use of leaven. Reform Jews rarely resort to this method and instead make leaven inaccessible in their homes.

20 The Mishnah (*P'sachim* 1:1, 3) sets forth the requirement to search for leaven on the night of the fourteenth of Nisan, using a light to aid in the search.

21 Maimonides, basing himself on the Mishnah (*P'sachim* 10:1), states that the Sages have forbidden the eating of matzah on the eve of Pesach in order to make its consumption at the seder a distinct event. In addition, one should come to the seder table hungry so that one may fully enjoy the seder meal (*Mishneh Torah, Hilchot Chameitz U'Matzah* 6:12).

22 See page 17, "The Mitzvah of Preparation." The changing of dishes for Pesach is a time-honored practice. Although many Reform Jews do not change their dishes for Pesach, some have separate dishes that are reserved

for Pesach. Their use sets Pesach apart from the other days of the year.

23 *A Passover Haggadah*, page 26. See page 169, note 22.

24 *Gates of Mitzvah*, pages 39–40, E-5, and "*Tzedakah*," pages 162–164.

25 The term *ma-ot chitin* means "money for wheat," indicating that originally the funds were collected so that the poor could buy matzah for Pesach. Already in Mishnaic times special provisions were made so that even the poor could celebrate Pesach properly (*Mishnah P'sachim* 10:1).

26 The yearly recitation at the seder of the Pesach story is derived from the Rabbinic understanding of Exodus 13:8, "You shall explain to your child on that day, 'It is because of what the Eternal did for me when I went free from Egypt" (*M'chilta Pischa* 3, ed. Lauterbach, page 149). The Haggadah itself reminds us that "even if all of us were wise, all of us people of understanding, all of us learned in Torah, it would still be our obligation to tell the story of the Exodus from Egypt" (*A Passover Haggadah*, page 34).

27 *Mishnah P'sachim* 10:5, based on Exodus 13:8; *A Passover Haggadah*, page 56.

28 *Shulchan Aruch, Orach Chayim* 473:4. *A Passover Haggadah*, page 15, lists all the items to be included on the seder plate.

29 Four cups of wine are required for the seder (see page 59, "The Mitzvah of Four Cups"). However, there is a controversy among the Rabbis concerning the drinking of a fifth cup (BT *P'sachim* 118a; *Mishneh Torah, Hilchot Chameitz U'Matzah* 8:10). Therefore, the cup was filled but not drunk. Since in the future Elijah was supposed to solve all legal controversies (*Mishnah Eduyot* 8:7; *Tosefta Eduyot* 3:4), the cup became associated with him and became known as Elijah's cup (*kos shel Eliyahu*).

Later the custom became associated with the belief that Elijah did not die but ascended to heaven alive (II Kings 2:11) and that he returned to earth from time to time to befriend the helpless, and in the future he would announce the coming of the Messiah (Malachi 3:23; *Pirkei D'Rabbi Eliezer* 43). Further, it was believed that as the first redemption took place in Nisan, so the future redemption would take place in Nisan (BT *Rosh HaShanah* 11b). So the popular notion arose that a cup should be placed on the table to welcome the prophet as he visits each seder.

30 BT *Taanit* 9a; BT *Chulin* 92a.

31 *A Passover Haggadah*, page 55, based on Exodus 12:39.

32 During the rest of the week the eating of matzah is optional (BT *P'sachim* 120a). Although matzah need not be eaten, one still abstains from eating leaven throughout Pesach (see page 53–54, "The Mitzvah of Abstaining from Eating Leaven [*Chameitz*]").

33 *A Passover Haggadah*, page 56, based on Exodus 1:14.

34 According to the Torah (Numbers 9:11), the Passover sacrifice was to be eaten with unleavened bread and bitter herbs.

35 The Mishnah (*P'sachim* 10:1) stipulates that even the poorest Jew be given no fewer than four cups of wine for the seder. The Talmud (JT *P'sachim* 10:1, 37b–c) relates the four cups to the four promises of redemption in Exodus 6:6–7: *V'hotzeiti*, "I will bring you out"; *v'hitzalti*, "I will save you"; *v'gaalti*, "I will redeem you"; *v'lakachti*, "I will take you." It also suggests that they are allusions to the four kingdoms mentioned in Daniel 7 or to the four cups of punishment poured out against Pharaoh that will be matched in the future with four cups of comfort for Israel.

The four cups correspond to four parts of the seder: *Kiddush* and the blessing of redemption before the meal, and *Birkat HaMazon* and *Birkat HaShir* (Blessing of the Song, also called *Nishmat*) after the meal (*A Passover Haggadah*, pages 22–25, 60, 61–67, 75–76, 93).

36 *Mishnah P'sachim* 10:4. The current Haggadah has a different version of the Four Questions. While contemporary Haggadot have a set formula for the Four Questions, spontaneity is to be encouraged. As Maimonides writes, "One should make some changes in procedures on this night of the fifteenth of Nisan in order that one's children will notice and ask, 'What makes this night different from other nights?'—to which one replies, 'This and this is what happened, and this and this is what took place'" (*Mishneh Torah, Hilchot Chameitz U'Matzah* 7:5).

37 *Mishnah P'sachim* 10:1.

38 The middle matzah is broken in two and the larger piece set aside. This is called the *afikoman*. The word *afikoman* is of Greek origin, but its etymology is problematic. It has been variously interpreted to mean either "after-meal entertainment" or "a dessert." The Mishnah (*P'sachim* 10:8) states, "One may not add *afikoman* after the paschal meal." The Talmud (BT *P'sachim* 119b–120a) understands this to mean that the last food that is to be eaten at the seder is the paschal lamb. However, since the destruction of the Temple, the *afikoman* has become a symbolic reminder of the sacrifice, and one concludes the seder with a piece of *afikoman*.

39 Exodus 12:15 specifies that *chameitz* may not be eaten during the entire seven days.

40 The five small biblical books—Song of Songs, Ruth, Lamentations, *Kohelet* (Ecclesiastes), and Esther are known as the Five Scrolls (*Chameish M'gilot*). Each scroll is read on a particular festival or holy day: Song of Songs on the intermediate Shabbat of Pesach; Ruth on Shavuot; Lamentations on Tishah B'Av; *Kohelet* on the intermediate Shabbat of Sukkot; and Esther on Purim.

The custom of reading Song of Songs in connection with Pesach and Ruth in connection with Shavuot is mentioned in *Masechet Sof'rim* 14:16, while the custom of reading *Kohelet* in connection with Sukkot apparently developed later.

41 See page 43, "The Mitzvah of *Yizkor* (Memorial Service); and page 178, note 45.

42 Traditionally the time of the *s'firah* is considered a period of semi-mourning because, according to the Talmudic tradition (BT *Y'vamot* 62b), twelve thousand pairs of Rabbi Akiva's disciples were killed between Pesach and Shavuot during the Hadrianic persecution which followed the Bar Kochba revolt (c. 135 CE).

Because of this designation of the *s'firah* as a time of semi-mourning, many rabbis will not officiate at weddings during most of this period, with the exception of Lag BaOmer (thirty-third day of the Omer), Rosh Chodesh (New Month), and the last three days of the counting. While some will perform weddings during this period, in seeking a wedding date the rabbi should be consulted (see *Gates of Mitzvah,* page 31, B-2). It is also recommended that weddings not be scheduled for Yom HaShoah (Holocaust Remembrance Day) which falls during this period (see "Yom HaShoah," page 83).

SHAVUOT

43 The biblical verse (Leviticus 23:15) states that the counting of the fifty-day period from Pesach until Shavuot begins on "the day after the Sabbath." According to the Talmud (BT *M'nachot* 65a–b), the Sadducees (Boethusians) took the word "Sabbath" literally and began to count from the day after the Sabbath that occurred during Pesach, which meant that the date of Shavuot varied from year to year. However, the Pharisees understood the word "Sabbath" to refer to the first day of Pesach and therefore began the counting on the second day of Pesach, thus establishing a fixed date for Shavuot.

44 BT *Shabbat* 86b.

45 See page 182, note 40.

46 This custom has probably developed from Shavuot's association with the harvest (Exodus 23:16) and the first fruits (Exodus 34:22). The Mishnah (*Rosh HaShanah* 1:2) and the Talmud (BT *Rosh HaShanah* 16a) identify Shavuot as the time when God blesses the fruit of the tree.

47 BT *Shabbat* 86b. Jewish tradition considers the mitzvah of *talmud Torah* (Torah study) to be of overarching significance:

These are things that are limitless, of which a person enjoys the fruit of the world, while the principal remains in the world to come. They are: honoring one's father and mother, engaging in deeds of compassion, arriving early for study, morning and evening, dealing graciously with guests, visiting the sick, providing for the wedding couple, accompanying the dead for burial, being devoted in prayer, and making peace among people. But the study of Torah encompasses them all. (BT *Shabbat* 127a, as cited in *Mishkan T'filah,* page 206)

The study of Torah is not merely an intellectual endeavor but the means to discover how to live. Torah study leads the Jew to live a life of holiness.

48 Solomon Alkabetz and his circle of sixteenth-century kabbalists developed the custom in Salonica, and Alkabetz subsequently introduced it wherever he lived (R. J. Wesblowsky, *Joseph Karo: Lawyer and Mystic* [London: Oxford University Press, 1962], pages 109–110).

49 Solomon B. Freehof, *Reform Jewish Practice*, vol. 1 (New York: UAHC, 1964), pages 25–26; *CCAR Resolutions*, page 11. It should be noted that some Reform congregations hold confirmation on the Shabbat nearest Shavuot rather than on Shavuot itself.

50 See Pesach, page 182, note 40.

51 *Abudarham HaShalem*, page 240. Another reason given for reading Ruth on Shavuot is based on the Talmudic legend that David, Ruth's great-grandson, died on Shavuot (JT *Beitzah* 2:4, 61c ; Midrash *Ruth Rabbah* 3:2).

52 Midrash *D'varim Rabbah* 7:3; *Shir HaShirim Rabbah* 1:3.

SUKKOT (INCLUDING SH'MINI ATZERET–SIMCHAT TORAH)

53 In the Torah (Exodus 23:16, 34:22) Sukkot is called Chag HaAsif, the Festival of Ingathering. It was so important in biblical times that it was also called HeChag, *The* Festival (I Kings 8:2).

54 "On the eighth day you shall observe a sacred occasion . . . it is a solemn gathering: you shall not work at your occupations" (Leviticus 23:36). The Talmud (BT *Sukkah* 47b–48a) also designates Sh'mini Atzeret–Simchat Torah as a separate festival, e.g., one no longer celebrates in the sukkah or takes up the *lulav* and *etrog*. In addition, the *Kiddush* for Sh'mini Atzeret–Simchat Torah night specifically mentions the name of the festival (*HaSh'mini, chag HaAtzeret hazeh*), indicating it has its own special mitzvot, as do Sukkot, Pesach, and Shavuot.

55 In Leviticus 23:40 and Deuteronomy 16:14, the Torah designates rejoicing as one of the characteristic mitzvot of Sukkot.

56 See "The Mitzvah of *Lulav* and *Etrog*," page 67.

57 See "Tzedakah," pages 162–164.

58 The sukkah is a temporary structure that is open to the sky. It has four walls and is covered with cut branches and plants. This covering is called the *s'chach*. The *s'chach* must be loosely arranged so as to allow the sky to be seen. The sukkah is usually decorated with fruits and vegetables of the harvest. According to the Talmud (BT *Shabbat* 133b), we should strive to make the sukkah as beautiful as possible. The enjoyment of the mitzvah is enhanced when we pay attention to the aesthetic dimensions of a mitzvah (see "*Hidur Mitzvah*: The Aesthetics of Mitzvot," pages 107–109).

The basic regulations for the construction of a sukkah are discussed in the Mishnah (*Sukkah* 1:1–2:4) and elaborated in the codes (*Mishneh Torah*,

Hilchot Sukkah 4–5; *Shulchan Aruch, Orach Chayim* 625ff.). Instructions for building a sukkah can be found in *Jewish Living: A Guide to Contemporary Reform Practice* by Mark Washofsky (New York: URJ Press, 2011). A number of synagogues, websites, and Jewish bookstores also sell prefabricated sukkot.

59 When the *lulav* and *etrog* are taken up, they are held together with the *lulav* in the right hand and the *etrog* in the left hand (though it is reversed for those who are left-handed) (BT *Sukkah* 37b). It is customary, while the blessing is being recited, to hold the *etrog* with its stem facing upward, and after the blessing, when it is waved, to hold it with stem facing downward as it grows (*Shulchan Aruch, Orach Chayim* 651:5).

60 "Rabbi Yochanan explained, "[One waves them] to and fro [in honor of] God to whom the four directions belong, and up and down [in honor of] God to whom are heaven and earth" (BT *Sukkah* 37b).

61 "The product of the *hadar* tree" is the *etrog* (BT *Sukkah* 35a), and "the boughs of leafy trees" are the myrtle (ibid., 32b).

62 *Mishnah Sukkah* 3:4, 3:8; BT *Sukkah* 37b.

63 The palm, myrtle, and willow should be fresh and green. It is customary to take special care in selecting the *etrog*. It should be yellow with no discoloration on its skin. The tip (*pitom*) should not be broken.

64 See page 17, "The Mitzvah of Hospitality (*Hachnasat Or'chim*)."

65 See page 182, note 40.

66 The seventh day of Sukkot is known as Hoshana Rabbah. Reform congregations take no special note of the day, treating it like all the other intermediate days. However, since the Middle Ages, the day has been known in the tradition as Yom Kippur Katan, "a small Yom Kippur," and is seen as an opportunity for those who have not completed their repentance to do so. In addition, special clusters of willows, known as *hoshanot*, are beaten against the ground.

67 See page 184, note 54.

68 Simchat Torah in its present form developed in the post-Talmudic period. In the Talmud (BT *M'gilah* 31a), we learn that the end of Deuteronomy was assigned as the Torah reading for the second day of Sh'mini Atzeret. Gradually, as the annual Torah-reading cycle that was dominant in the Babylonian Jewish community replaced the earlier Palestinian triennial cycle, the second day of Sh'mini Atzeret became a joyous celebration of the completion of the Torah-reading cycle (*siyum haTorah*). Later, the reading from the first chapter of Genesis was added.

69 See page 178, note 45.

70 Some Reform congregations hold consecration on the Shabbat during Sukkot rather than on Sh'mini Atzeret–Simchat Torah. Consecration probably developed from the custom of calling all the children to the

Torah on Sh'mini Atzeret–Simchat Torah, which is based on Deuteronomy 31:12. Moses is commanded to gather the people on Sukkot during the Sabbatical year to hear the reading of the Torah. The verse reads, "Gather the people—men, women, children, and the strangers in your communities—that they may hear and so learn to revere the Eternal your God and to observe faithfully every word of this Teaching." (See Solomon B. Freehof, *Reform Jewish Practice*, vol. 1 [New York: UAHC, 1964], pages 26–27.)

CHANUKAH AND PURIM

1 I Maccabees 4:59. The Books of Maccabees are part of an extracanonical collection called the Apocrypha. It is found only in Protestant and Catholic Bibles, but not in the Hebrew Bible.

2 BT *Shabbat* 21b.

3 Ibid. Part of the celebration of Chanukah was to display the menorah so that it could be seen from outside the house (see page 75, "Displaying the *Chanukiyah*").

4 Zechariah 4:1–7 is the haftarah for the first Shabbat during Chanukah.

5 BT Shabbat 21b. Shivah is *not* suspended during Chanukah, but tradition suggested that the formal eulogy be omitted at funerals.

6 Although Chanukah is not a biblical festival, the Rabbis required that blessings be recited over the lighting of Chanukah lights and used the same formula as is used for biblical mitzvot: "Blessed are You, Adonai our God, Sovereign of all, who hallows us with mitzvot, commanding us . . ." (BT *Sukkah* 46a).

7 In Masechet *Sof'rim* 20:6 it is stated that we are only permitted to look at the Chanukah candles but not use them, as they are exclusively a symbol of thanksgiving for the miracle of deliverance that Chanukah commemorates.

8 Since the lighting of Shabbat candles ushers in Shabbat (see pages 18–19, "The Mitzvah of Kindling Shabbat Candles") and because of the traditional prohibition against lighting a fire on Shabbat, the Chanukah candles are lit before Shabbat candles. For the same reason, the Chanukah candles are lit after *Havdalah* on Saturday night.

9 BT *Shabbat* 24a.

10 The eating of dairy dishes is associated with the story of Judith, who slew the Assyrian leader Holofernes after he laid siege to the town of Bethulea near Jerusalem. It is reported that Judith prepared a meal of wine and cheese and brought it to Holofernes's tent. When the general had fallen into a drunken stupor, Judith killed him. Eventually this story was joined to the lore of the bravery of the Hasmoneans. Dishes cooked in oil are associated with the story of the cruse of oil, which according to the Talmudic legend lasted eight days (see Rama on *Orach Chayim* 670:2).

11 Legend tells that during the time of the Hellenistic and Roman persecu-

tion, when the study of Torah was forbidden by the ruling powers, students used the game of dreidel as a subterfuge to hide their studying. *Dreidel* is a Yiddish word from *drehn*, "to spin"; *s'vivon* is its Hebrew equivalent.

12   The fifteenth of Adar is known as Shushan Purim, because according to the Book of Esther (9:18), the Jews of Shushan (the capital) celebrated Purim on the fifteenth of Adar rather than on the fourteenth. The Mishnah (*M'gilah* 1:1) therefore ordained that cities that were surrounded by walls in the time of Joshua should observe Purim on the fifteenth. Jerusalem is considered to be one such city, and thus the Jews of Jerusalem observe Purim on the fifteenth.

The Shabbat preceding Purim is called Shabbat Zachor (Sabbath of Remembrance), because the additional Torah reading for that Shabbat (Deuteronomy 25:17–19) begins with the words *Zachor eit asher asah l'cha Amalek*, "Remember what Amalek did to you." In Jewish tradition Amalek is identified with Haman, the villain of the Purim story. Shabbat Zachor serves as preparation for Purim.

13   While this is the popular understanding of the meaning of Purim, the original meaning of the Book of Esther (which became overshadowed by later history) was to tell the story of two assimilated Jews who tried to make it as gentiles but could not. This understanding of the story remains relevant for Jews today. Assimilation did not protect the Jews of Europe from becoming victims of the Shoah. Judaism, the Jewish people, and the world are better served by Jews who proudly acknowledge their heritage and actively oppose anti-Semites. The story further emphasizes the tragic necessity of Jews to defend themselves against those who would kill them.

14   The Jews of Jerusalem observe Purim on the fifteenth of Adar. See note 13 above.

15   The Talmud (BT *M'gilah* 4a) prescribes the reading of *M'gilat Esther* at both the evening and morning services.

16   *Shulchan Aruch, Orach Chayim* 690:18.

17   Esther 9:22 designates Purim as "days of festive joy, feasting, and merrymaking." The mood on Purim is so joyous that the Talmud (BT *M'gilah* 7b) is permissive concerning the drinking of intoxicants on Purim: "As Rava said, 'A person should be so merry [with drink] on Purim that he does not know the difference between 'cursed be Haman' and 'blessed is Mordecai.'" On no other occasion is such conduct encouraged. While we are not encouraging intoxication, it should be clear that the atmosphere on Purim is unlike that of any other holiday. The celebration is unrestrained, with laughter and merrymaking the order of the day.

18   The wearing of costumes, especially of the characters in the Purim story, is part of the celebration. Purim is the one occasion when men and women are permitted to wear each others' clothes (Rama on *Orach Chayim* 696:8).

In Israel, Purim is celebrated with a carnival called *Adlayada*, which includes costume parades, floats, and bands. The term is based on the Talmudic phrase *Ad d'la yada bein arur Haman l'varuch Mordechai*, "A person should be so merry on Purim that he cannot discern between 'cursed is Haman' and 'blessed is Mordecai'" (BT *M'gilah* 7b).

19 See Esther 9:22. Gifts to the poor at this season are particularly significant, because they recognize that the survival of Jews is in part dependent upon other Jews expressing care and concern.

The giving of *tzedakah* on Purim can also be linked to the ancient half-shekel tax paid to support the Temple (Exodus 30:13). The Rabbis ordained that the Shabbat immediately preceding the first of Adar contain a warning that the tax was coming due (*Mishnah Sh'kalim* 1:1). Therefore Exodus 30:11–16 is read in addition to the weekly portion. The Shabbat is known as Shabbat Sh'kalim.

Other Special Days
ROSH CHODESH

20 See, e.g., I Samuel 20; II Kings 4:23; Isaiah 1:13; Amos 8:5; Psalm 81:4; and Ezra 3:5.

21 *Mishnah Rosh HaShanah* 2:5–7.

22 While Reform Jews consider the first day of each month as Rosh Chodesh, traditional observance also includes the thirtieth day of the preceding month where the preceding month has thirty days (as opposed to twenty-nine). Thus, in other congregations, Rosh Chodesh will be observed either one or two days, depending on the length of the preceding month.

23 JT *Taanit* 1:6; *Tosafot, Rosh HaShanah* 23a, s.v. "*Mishum bitul m'lacha laam sh'nei yamim*"; *Aruch HaShulchan, Orach Chayim* 417:10.

24 *Targum Yonatan* to Exodus 32:3.

25 The connection between women and Rosh Chodesh probably has its origin in the parallel between the lunar cycle and the female menstrual cycle.

YOM HASHOAH (HOLOCAUST MEMORIAL DAY)

26 *CCAR Yearbook*, vol. 87 (1977), page 87.

YOM HAATZMA-UT (ISRAEL INDEPENDENCE DAY)

27 *CCAR Yearbook*, vol. 80 (1970), page 39; see also *CCAR Yearbook*, 1969, page 143.

28 Deuteronomy 8:1–18, 11:8–21, 26:1–11, and 30:1–16 have all been designated possible Yom HaAtzma-ut Torah readings. The designated haftarah reading is Isaiah 60:1–22.

29 In the Mishnah (*Taanit* 4:6), a number of tragic events are said to have happened on the ninth of Av: "It was decreed against our ancestors that they should not enter the Land of Israel, the Temple was destroyed the first and second time, and Betar was captured, and the city [Jerusalem] was ploughed up."

30 For example, in 1290, King Edward I signed the edict expelling the Jews from England; in 1914, Archduke Ferdinand of Austria was shot on the eve of Tishah B'Av, leading to the mobilization for World War I on the next day.

TU BISH'VAT

31 *Mishnah Rosh HaShanah* 1:1. *Tu* is the number fifteen written in Hebrew letters. Each alphabet letter in Hebrew is also a number. *Tet*, ט, equals nine; *vav*, ו, equals six. When they are written together, [ט"ו], they may be pronounced *tu*.

32 An old kabbalistic text, *Sefer P'ri Eitz Hadar*, attributed to Chayim Vital, contains a fully written version of the seder. Some Reform congregations have revived this old tradition, and a number of rabbis have produced their own texts for the seder.

ESSAYS

What Is a Mitzvah?

1 Herbert Bronstein, "Mitzvah and Autonomy," in *Duties of the Soul: The Role of Commandments in Literature*, ed. Niles E. Goldstein and Peter S. Knobel (New York: URJ Press, 1999), pages 65–66.

2 Elyse Frishman, "A Voice in the Dark: How Do We Hear God?" in *Duties of the Soul*, pages 115–125.

3 From Richard Levy, in *The Many Faces of God: A Reader of Modern Jewish Theologies*, ed. Rifat Sonsino (New York: URJ Press, 2004), pages 217–218.

4 Adapted from "A Progressive Reform Judaism" by Rabbi Evan Moffic, in *Jewish Theology in Our Time: A New Generation Explores the Foundations & Future of Jewish Belief*, ed. Rabbi Elliot J. Cosgrove (Woodstock, VT: Jewish Lights, 2010).

Hidur Mitzvah: The Aesthetics of Mitzvot

1 Midrash, *M'chilta*, *Shirata* 3, ed. Lauterbach, page 25.

2 BT *Shabbat* 133b.

3 BT *Bava Kama* 9b.

4 Midrash, *Shir HaShirim Rabbah* 1:15.

5 C. G. Montefiore and H. Loewe, *A Rabbinic Anthology* (London: Macmillan, 1938), note by H. Loewe, page 118.

Approaching the High Holy Days

1   Based on Alan Lew, *This is Real and You Are Totally Unprepared: The Days of Awe as a Journey of Transformation* (New York: Hachette Book Group, 2003), p. 29.

2   Ibid., p. 29.

3   Bernard Bamberger, "A Concern for Man" in *The Rabbis Speak : A Quarter Century of Sermons for the High Holy Days*, ed. Saul L. Teplitz (New York: New York Board of Rabbis, 1986).

M'nuchah and *M'lachah*: On Observing the Sabbath in Reform Judaism

1   The Torah states this explicitly in both appearances of the Decalogue (the Ten Commandments): Exodus 20:8–11 and Deuteronomy 5:12–15. See also Exodus 23:12, 31:14–15, 35:2; Leviticus 23:3.

2   The Torah does not call the Festivals days of "rest" but rather days of "rejoicing" (*simchah*; Deuteronomy 16:14). Still, most forms of work are prohibited on the festival day; see Exodus 12:16 and numerous verses in Leviticus 23 and Numbers 28–29.

3   Work prohibited on Shabbat and Yom Kippur consists of thirty-nine general categories of activity (*avot*; *Mishnah Shabbat* 7:2). Each of these is subdivided into many subcategories (*tol'dot*). Other prohibitions are added by Rabbinic decree. The list, with some important exceptions, is the same for *Yom Tov*.

4   W. Gunther Plaut, *A Shabbat Manual* (New York: CCAR Press, 1972); Peter Knobel, ed., *Gates of the Seasons: A Guide to the Jewish Year* (New York: CCAR Press, 1983); and Mark Dov Shapiro, *Gates of Shabbat: A Guide for Observing Shabbat* (New York: CCAR Press, 1991).

5   Knobel, *Gates of the Seasons*, page 17.

6   For descriptions and materials, see http://urj.org/holidays/shabbat/congregation.

7   In Shapiro, *Gates of Shabbat*, pages 55–56.

8   Rabbi Eric H. Yoffie, Presidential Sermon, Sixty-Ninth General Assembly (Biennial) of the Union for Reform Judaism, December 15, 2007, http://urj.org//holidays/shabbat/congregation//?syspage=article&item_id=4130.

9   See Shapiro, *Gates of Shabbat*, pages 49–59.

10 "In creating a contemporary approach to Shabbat, Reform Jews do not function in a vacuum. Although we may depart from ancient practices, we live with a sense of responsibility to the continuum of Jewish experience" (Knobel, *Gates of the Seasons*, page 57).

11 This trend of thought appears in a long line of responsa. See, as an example, "The Synagogue Thrift Shop and Shabbat," in *Reform Responsa for the Twenty-First Century*, ed. Mark Washofsky (New York: CCAR, 2010), vol. 1, pages 41–48. The endnotes to that responsum refer the reader to the entire line of opinions in this vein.

Eating Our Values

1 BT *P'sachim* 109a.
2 Fair Trade USA, http://www.transfairusa.org/.
3 Magen Tzedek, http://magentzedek.org/.
4 Bema'aglei Tzedek, http://www.mtzedek.org.il/english/TavChevrati.asp.
5 Uri L'Tzedek, http://www.utzedek.org/tavhayosher.html.
6 BT *Bava M'tzia* 32a–b.

The Journey to Judaism: Choosing Judaism, Choosing Mitzvot

1 Address to the ULPS of Great Britain (London, England, February 13, 1995).
2 *Pirkei Avot* 1:6.
3 Arnold Jacob Wolf, *The Condition of Jewish Belief: A Symposium*, compiled by the editors of *Commentary Magazine* (New York: Macmillan, 1966), page 268.

Tzedakah

1 BT *Gittin* 7b.
2 *Mishneh Torah, Hilchot Mat'not Aniyim* (Laws about Giving to Poor People) 10:7–14.
3 *Pirkei Avot* 1:2.

Glossary

Adar. The twelfth month of the Jewish calendar. In a leap year, a thirteenth month—called Adar II—is added.

Adlayada. Purim carnival. The term comes from the Aramaic words *ad d'la yada* ("until he could not discern") included in the Talmudic phrase "A person should be so merry on Purim that *he cannot discern* between 'cursed is Haman' and 'blessed is Mordecai.'"

afikoman. Name for half of the middle of the three matzot on the Passover seder plate. It is eaten at the conclusion of the seder meal. The word *afikoman* is of Greek origin, but its exact etymology is unclear. It has been interpreted as "after-meal entertainment" or "dessert."

Ahasuerus. Revelry-loving king of Persia from the story of Purim in the biblical book of Esther, who saves Queen Esther and the Jewish people after Haman's evil plot to exterminate them is revealed.

am b'rit. "People of the covenant." The Jewish people.

Amidah. Literally, "standing." The core and main element of each of the prescribed daily services. Also known as *T'filah* and (among Ashkenazim) as *Sh'moneh Esreih* (Eighteen) because of the eighteen benedictions that it originally comprised.

Aramaic. A Semitic language, closely related to Hebrew, that was widely used in Talmudic times.

aravah (**pl.:** *aravot*). "Willow." One of the four species gathered on Sukkot.

arbaah minim. "Four species." The four species gathered during the Festival of Sukkot: citron (*etrog*), palm (*lulav*), myrtle (*hadas*), and willow (*aravah*).

Arba Parashiyot. "Four portions [of the Torah]" read in addition to the weekly portion on four of the Sabbaths preceding Pesach.

Aseret Y'mei T'shuvah. "Ten Days of Repentance." The ten-day period from Rosh HaShanah through Yom Kippur. The period is also called *Yamim Noraim* (Days of Awe).

Ashkenazi (pl.: Ashkenazim). "German." A Jew from Central or Eastern Europe descendants of these Jews.

Atzeret. "Festive meeting." See **Sh'mini Atzeret.**

Av. The fifth month of the Jewish calendar.

Aviv. Spring. In the Bible, also the name of the month in which Pesach occurs.

avodah shebalev. "Service of the heart." The Talmudic Sages understood the biblical command "You shall serve God with your whole heart" (Deuteronomy 11:13) as an injunction regarding prayer, for "What service is performed with the heart? This is prayer" (BT *Taanit* 2a).

bal tashchit. "Do not destroy." Stemming from the prohibition of Deuteronomy 20:19–20 that forbids the destruction of fruit trees, even in a time of war, *bal tashchit* has since become the Jewish ethical imperative for environmentalism and ecological sustainability.

b'dikat chameitz. "Search for *chameitz* [leaven]." A symbolic search for the last remains of leaven conducted on the night before the first Passover seder.

beitzah (pl.: beitzim). "Egg." One of the items on the Passover seder plate. The egg represents the festival offering; it symbolizes the potentiality of life and the triumph of life over death.

bikur cholim. [The mitzvah of] visiting the sick.

bikurim. "First fruits." An ancient custom of bringing the first seasonal fruits to the Temple in Jerusalem.

Birkat HaMazon. "Blessing after Eating." Prayers recited after eating.

Birkat HaShir. "Blessing of the Song." A prayer recited at Shabbat and Festival morning services at the end of the preliminary section known as *P'sukei D'zimrah* (Poems of Praise). It is also a part of the Passover Haggadah. Also known as *Nishmat*, because it begins with the words *Nishmat kol chai* ("Let the soul of everything alive [bless Your name]").

bokser. Fruit of the carob tree. Eaten on Tu BiSh'vat.

***b'rachah* (pl.: *b'rachot*).** "Blessing."

b'rit. "Covenant." A promise between God and people, such as the rainbow following the Flood in Genesis 9, or a promise between people and people. Also refers to *b'rit milah*, the covenant of circumcision.

***chag* (pl.: *chagim*).** Holiday, festival.

Chag HaAsif. "The Festival of Ingathering." Sukkot.

Chag HaAviv. "The Spring Festival; the Festival of the Month Aviv." Passover.

Chag HaBikurim. "The Festival of First Fruits." Shavuot.

Chag HaKatzir. "The Harvest Festival." Shavuot.

Chag HaMatzot. "The Festival of Unleavened Bread." Passover.

Chag HaPesach. "The Festival of the Paschal Offering." Passover.

***chagigah* (pl.: *chagigot*).** Celebration. Also festive offering brought by visitors to the Temple on the Festivals.

challah (pl.: challot). Special holiday bread. The name is derived from the special dough offering that was set aside for the priests during the existence of the Temple. After the destruction of the Temple, people continued the practice of setting aside part of the dough when they baked holiday loaves. Eventually the term *challah* was applied to the holiday loaves themselves.

Chameish M'gilot. "The Five Scrolls." Five biblical books that are read on holidays and festivals. Song of Songs (*Shir HaShirim*) is read on the intermediate Shabbat of Passover; Ruth is read on Shavuot; Lamentations (*Eichah*) is read on Tishah B'Av; Ecclesiastes (*Kohelet*) is read on the intermediate Shabbat of Sukkot; and Esther is read on Purim.

chameitz. "Leaven." Leavened products that are not to be eaten during Passover.

Chamishah-Asar BiSh'vat. "The Fifteenth of Shevat." See **Tu BiSh'vat.**

Chanukah. "Dedication; consecration." The Feast of Lights. Chanukah begins on the twenty-fifth day of Kislev and lasts for eight days. It commemorates the victory of Judah Maccabee and his followers over the forces of the Syrian tyrant Antiochus Epiphanes (165 BCE) and the rededication of the Temple in Jerusalem.

chanukiyah (pl.: *chanukiyot*). Eight-branched Chanukah candelabrum, with an additional ninth candle called a *shamash*. Also known as "menorah."

charoset. One of the items on the Passover seder plate. A mixture of ground nuts, fruits, spices, and wine used to sweeten the bitter herbs eaten on Passover night. Symbolic of the mortar that our ancestors used for Pharaoh's labor.

chasidei umot haolam. "The righteous of the nations." Benevolent gentiles who risked or gave their lives to save Jews during the Shoah (Holocaust).

chavurah (pl.: *chavurot*). "Fellowship; community." An informal, usually small association, sometimes (but not necessarily) formed within a congregation, whose purpose is the enhancement of personal Judaism through shared prayer, study, and the adoption of new practices within a Jewish lifestyle.

chazeret. "Bitter vegetable." Often placed in addition to the *maror* as a bitter herb on the seder plate. The authorities are divided on the requirement of *chazeret,* so not all communities use it. Since the commandment (in Numbers 9:11) to eat the paschal lamb "with unleavened bread and bitter herbs" uses the plural ("bitter herbs") many seder plates have a place for *chazeret* in addition to *maror*.

Cheshvan. The eighth month of the Jewish calendar.

chol hamoeid. The intermediate days (between the first and last days) of Pesach and Sukkot.

citron. *Etrog,* one of the four species gathered on Sukkot.

confirmation. Originally a substitution for the bar/bat mitzvah ceremony, today it is held in Reform congregations partway through high school on or near Shavuot as a group ceremony of commitment to the covenant. Also called *Kabbalat Torah* in Hebrew.

consecration. Special ceremony for children entering religious school for the first time. Most congregations hold it on Simchat Torah.

counting of the Omer: see *S'firat HaOmer*; **Omer.**

covenant. See *b'rit.*

cup of Elijah. See *kos shel Eliyahu.*

Days of Awe. See *Yamim Noraim.*

Decalogue. The Ten Commandments, found in Exodus 20:2–14 as well as in Deuteronomy 5:6–18.

Diaspora. The scattering of the Jewish community across the world, beginning with exile from the Land of Israel during the Babylonian conquest of 587 BCE.

dreidel. A four-sided spinning top used in Chanukah games.

d'var Torah **(pl.** *divrei Torah***).** "Word(s) of Torah." A sermon, or presentation of the salient points for the weekly Torah portion.

eifah. An ancient measure of grain.

Ein m'ar'vin simchah b'simchah. "One may not mix two joyous occasions." The Talmudic prohibition of holding marriages on Shabbat and festival days.

Elijah. Israelite prophet active during the reign of Ahab and Ahaziah (ninth century BCE). According to Jewish folklore, Elijah appears on the eve of Passover to bring his message of redemption.

El Malei Rachamim. "Fully compassionate God." Prayer for the dead.

Elul. The sixth month of the Jewish calendar.

erev **(pl.:** *aravim***).** "Evening, eve." The time prior to the start of Shabbat or the festival. All Jewish holidays begin at night. Thus, for example, "Erev Shabbat" refers to Friday, especially the afternoon and early evening before the beginning of Shabbat; "Erev Sukkot" is the day before the first day of Sukkot. However, in popular parlance the first night of the holiday is often referred to as "Erev Sukkot," etc.

Esther. Heroine of the story of Purim, recounted in the Book of Esther. Also known in Hebrew as Hadassah. Through her courageous actions, Haman's plan to annihilate the Jewish people was thwarted.

etrog (pl.: *etrogim*). "Citron." One of the four species gathered on Sukkot.

Feast of Weeks. See **Shavuot**.

Five Scrolls. See *Chameish M'gilot*.

Four Questions. Part of the Passover Haggadah that asks, "Why is this night different from all other nights?" It is customary for the youngest participant(s) in the seder to recite the Four Questions.

four species. See *arbaah minim*.

gefilte fish. "Filled fish." Chopped fish mixed with crumbs, eggs, and seasonings, cooked in a broth, and usually served chilled in the form of balls or oval-shaped cakes. Part of the traditional Shabbat evening meal.

G'mar chatimah tovah. "May the final decree be good." Greeting for Yom Kippur.

g'milut chasadim. "Acts of loving-kindness." The Talmud teaches that such acts of *g'milut chasadim* are gestures "whose worth is beyond measure" (Mishnah *Pei-ah* 1:1), even greater than *tzedakah*, because it can be done for both poor and rich, living and dead, with acts or gifts (BT *Sukkah* 49b).

grager. A noisemaker used to drown out the sound of Haman's name during the reading of the Scroll of Esther on Purim.

hachnasat or'chim. [The mitzvah of] hospitality to guests.

hadar. "Beautiful." Rabbinic interpretation identifies the fruit of the "*hadar* tree" (Leviticus 23:40) as the *etrog* (citron). It is one of the four species gathered on Sukkot.

hadas (pl.: *hadasim*). "Myrtle." One of the four species gathered on Sukkot.

hadlakat nerot. [The mitzvah of] kindling the candles [on the eve of Shabbat and the Festivals].

haftarah (pl.: **haftarot**). "Conclusion." A section from the prophetic books of the Bible read on Shabbat and holidays after the reading of the Torah.

Haggadah (pl.: Haggadot). "Narrative." The tale of the Exodus from Egypt, read on Passover night.

hakafah (pl.: *hakafot*). From "to encircle." Portion of the Torah service where the Torah is carried in a procession around the prayer space, so that everyone has access to touch or kiss the scroll.

halachah. "The path." Collective body of Jewish ritual and ethical law, as determined by textual sources such as biblical law, Talmudic law, and later Rabbinic law codes.

Hallel. Psalms 113–118 recited on Rosh Chodesh and the Festivals.

Haman. Villain of the story of Purim, whose name is symbolically drowned out by the noise of *gragers* during the reading of the Book of Esther. Haman, the vizier in the court of King Ahasuerus, sought the annihilation of the Jewish people because Mordecai, Queen Esther's cousin, refused to prostrate himself before him.

hamantaschen. Three-cornered pastry filled with prunes, poppy seeds, apricots, or other fruits. A Purim dessert symbolizing Haman's ears or pockets. In Hebrew, *oznei haman*.

hama-or hagadol. "The bigger light." The sun.

hama-or hakatan. "The lesser light." The moon.

HaMotzi. "Who brings forth [bread]." The benediction recited over bread and before eating.

Havdalah. "Separation." The ceremony that marks the end of Shabbat and festivals. The *Havdalah* blessing separates the holy from the ordinary.

HeChag. "The Festival." Sukkot.

hidur mitzvah. The principle of enhancing a mitzvah through aesthetics. This, in turn, enhances the individual's practice and gladdens God through the commitment to the joy that beauty brings to ritual.

hin. An ancient measure of liquid.

Holiness Code. Refers to Leviticus 17–26, a section outlining a series of ritual and ethical purity laws, seen as a discrete unit in this biblical book.

Hoshana Rabbah. The seventh day of Sukkot.

hoshanot. Clusters of willows carried in procession on the last day of Sukkot.

Iyar. The second month of the Jewish calendar.

Jubilee. In the Bible, a year of rest to be observed by the Israelites every fiftieth year.

Judah HaNasi. "Judah the Prince" (later half of the second century CE). Editor of the Mishnah. Also known as "Rabbi."

kaparah (pl.: *kaparot*). "Forgiveness, absolution, expiation." The setting aside of charity money before sunset on the eve of Yom Kippur. Implicit in this act of *kaparah* is the idea that the charity money serves as atonement for one's sins. The concept of *kaparah* is probably based on the ancient scapegoat ritual for Yom Kippur (Leviticus 16:5–22).

karpas. "Parsley, green herbs." One of the items on the Passover seder plate. It symbolizes the rebirth of springtime and the green of hope and renewal.

kashrut. "Fitness." The term is most often applied to the traditional Jewish dietary laws, but it can also refer to the fitness of religious objects.

kavanah. "Directed intention." The ideal state of mental concentration and devotion at prayer and during the performance of mitzvot.

k'doshim (sing.: *kadosh*). "Holy ones." Jewish martyrs.

k'dushah. "Holiness." The Hebrew word also has the connotation of separation, setting aside.

ketubah (pl.: *k'tubot*). The Jewish marriage contract.

Kiddush. "Sanctification." Prayers recited, usually over wine, to mark the holiness of Shabbat or the Festivals. The word is also used as a general term for the festive table after a morning service on such days.

kippah (pl.: *kippot*). Ritual head-covering traditionally worn during prayer to show respect and deference to God (BT *Shabbat* 156b). Also known in Yiddish as a *yarmulke.*

Kislev. The ninth month of the Jewish calendar.

kitniyot. "Legumes." A category of foods prohibited during Peach by Ashkenazic tradition in addition to *chameitz. Kitniyot* include corn, rice, peas, lentils, beans, and for some, peanuts.

Kol Nidrei. "All Vows." A declaration of annulment of all vows that begins the evening service of Yom Kippur.

kos shel Eliyahu. "Cup of Elijah." A cup of wine placed on the Passover seder table for the prophet Elijah, the herald of redemption, who, by tradition, is believed to visit every Jewish home on the first night of Passover.

kreplach. Three-cornered meat-filled dumplings served in soup.

Lag BaOmer. The thirty-third day of the counting of the Omer (falling on the eighteenth day of Iyar). A semi-holiday during the mourning period between Passover and Shavuot.

lashuv. "To return; to repent."

latkes. Potato pancakes traditionally served during Chanukah.

leap year. For the Jewish calendar, a year in which a second month of Adar is added. This occurs seven times in a nineteen-year period.

lechem mishneh. "Two loaves." The two traditional loaves set out in the ancient Temple during Shabbat and the Festivals to commemorate the double portion of manna the Children of Israel received as their Sabbath portion while wandering in the desert (Exodus 16:22–27).

L'shanah tovah teichateimu. "May you be sealed [in the Book of Life] for a good year." Greeting after Rosh HaShanah.

L'shanah tovah tikateivu. "May you be inscribed [in the Book of Life] for a good year." Greeting for Rosh HaShanah.

lulav (pl.: *lulavim*). "Palm branch." One of the four species gathered on Sukkot. Also refers to the combination of the palm, myrtle, and willow that are taken up and waved together.

Maccabee. The additional name given to Judah, the military leader of the revolt against Syria in 168 BCE. The name Maccabee, meaning "hammer," is also applied loosely to other members of the family, as well as to the Hasmonean dynasty as a whole.

Maimonides. Rabbi Moses ben Maimon (1135–1204), also known by the acronym Rambam. The foremost Jewish thinker and rabbinic authority of the Middle Ages. His writings include the *Guide of the Perplexed*, the *Mishneh Torah* (also known as the *Yad*), and *Sefer HaMitzvot*.

Malchuyot. "Sovereign Verses." The first of the three central benedictions of the Shofar Service on Rosh HaShanah morning. (The other two benedictions are known as *Zichronot* and *Shofarot*.)

ma-ot chitin. "Wheat money." Collection made before Passover to ensure a supply of flour for matzot for the poor.

marit ayin. "Appearance of the eye." The avoidance of acts that although not in fact prohibited by the halachah, give the appearance of a violation.

maror. "Bitter herbs." One of the items on the Passover seder plate. The top part of the horseradish root, symbolic of the bitterness that our ancestors experienced in Egypt.

matan Torah. "The giving of the Torah." The Revelation on Mount Sinai.

matzah (pl.: matzot). Unleavened bread eaten during Passover and especially at the seder.

menorah. "Candelabrum." The name given to the seven-branched candelabrum that was a prominent feature in the Tabernacle as well as in the Jerusalem Temple. Also, one of the names for the eight-branched Chanukah lamp (*chanukiyah*).

mezuzah (pl.: mezuzot). "Doorpost." A scroll with biblical verses, usually in a wooden or metal container, affixed to the doorpost of a Jewish home.

M'gilah (pl.: M'gilot). "Scroll." Commonly refers to *M'gilat Esther*, the Scroll of Esther read on Purim. See also ***Chameish M'gilot***.

milah. "Circumcision." Ritual ceremony traditionally performed on the eighth day after a male infant is born, welcoming him as part of the *b'rit*, the covenant.

Miriam's cup. A modern feminist symbol, Miriam's cup is a new ritual object placed next to Elijah's cup on the Passover seder table, filled with water to represent Miriam's well, which according to the midrash nourished the Israelites during their wanderings in the desert.

mishlo-ach manot. "Sending of portions." A Purim custom of exchanging gifts of food or pastries with friends and family. Also known as *shalachmanos.*

mitzvah (pl.: mitzvot). Literally, a commandment or religious obligation. Sometimes understood colloquially as good deed, though this is not the true meaning.

m'lachah. "Work." Traditionally, the Rabbis defined thirty-nine major categories of work that are forbidden on the Sabbath in order to make it a true *Shabbat m'nuchah* (Sabbath of rest).

m'nuchah. "Rest." Shabbat is a day of rest.

moeid (pl.: mo-adim). Season; festival.

Mordecai. One of the heroes of the story of Purim, who acted as foster father to his beautiful cousin Esther. Mordecai encouraged Esther to attract the attention of the king. He was the only one who refused to bow down to Haman, the king's vizier, and the one who inspired Esther to reveal her true identity to the king in order to save the Jewish people.

myrtle. *Hadas,* one of the four species gathered on Sukkot.

Naaseh v'nishma. "We will faithfully do," or literally, "We will do and we will hear." Part of the phrase in Exodus 24:7, "And they [the people of Israel] said, 'All that the Eternal has spoken, we will faithfully do,'" indicating the Israelites' acceptance of the Torah at Mount Sinai. This phrase is identified as the basis for the understanding that Judaism is a religion of "deed, not creed," based on the ordering of the verbs.

Neis gadol hayah po. "A great miracle happened here." In Israel, the four Hebrew letters *nun, gimel, hei,* and *pei* on the dreidel stand for *Neis gadol hayah po.*

Neis gadol hayah sham. "A great miracle happened there." In the Diaspora, the four Hebrew letters *nun, gimel, hei,* and *shin* on the dreidel stand for *Nes gadol hayah sham.*

ner (pl.: nerot). Candle.

ner(ot) shel Chanukah. Chanukah candle(s).

ner(ot) shel Shabbat. Shabbat candle(s).

N'ilah. "Conclusion, closing." The concluding prayer, recited close to sunset, on Yom Kippur.

Nisan. The first month of the Jewish calendar.

Nishmat (kol chai). See **Birkat HaShir.**

n'shamah y'teirah. "An additional soul." According to Rabbinic legend, an additional soul dwells in each Jew during Shabbat.

Omer. "Sheaf; wave offering." The sheaf offering of barley brought to the Temple on the sixteenth day of Nisan, and thus the name of the forty-nine-day period between Passover and Shavuot. Traditionally, the forty-nine days of the Omer are considered a period of semi-mourning because, according to the Talmud, twenty-four thousand of Rabbi Akiva's disciples died between Passover and Shavuot during the Hadrianic persecution that followed the Bar Kochba revolt.

oneg. "Joy, delight." Shabbat is a day of *oneg.* The term also refers to the social gathering after a Shabbat evening service or to a study session and get-together on Shabbat afternoon.

oznei Haman. "Haman's ears." Hebrew name for hamantaschen.

palm. *Lulav,* one of the four species gathered on Sukkot.

Pesach. "Passover." Spring festival, beginning on the fifteenth day of Nisan and lasting for seven days. It commemorates the Israelite Exodus from Egypt, with the concept of freedom as its main theme. It is called "Pesach" or "Passover" because God "passed over" or protected the houses of the Children of Israel. *Pesach* is also the paschal lamb that was offered as a sacrifice on the eve of the feast in Temple times.

pikuach nefesh. "Saving a life." Ethical mandate in Jewish law dictating that the act of saving a life takes ultimate precedence and overrides nearly any other consideration.

Pilgrimage Festivals. See **Three Pilgrimage Festivals.**

Pirkei Avot. "Ethics of the Ancestors." The tractate *Avot* of the Mishnah.

Purim. "Lots." The holiday commemorating the deliverance of the Jews of ancient Persia from Haman's plot to kill them, through the efforts of Mordecai and Queen Esther. Purim is so called after the lots cast by Haman in order to determine the month in which the slaughter was to take place. The holiday is celebrated on the fourteenth day of Adar (in leap years during Adar II).

raashan **(pl.:** *raashanim***).** "Noisemaker." Hebrew name for *grager*.

Rama. Rabbi Moses Isserles (1520–1572). Best known for his commentary on the *Shulchan Aruch* called the *Mapah*. He provides Ashkenazic traditions to Caro's work.

Rosh Chodesh. "The New Moon; the New Month." The first day of the month.

Rosh HaShanah. The Jewish New Year. Celebrated on the first day of Tishrei. The holiday initiates a period of soul searching and reflection that culminates on Yom Kippur.

Sabbatical Year. In Hebrew, *Sh'mitah* or *Sh'vi-it*. The seventh year of a seven-year agricultural cycle in which the Torah dictates that all land must lie fallow and debts must be remitted.

s'chach. "Thatch." The branches and plants covering the sukkah.

seder (pl.: s'darim). "Order, arrangement." The family meal and home ritual for Passover.

Sephardi (pl.: Sephardim). "Spaniard." A Jew with roots in the Iberian peninsula. The term is often erroneously used to designate all Jews who are non-Ashkenazi.

S'firat HaOmer. "Counting of the Omer." Counting the forty-nine days between the second day of Passover and Shavuot.

Shabbat (pl.: Shabbatot). The Sabbath; Saturday; the seventh day of the week; an occasion for rest and spiritual refreshment, abstention from the concerns of the workaday world, and participation in home and synagogue religious observances.

Shabbat HaChodesh. "Sabbath of the Month." The Shabbat immediately preceding the month of Nisan. It announces the arrival of Nisan and serves as part of the preparations for Passover.

Shabbat HaGadol. "The Great Sabbath." The Shabbat immediately preceding Passover.

Shabbat Parah. The Shabbat preceding Shabbat HaChodesh. It recalls the purification ritual of the red heifer (*parah adumah*).

Shabbat Shabbaton. "Sabbath of Sabbaths." The Bible refers only to Shabbat and Yom Kippur by this name.

Shabbat Sh'kalim. The Shabbat immediately preceding the month of Adar. During this Shabbat, Exodus 30:11–16 is read in addition to the weekly Torah portion. These verses contain the warning that the half-shekel tax to support the Sanctuary was due. The giving of *tzedakah* at Purim is linked to the ancient half-shekel tax.

Shabbat Shuvah. The Shabbat between Rosh HaShanah and Yom Kippur. Its name is derived from the first word of the haftarah (Hosea 14:2–10), which begins, *Shuvah Yisrael*, "Return, O Israel."

Shabbat Zachor. "Sabbath of Remembrance." The Shabbat immediately preceding Purim. The additional Torah reading for this Shabbat (Deuteronomy 25:17–19) begins, *Zachor eit asher asah l'cha Amalek*, "Remember what Amalek did to you." In Jewish tradition Amalek is identified with Haman, the villain of the Purim story. Shabbat Zachor serves as a preparation for Purim.

shalachmanos. See *mishlo-ach manot*.

Shalosh R'galim. See **Three Pilgrimage Festivals**.

shamash. "Servant." The auxiliary candle used to light the eight Chanukah candles.

shamor. "Observe." In Deuteronomy 5:12 we are commanded, *Shamor et yom haShabbat l'kad'sho*, "Observe the Sabbath day and keep it holy."

shavua tov. "Have a good week!" A greeting at the end of the *Havdalah* service at the conclusion of Shabbat.

Shavuot. "Weeks." A festival celebrated on the sixth day of Sivan, seven weeks ("a week of weeks") after Passover. The holiday is also called Chag HaKatzir (the Harvest Festival), Chag HaBikurim (the Festival of First Fruits), and *z'man matan Tora-teinu* (the season of the giving of the Torah).

Shehecheyanu. "Who has kept us alive." Key word in the special blessing of gratitude recited on holidays and occasions of joy.

shivah. "Seven." The seven most intense days of mourning for family members.

Sh'mini Atzeret. "The eighth day of the festive meeting." The day immediately following the Festival of Sukkot, coinciding in Reform Judaism and in Israel with the holiday of Simchat Torah. (Orthodox and Conservative Jews observe Simchat Torah on the ninth day.) Also known as Atzeret.

shofar **(pl.: *shofarot*).** A ram's horn prepared for use as the ritual horn on Rosh HaShanah and Yom Kippur.

Shofarot. "Shofar Verses." The last of the three central benedictions of the Shofar Service on Rosh HaShanah morning. (The other two benedictions are *Malchuyot* and *Zichronot*.)

Shushan Purim. The fifteenth day of Adar, so called because, according to the Book of Esther, the Jews of Shushan celebrated Purim on the fifteenth rather than the fourteenth day of Adar.

Sh'vat. The eleventh month of the Jewish calendar.

siddur (pl.: siddurim). "Arrangement." Prayer book.

sidrah **(pl.: *sidrot*).** "Order; arrangement." Popular term for the sections of the Torah read publicly in the synagogue on Shabbat.

simchah **(pl.: *s'machot*).** Joy, rejoicing, happiness; festivity, joyful occasion.

Simchat Torah. "Rejoicing of the Torah." The festival marking the annual completion and recommencing of the Torah-reading cycle. In Reform Judaism and in Israel, it coincides with Sh'mini Atzeret.

Sivan. The third month of the Jewish calendar.

siyum haTorah. "Completion of the Torah." Completion of the Torah-reading cycle on Sh'mini Atzeret–Simchat Torah.

S'lichot **(sing.: *s'lichah*).** In the singular, the word means "forgiveness." In the plural, it designates special penitential prayers that are recited during the penitential season, which begins before Rosh HaShanah and concludes with Yom Kippur. A special *S'lichot* service is recited late on the Saturday before Rosh HaShanah.

s'udah mafseket. The last meal before the Yom Kippur fast begins.

sufganiyah (pl.: sufganiyot). "Doughnut." Jelly doughnut served on Chanukah.

sukkah (pl.: sukkot). "Booth." Booth erected for the Festival of Sukkot in accordance with the biblical commandment, "You shall dwell in booths seven days" (Leviticus 23:42).

Sukkot. "Booths, Tabernacles." The autumn harvest festival that begins on the fifteenth day of Tishrei and concludes on the twenty-second with Sh'mini Atzeret–Simchat Torah. It commemorates the sukkot in which the Children of Israel dwelt in the wilderness after the Exodus from Egypt.

s'vivon (pl.: s'vivonim). Hebrew word for dreidel.

tallit (pl.: tallitot). "Prayer shawl." The tallit is traditionally white with blue stripes, and made of wool, cotton, or silk. Today tallitot come in a large range of colors, fabrics, and styles. At the four corners of the tallit, tassels are attached in fulfillment of the biblical commandment of *tzitzit.*

talmud Torah. "The study of Torah." The mitzvah of Jewish study. The term is also applied to the school where one studies Torah and about Judaism.

Tammuz. The fourth month in the Jewish calendar.

Tashlich. "You shall cast off." The custom of going to a body of water on the afternoon of Rosh HaShanah and symbolically casting off one's sins in the form of breadcrumbs or another symbol.

Ten Days of Repentance. See *Aseret Y'mei T'shuvah.*

Tevet. The tenth month of the Jewish calendar.

t'filah (pl.: t'filot). Prayer. Also, *T'filah,* another name for the *Amidah.*

t'fillin. "Phylacteries." Two black leather boxes containing scriptural passages, bound by black leather straps on the left arm and on the head (though it is worn on the right arm by those who are left-handed) and worn for the morning services on all days except Shabbat and scriptural holidays.

Three Pilgrimage Festivals. *Shalosh R'galim*, a collective name for Passover, Shavuot, and Sukkot (including Sh'mini Atzeret–Simchat Torah), on which pilgrims used to ascend to Jerusalem.

Tikkun Leil Shavuot. Torah study late into the Shavuot night.

tikkun olam. "Repairing the world." Healing our broken universe through acts of compassion and justice.

Tishah B'Av. "Ninth of Av." A day of mourning commemorating the destruction of the First and Second Temples in Jerusalem as well as other tragic events in Jewish history.

Tishrei. The seventh month of the Jewish calendar.

Tosefta. "Addition." A collection of Rabbinic material contemporaneous with the Mishnah but not included in it.

t'shuvah. "Return." Repentance, denoting a return to God after sinning.

Tu BiSh'vat. "The fifteenth of Sh'vat." A minor holiday. This day was designated in the Mishnah as the "New Year of Trees." Also known as "Chamishah-Asar BiSh'vat."

tzedek. Righteousness, justice.

tzedakah. "Righteous act; charity." A gift given as an act of justice and moral behavior.

tzitzit. Tassels attached to the four corners of the tallit.

ushpizin. "Guests." According to kabbalistic tradition, the seven mystical "guests" (Abraham, Isaac, Jacob, Moses, Aaron, Joseph, and David) who visit the sukkah during Sukkot. Reform Judaism includes also Sarah, Rebecca, Rachel, Leah, Miriam, Hannah, and Deborah.

Vidui. "Confession." Confessional prayers that form a central part of the Yom Kippur and *S'lichot* liturgy.

V'initem et nafshoteichem. "You shall afflict your souls [on Yom Kippur]" (Leviticus 23:27). It is from this verse that the mitzvah of fasting on Yom Kippur is derived.

V'shamru. Part of the *Kiddush* for the Shabbat noon meal, which begins, *V'shamru v'nei Yisrael et haShabbat,* "The Israelite people shall keep the Sabbath" (Exodus 31:16–17). It is also part of the middle blessing of the *Amidah* on Shabbat.

Willow. *Aravah,* one of the four species gathered on Sukkot.

Yamim Noraim. "Days of Awe." The period from the first day of Rosh HaShanah until Yom Kippur, and these two days in particular. The period is also called *Aseret Y'mei T'shuvah* (Ten Days of Repentance), a time when individuals seek forgiveness and engage in repentance and reconciliation for wrongs they have committed against God and against other human beings.

Yiddish. Language of medieval origin developed by Ashkenazic Jews and derived from German and Eastern European dialects.

Yizkor. "God shall remember." Service of remembrance for the martyrs of our people as well as for our own relatives and friends, recited on Yom Kippur, the last days of Sukkot and Passover, and on Shavuot.

yom (pl.: yamim). Day.

Yom HaAtzma-ut. "Independence Day." Israel's Independence Day, celebrated on the fifth of Iyar.

Yom HaDin. "Day of Judgment." Rosh HaShanah.

Yom HaShoah. Holocaust Remembrance Day. The 27th day of Nisan, set aside as a memorial to the victims of the Holocaust.

Yom HaZikaron. "Remembrance Day." Another name for Rosh HaShanah. In Israel, Yom HaZikaron also refers to a memorial day for those who fell during active duty in the Israeli War of Independence, which is observed on the fourth of Iyar (the day before Yom Ha-Atzma-ut).

Yom Kippur. "Day of Atonement." A solemn day of fasting and prayer concluding the Ten Days of Repentance, which begin on Rosh HaShanah. Considered by some to be the most important day in the Jewish liturgical year.

Yom Kippur Katan. "Small Yom Kippur." The seventh day of

Sukkot (also known as Hoshana Rabbah). Tradition sees this day as an opportunity for those who have not yet completed their repentance to do so. This term can also refer to the eve of a new month, observed by the kabbalists as a time for fasting and repentance.

yom shekulo Shabbat. "A day of eternal Shabbat." One of the traditional descriptions of the messianic era.

Yom Tov. "Good Day," "Holiday." A festival of biblical origin.

zachor. "Remember." In Exodus 20:8 we are commanded, *Zachor et yom haShabbat l'kad'sho*, "Remember the Sabbath day to keep it holy."

Zachor eit asher asah l'cha Amalek. See **Shabbat Zachor.**

zeicher litziat Mitzrayim. "Memorial to the Exodus from Egypt." One of the themes of the *Kiddush* for Shabbat.

Zichronot. "Remembrance Verses." The second of the three central benedictions of the Shofar Service on Rosh HaShanah morning. (The other two benedictions are known as *Malchuyot* and *Shofarot*.)

zikaron l'maaseih v'reishit. "Commemoration of the creation of the world." One of the themes of the *Kiddush* for Shabbat.

z'man cheiruteinu. "The season of our liberation." Passover.

z'man matan Torateinu. "The season of the giving of the Torah." Shavuot.

z'man simchateinu. "The season of our rejoicing." Sukkot.

z'mirot. "Songs." Special musical selections sung at the table on Shabbat and festivals.

Zochreinu l'chayim. "Remember us unto life." A Rosh HaShanah prayer.

z'roa. A roasted shank bone, burned or scorched, representing the ancient Passover sacrifice. One of the items on the seder plate.

zuz (pl.: zuzim). Silver coin; value of a quarter-shekel.

The Classic Texts of Judaism

Apocrypha and Pseudepigrapha. Known in Hebrew as "hidden" works, both terms refer to collections of intertestamental literature, ca. 200 BCE to 200 CE, primarily of Jewish authorship. They are hidden by exclusion from the Hebrew canon. Books of the Apocrypha and Pseudepigrapha, like Maccabees and Judith, are included in some Christian Bibles.

Arbaah Turim. A comprehensive compilation of private and public law, by Jacob ben Asher (1270?–1340), chiefly following the legal opinions of Maimonides and universally accepted as authoritative. The code served as the basis for Joseph Caro's monumental *Beit Yosef* and later his *Shulchan Aruch.*

Gemara. (Lit., "learning.") A word popularly applied to the Talmud as a whole or, more particularly, to the discussions and elaborations on the Mishnah by Rabbinic authorities of the third to fifth centuries CE. There is a Gemara to both the Babylonian and Jerusalem Talmuds, although not to all or to the same tractates.

midrash. The method of interpreting Scripture to elucidate legal points (*midrash halachah*) or to bring out lessons through stories or homiletics (*midrash aggadah*). Midrash is also the designation of a particular genre of Rabbinic literature extending from pre-Mishnaic times to the tenth century. Taken together, the body of works known as midrash constitutes an anthology of homilies consisting of both biblical exegesis and sermonic material. Among the more important midrashic works are *Midrash Rabbah*[1] (separate works on each volume of the Pentateuch, ca. 400–1000); *Tanchuma* (a group of homiletical midrashim edited later than ca. 800); and *P'sikta D'Rav Kahana*[2] (a homiletical midrash, probably ca. 500, on portions of scriptural readings for festivals and special Sabbaths). Among the *midr'shei halachah*, dealing primarily with law as derived from the Torah, are the *M'chilta* on Exodus,[3] *Sifra* on Leviticus, and *Sifrei* on Numbers and Deuteronomy. All were edited ca. fourth to fifth century CE.

Mishnah. The first legal codification of basic Jewish law, arranged
and redacted by Rabbi Judah HaNasi about 200 CE. The Mishnah[4] is the nucleus for all halachah and contains the basic Oral
Law as evolved through generations. The Mishnah is divided
into six orders: *Z'raim* (seeds), *Moeid* (seasons), *Nashim* (mat-
rimonial law), *N'zikin* (civil law), *Kodashim* (holy things), and
Tohorot (ritual purity), each order being divided into separate
tractates.

Mishneh Torah. An encyclopedic legal code in fourteen volumes,
also called *Yad HaChazakah*, by Moses ben Maimon (Maimonides, Rambam; 1135–1204). The *Mishneh Torah*[5] covers all
halachic subjects discussed in the Talmud and gives clear rul-
ings where there are conflicting opinions.

responsa (Heb.: *sh'eilot ut'shuvot*; sing.: responsum). Replies sent
by halachic authorities to questioners who addressed them in
writing. These responses cover every aspect of Jewish belief and
practice and are the main source for the development of Jewish
law since the close of the Talmud and a primary source for Jewish and general history. The writing of responsa continues to our
own day in all branches of the Jewish community.

Shulchan Aruch. (Lit., "A Prepared Table.") The basis for Jewish
law today, by Joseph Caro (1488–1575), codifying Sephardic
custom and to which was added Moses Isserles's *Mapah* (lit.,
"Tablecloth"), codifying Ashkenazic custom. Usually referred
to as the *Code of Jewish Law*, the *Shulchan Aruch* contains four
main subdivisions: *Orach Chayim, Yoreh Dei-ah, Even HaEizer,*
and *Choshen Mishpat.*

Talmud. (Lit., "study" or "learning.") The body of teaching that
comprises the commentary and discussions of the early Rabbis
on the Mishnah of Rabbi Judah HaNasi. Divided into the same
orders and tractates as the Mishnah, the Talmudic discussions
are always printed together with their corresponding parts of
the Mishnah. The Babylonian Talmud[6] is the interpretation and

elaboration of the Mishnah as developed in the great academies of Babylonia between the third and fifth centuries CE and is considered more authoritative than the smaller Jerusalem Talmud,[7] developed in the great academies of Palestine before the fifth century. The Babylonian Talmud, especially as a storehouse of Jewish history and customs as well as law, has exerted an unparalleled influence on Jewish thought and is the foundation of Judaism as we know it today.

Tanach. The traditional Hebrew acronym designating the Hebrew Bible, composed of the initial letters of the words *Torah* (Pentateuch)[8], *N'vi-im* (Prophets),[9] and *K'tuvim* (Writings, Hagiographa).[10]

Torah. (Lit., "teaching, doctrine, instruction.") The scroll consisting of the first five books of the Hebrew Bible. "Torah" is also used to describe the entire body of traditional Jewish teaching and literature.

Endnotes to The Classic Texts of Judaism

1   H. Freedman and M. Simon, eds., *The Midrash* (London: Soncino Press, 1951), 10 vols.

2   W. Braude and I. Kapstein, trans., *Pesikta deRab Kahana* (Philadelphia: Jewish Publication Society, 1975).

3   J. Lauterbach, trans., *Mekilta* (Philadelphia: Jewish Publication Society, 1961), 3 vols.

4   H. Danby, *The Mishnah* (Peabody, MA: Hendrickson Publishers, 2012).

5   Julian Oberman, ed., *The Code of Maimonides* (New Haven: Yale University Press, 1957).

6   Adin Steinsaltz, ed., *The Talmud, Steinsaltz Edition* (New York: Random House, 1965–2010).

7   J. Neusner, ed., *The Talmud of the Land of Israel.* (Chicago: University of Chicago Press, 1980).

8   W. Gunther Plaut, ed., *The Torah: A Modern Commentary*, Revised Edition (New York: URJ Press, 2005); Tamara Cohn Eskenazi and Andrea Weiss, eds., *The Torah: A Women's Commentary* (New York: URJ Press, 2007).

9   *The Prophets* (Philadelphia: Jewish Publication Society, 1978).

10 *The Writings* (Philadelphia: Jewish Publication Society, 1982).

For Further Reading

Related Titles from the
Central Conference of American Rabbis

Available at www.ccarpress.org or 212-972-3636 x 243

A Children's Haggadah. By Howard Bogot. New York: CCAR Press, 1994.

Gates of Forgiveness: The Union S'lichot Service; A Service of Preparation for the Days of Awe. Edited by Chaim Stern. New York: CCAR Press, 1993.

Gates of Mitzvah: A Guide to the Jewish Life Cycle. Edited by Simeon J. Maslin. New York: CCAR Press, 1979.

Gates of Repentance: The New Union Prayerbook for the Days of Awe. Rev. ed. Edited by Chaim Stern. New York: CCAR Press, 1996.

Gates of Shabbat: A Guide for Observing Shabbat. Edited by Mark Dov Shapiro. New York: CCAR Press, 1996.

Gates of Understanding. Edited by Lawrence A. Hoffman. 2 vols. New York: CCAR Press, 1984–1997.

Machzor Challenge and Change. New York: CCAR Press, 2009.

Mishkan T'filah: A Reform Siddur. Edited by Elyse D. Frishman. New York: CCAR Press, 2007.

Mishkan T'filah: The Journal Edition. By Michelle Shapiro Abraham and Joel Abraham. New York: CCAR Press, 2010.

Mishkan T'filah for Gatherings: A Reform Siddur. Edited by Elyse D. Frishman. New York: CCAR Press, 2009.

Mishkan T'filah for Travelers: A Reform Siddur. Edited by Elyse D. Frishman. New York: CCAR Press, 2009.

Mishkan T'filah: The World Union Edition; A Progressive Siddur. New York: CCAR Press, 2010.

On the Doorposts of Your House: Prayers and Ceremonies for the Jewish Home. Rev. ed. Edited by Chaim Stern, Donna Berman, Edward Graham, and H. Leonard Poller. New York: CCAR Press, 2010.

The Open Door: A Passover Haggadah. Edited by Sue Levi Elwell. New York: CCAR Press, 2002.

A Passover Haggadah. Rev. ed. Edited by Herbert Bronstein. New York: CCAR Press, 1994.

Seder Tu Bishevat: The Festival of Trees. By Adam Fisher. New York: CCAR Press, 1989.

Sharing the Journey: The Haggadah for the Contemporary Family. By Alan S. Yoffie. New York: CCAR Press, 2012.

Sharing the Journey: Leader's Guide (with two CDs of seder music). By Alan S. Yoffie. New York: CCAR Press, 2012.

Additional Suggestions for Further Reading

Agnon, S. Y. *Days of Awe: A Treasury of Jewish Wisdom for Reflection, Repentance, and Renewal on the High Holy Days.* New York: Schocken Books, 1995.

Arnow, David. *Creating Lively Passover Seders.* Woodstock, VT: Jewish Lights, 2004.

Cardin, Nina Beth. *The Tapestry of Jewish Time: A Spiritual Guide to Holidays and Life-Cycle Events.* Springfield, NJ: Behrman House, 2000.

Cohen, Jayne. *Jewish Holiday Cooking: A Food Lover's Treasury of Classics and Improvisations.* Hoboken, NJ: Wiley, 2008.

Glazer, Phyllis, and Miriyam Glazer. *The Essential Book of Jewish Festival Cooking: 200 Seasonal Holiday Recipies and Their Traditions.* New York: William Morrow Cookbooks, 2004.

Goldstein, Niles E., and Peter S. Knobel. *Duties of the Soul: The Role of Commandments in Liberal Judaism.* New York: URJ Press, 1999.

Goodman, Philip. *The Passover Anthology.* Philadelphia: Jewish Publication Society, 2003.

_____. *The Purim Anthology.* Philadelphia: Jewish Publication Society, 2003.

_____. *The Rosh Hashanah Anthology.* Philadelphia: Jewish Publication Society, 2003.

_____. *The Shavuot Anthology.* Philadelphia: Jewish Publication Society, 1992.

_____. *The Sukkot/Simchat Torah Anthology.* Philadelphia: Jewish Publication Society, 2003.

_____. *The Yom Kippur Anthology.* Philadelphia: Jewish Publication Society, 1997.

Greenberg, Irving. *The Jewish Way: Living the Holidays.* Northvale, NJ: Jason Aronson, 1998.

Hammer, Jill. *The Jewish Book of Days: A Companion for All Seasons.* Philadelphia: Jewish Publication Society, 2006.

Heschel, Abraham Joshua. *The Sabbath: Its Meaning for Modern Man.* New York: Farrar, Straus and Giroux, 1951, 2005.

Hoffman, Lawrence. *My People's Passover Haggadah.* 2 vols. Woodstock, VT: Jewish Lights, 2008.

Klagsbrun, Francine. *A Book of Jewish Life and Culture around the Year.* New York: Farrar, Straus and Giroux, 1996.

Klein, Isaac. *A Guide to Jewish Religious Practice.* New York: Jewish Theological Seminary of America, 1979.

Kravitz, Leonard, and Kerry Olitzky. *Eichah: A Modern Commentary on the Book of Lamentations.* New York: URJ Press, 2008.

_____. *Esther: A Modern Commentary.* New York: URJ Press, 2010.

_____. *Jonah: A Modern Commentary.* New York: URJ Press, 2006.

_____. *Kohelet: A Modern Commentary.* New York: URJ Press, 2003.

_____. *Ruth: A Modern Commentary.* New York: URJ Press, 2005.

_____. *Song of Songs: A Modern Commentary.* New York: URJ Press, 2005.

Kula, Irwin, and Vanessa L. Ochs. *The Book of Sacred Jewish Practice: CLAL's Guide to Everyday & Holiday Rituals and Blessings*. Woodstock, VT: Jewish Lights, 2001.

Marks, Gil. *Olive Trees and Honey: A Treasury of Vegetarian Recipes from Jewish Communities around the World*. Hoboken, NJ: Wiley, 2005.

Miller, Phyllis Zimbler, and Karen L. Fox. *Seasons for Celebration: A Contemporary Guide to the Joys, Practices, and Traditions of the Jewish Holidays*. Book-Surge, 2008.

Nathan, Joan. *Joan Nathan's Jewish Holiday Cookbook*. New York: Schocken Books, 2004.

_____. *The Children's Jewish Holiday Kitchen*. New York: Schocken Books, 2000.

Olitzky, Kerry M., and Daniel Judson. *Jewish Holidays: A Brief Introduction for Christians*. Woodstock, VT: Jewish Lights, 2006.

Perelson, Ruth. *An Invitation to Shabbat*. New York: URJ Press, 1997.

Siegel, Richard, Michael Strassfeld, and Sharon Strassfeld. *The First Jewish Catalog: A Do-It-Yourself Kit*. Philadephia: Jewish Publication Society, 1973.

Steinberg, Paul. *Celebrating the Jewish Year: The Fall Holidays*. Philadelphia: Jewish Publication Society, 2007.

_____. *Celebrating the Jewish Year: The Spring and Summer Holidays*. Philadephia: Jewish Publication Society, 2009.

_____. *Celebrating the Jewish Year: The Winter Holidays*. Philadelphia: Jewish Publication Society, 2007.

Strassfeld, Michael. *Jewish Holidays*. New York: Harper Paperbacks, 1993.

Strassfeld, Michael, and Sharon Strassfeld. *The Second Jewish Catalog: Sources and Resources*. Philadelphia: Jewish Publication Society, 1976.

_____. *The Third Jewish Catalog: Creating Community*. Philadelphia: Jewish Publication Society, 1980.

Syme, Daniel B. *The Jewish Home: A Guide for Jewish Living*. New York: URJ Press, 2003.

Washofsky, Mark. *Jewish Living: A Guide to Contemporary Reform Practice*. New York: URJ Press, 2010.

Waskow, Arthur. *Seasons of Our Joy: A Modern Guide to the Jewish Holidays*. Boston: Beacon Press, 1991.

Wasserman, Tina. *Entrée to Judaism: A Culinary Exploration of the Jewish Diaspora*. New York: URJ Press, 2009.

Wolfson, Ron. *Hanukkah: The Family Guide to Spiritual Celebration*. Woodstock, VT: Jewish Lights, 2001.

_____. *Passover: The Family Guide to Spiritual Celebration*. Woodstock, VT: Jewish Lights, 2003.

_____. *Shabbat: The Family Guide to Preparing for and Welcoming the Sabbath*. Woodstock, VT: Jewish Lights, 2002.

Zamore, Mary L. *The Sacred Table: Creating a Jewish Food Ethic*. New York: CCAR Press, 2011.

Index

86–87, 189n32, **208**
tzaar baalei chayim. See animal rights
tzedakah, 18, 31–32, 40–41, 151–52,
162–64, 169n23, **208**. See also *ma-ot
chitin* funds; social action/justice
Chanukah and, 76
Maimonides's Eight Levels, 162–63
Purim and, 79, 188n19
repentance and, 177n38
sacred time and, 163–64
Sukkot and, 66
tzedek, **208**. See also social action/justice
tzitzit, **208**

ushpizin, 69, 136, **208**
utensils for Pesach, 155, 180–81n22

values. See mitzvot (s. mitzvah)
values, food. See food values
Vidui, **208**. See also confession and confessional prayers (*vidui*)
v'initem et nafshoteichem, **208**
visiting the sick, 23, 193
v'shamru, **209**

weddings, 23, 50, 86, 171–72n44, 183n42
willow, **209**
wine, 147–48. See also *Kiddush* (sanctification of Shabbat or festival)
Wolf, Arnold Jacob, 101, 105, 127, 160
women and Rosh Chodesh, 82, 188n25
work, 13, 16. See also *m'lachah*
work, refraining from
on Rosh HaShanah, 34
on Shabbat, 16, 127, 131–32, 168n15,
190n3
on Three Pilgrimage Festivals, 49, 116,
178n5
on Yom Kippur, 43, 190n3
worker's rights, 135–36, 149–50
worship, 22, 33, 43, 49. See also liturgy;
prayer

Yaaleh v'yavo prayer, 116
yamim (s. *yom*), **209**
Yamim Noraim, **209**
years, 6–8. See also leap years
Yiddish, **209**
Yizkor (memorial prayers), 118–19,
120–22, **209**
Pesach, 60

Shavuot, 64
Sukkot, 70
Yom Kippur, 43, 178n45
Yoffie, Eric, 127
Yom HaAtzma-ut (Israel Independence
Day), 85–86, **209**
Yom HaDin, **209**. See also Rosh HaSha-
nah
Yom HaShoah. See Holocaust Remem-
brance Day (Yom HaShoah)
Yom HaZikaron, **209**. See also Israel
Memorial Day (Yom HaZikaron); Rosh
HaShanah
Yom Kippur, 36–37, 38–44, **209**. See also
N'ilah (service)
fasting on, 123. See also meal before
the fast
greetings. See *G'mar chatimah tovah*
refraining from work, 43, 190n3
Yom Kippur Katan, **209–10**. See also
Hoshana Rabbah
yom shekulo Shabbat, **210**
yom tov, **210**. See also festivals

zachor, **210**
Zachor eit asher asah l'cha Amalek. See
Shabbat Zachor
Zecher, Elaine, 97–98
zeicher litziat Mitzrayim, **210**. See also
Exodus from Egypt
Zichronot, **210**
zikaron l'maaseih v'reishit, **210**. See also
Kiddush (sanctification of Shabbat or
festival)
z'man cheiruteinu, **210**. See also Pesach
z'man matan Torateinu, **210**. See also
Shavuot
z'man simchateinu, **210**. See also Sukkot
z'mirot, **210**
z'roa, **210**
zuzim, **210**